Today, a large and complex 'global humanitarian response system' with local, national, and international actors attempts to help tens of millions engulfed in wars and catastrophes. Understanding how this frontline of and for humanity works, succeeds, and fails is the core focus of this book.

With their impressive background as experts, academics and practitioners, Daniel Maxwell and Kirsten Gelsdorf are uniquely qualified to highlight the origins, growth, and challenges to contemporary humanitarian action. They outline the historical roots of the system, outline the main actors and explore how humanitarian work succeeds and fails under the extreme circumstances where it takes place. Interrogating the reasons why humanitarian operations, as well as actions undertaken in its name, remain the subject of so much controversy, they describe how humanitarian work is undertaken today and the ways it may develop in the future.

This book is therefore a much needed introductory text on how and why the United Nations agencies, the Red Cross and Red Crescent Movement and hundreds of international and national non-governmental organisations do what they do in times of crisis and conflict. It will be essential reading for students and practitioners, and others with an interest in humanitarian action, international humanitarian and human rights law, disaster management and international relations.

> Jan Egeland, Secretary General of the Norwegian Refugee Council and former United Nations Under-Secretary-General for Humanitarian Affairs and Emergency Relief Coordinator

Understanding the Humanitarian World is an informed and intelligent analysis of the complexities of humanitarian action today. Dan and Kirsten have done an excellent job in providing a resource that is equally valuable for students who aspire to humanitarian careers, whether academic or operational, as well as for experienced practitioners and policy makers who work at the sharp end of humanitarian response.

> Sara Pantuliano, Acting Executive Director, Overseas Development Institute, UK

Since Dan Maxwell and I published *Shaping the Humanitarian World* the humanitarian world has gotten a whole lot closer, as the end point of unsustainable development floods cities, forces communities to migrate, renders farmland barren and replaces coexistence with conflict. Understanding these crises, and how to respond to them to reset development in a more sustainable direction, is now a vital part of mainstream politics and economics. Whether you are teaching, learning or practicing, Understanding the Humanitarian World is the go to text to move from compassion to effective action.

> Peter Walker, Falk School of Sustainability and Environment, Chatham University, USA

Understanding the Humanitarian World

Conflict and disaster have been part of human history for as long as it has been recorded. Over time, more mechanisms for responding to crises have developed and become more systematized. Today a large and complex "global humanitarian response system" made up of a multitude of local, national, and international actors carries out a wide variety of responses. Understanding this intricate system, and the forces that shape it, are the core focus of this book.

Daniel Maxwell and Kirsten Gelsdorf highlight the origins, growth, and specific challenges to, humanitarian action and examine why the contemporary system functions as it does. They outline the historical underpinnings of the system through specific crisis case studies, outline the main actors, and explore how the ways humanitarian action is carried out. Interrogating major contemporary debates and controversies in the humanitarian system, and the reasons why actions undertaken in its name remain the subject of so much controversy, they provide an important overview of humanitarian action today and the ways it may develop in the future.

This book serves as a valuable introductory text to the way humanitarian action operates in the twenty-first century. It will be essential reading for students and practitioners or anyone with an interest in humanitarian action, international humanitarian and human rights law, disaster management and international relations.

Daniel Maxwell is the Henry J. Leir Professor in Food Security at the Feinstein International Center and the Friedman School of Nutrition Science and Policy, at Tufts University. He teaches humanitarian action, humanitarian policy, and food security in crisis situations. His recent research is on the re-emergence of famines in the 21st century, as well as food security in crises and livelihood systems under stress. He is the author, with Nisar Majid, of *Famine in Somalia: Competing Imperatives, Collective Failures* (Oxford University Press, 2016). Prior to joining the faculty at Tufts in 2016, he was the Deputy Director for Eastern and Central Africa for CARE International, and spent 20 years working in Eastern, Central and West Africa. He holds a B.Sc. from Wilmington College, a Master's degree from Cornell University, and a Ph.D. from the University of Wisconsin.

Kirsten Heidi Gelsdorf is a Professor of Practice of Public Policy and Leadership and the Director of Global Humanitarian Policy, at the University of Virginia (UVA). She teaches global humanitarian crisis response and humanitarian policy development. Her recent research focuses on effectiveness, advocacy, and innovation in the humanitarian sector. She has worked for over 20 years in the humanitarian sector, most recently serving as the Chief of Policy Analysis and Innovation at the United Nations Office for the Coordination of Humanitarian Affairs. Her career includes serving on responses to major emergencies including the Ethiopian Famine, the Liberian War, the tsunami in Indonesia, Hurricane Katrina, the Pakistan earthquake and the Haiti earthquake. She holds a Bachelor's degree from Dartmouth College, and a Master's degree from the Fletcher School of Law and Diplomacy at Tufts University.

Global Institutions

Edited by Thomas G. Weiss
The CUNY Graduate Center, New York, USA
and Rorden Wilkinson
University of Sussex, Brighton, UK

The "Global Institutions Series" provides cutting-edge books about many aspects of what we know as "global governance". It emerges from our shared frustrations with the state of available knowledge—electronic and print-wise—for research and teaching. The series is designed as a resource for those interested in exploring issues of international organization and global governance. And since the first volumes appeared in 2005, we have taken significant strides toward filling many conceptual gaps.

The series consists of two related "streams" distinguished by their blue and red covers. The blue volumes, comprising the majority of the books in the series, provide user-friendly and short (usually no more than 50,000 words) but authoritative guides to major global and regional organizations, as well as key issues in the global governance of security, the environment, human rights, poverty, and humanitarian action among others. The books with red covers are designed to present original research and serve as extended and more specialized treatments of issues pertinent for advancing understanding about global governance.

The books in each of the streams are written by experts in the field, ranging from the most senior and respected authors to first-rate scholars at the beginning of their careers. In combination, the components of the series serve as key resources for faculty, students, and practitioners alike. The works in the blue stream have value as core and complementary readings in courses on, among other things, international organization, global governance, international law, international relations, and international political economy; the red volumes allow further reflection and investigation in these and related areas.

The books in the series also provide a segue-way to the foundation volume that offers the most comprehensive textbook treatment available dealing with all the major issues, approaches, institutions, and actors in contemporary global governance. The second edition of our

Contents

List of illustrations   x
Preface   xi
Acknowledgements   xiv
List of abbreviations   xvi

Introduction   1

1 The origins of contemporary humanitarian action: From the early beginnings to World War II   14

2 Humanitarian action in the Cold War and its aftermath   31

3 Humanitarian action in the twenty-first century   53

4 Contemporary humanitarian actors   88

5 Contemporary humanitarian architecture and action   120

6 Changes in policy and practice   146

7 Unresolved (and unresolvable?): Understanding the humanitarian world in the twenty-first century   172

Epilogue   181

Bibliography   183
Index   185

Illustrations

Figures

I.1 The humanitarian world   7
I.2 Fuzzy boundaries   8
4.1 Humanitarian actors   90
5.1 Coordination structures   123
5.2 The IASC   124

Tables

I.1 UN Consolidated Appeals Process (CAP)* appeals: People
     in need, funding requests, and gaps   4
4.1 UN agencies, funds, and programs engaging in
     humanitarian action   98
5.1 The cluster system   126
5.2 Examples of cluster objectives and activities   131

Boxes

4.1 UN General Assembly Resolution 46/182   94
4.2 Overview of some INGOs   99
4.3 Overview of some humanitarian government donors   102
5.1 What is the definition of "humanitarian action"?   129
5.2 Selection of formal funding mechanisms and tools   135
5.3 Humanitarian Needs Overview (HNO) and Humanitarian
     Response Plans (HRPs) and appeals   137
6.1 The nine commitments of the Core Humanitarian Standard 157
6.2 Sexual abuse and exploitation   158

edited work International Organization and Global Governance (2018) contains essays by many of the authors in the series.

Understanding global governance—past, present, and future—is far from a finished journey. The books in this series nonetheless represent significant steps toward a better way of conceiving contemporary problems and issues as well as, hopefully, doing something to improve world order. We value the feedback from our readers and their role in helping shape the on-going development of the series.

A complete list of titles can be viewed online here: https://www.routledge.com/Global-Institutions/book-series/GI.

Negotiating Trade in Uncertain Worlds
Misperceptions and Contestation in EU-West Africa Relations
by Clara Weinhardt

Coping with Nuclear Weapons
Issues and Global Institutions
by W. Pal Sidhu

Understanding the Humanitarian World
by Daniel Maxwell and Kirsten Heidi Gelsdorf

Global Energy and Climate Governance
Towards an Integrated Architecture
by Harald Heubaum

The United Nations High Commissioner for Refugees (UNHCR)
The Politics and Practice of Refugee Protection, 3rd Edition
by Alexander Betts, Gil Loescher and James Milner

Regional Development Banks
Lending with a regional flavour
Edited by Jonathan Strand

The International Organization for Migration
Challenges and Complexities of a Rising Humanitarian Actor
by Megan Bradley

Towards a Global Consensus Against Corruption
by Mathis Lohaus

Understanding the Humanitarian World

Daniel Maxwell and
Kirsten Heidi Gelsdorf

Routledge
Taylor & Francis Group

LONDON AND NEW YORK

First published 2019
by Routledge
2 Park Square, Milton Park, Abingdon, Oxon OX14 4RN

and by Routledge
52 Vanderbilt Avenue, New York, NY 10017

Routledge is an imprint of the Taylor & Francis Group, an informa business

British Library Cataloguing in Publication Data
A catalogue record for this book is available from the British Library

Library of Congress Cataloging-in-Publication Data
A catalog record has been requested for this book

ISBN: 9780367232931 (hbk)
ISBN: 9780367233013 (pbk)
ISBN: 9780429279188 (ebk)

Typeset in Times New Roman
by Taylor & Francis Books

Preface

Almost ten years ago, Peter Walker and Dan Maxwell wrote *Shaping the Humanitarian World*. That book proved to be an essential addition to an expanding field of scholarship on the global humanitarian system. However, increased research, shifting policy priorities, altered political landscapes, and the rapid growth of humanitarian action worldwide have all rendered that book outdated. While the underlying institutional architecture of the humanitarian system remains largely the same, the expanding needs of populations caught in crisis, the duration of humanitarian crises, a more fraught operating environment, and a redefinition of who is a humanitarian actor and what defines humanitarian action have transformed how our humanitarian world is understood and what it may look like in the future.

In the ten years since *Shaping the Humanitarian World* was published, the number of people in need of formal humanitarian assistance globally has increased fivefold. The global humanitarian budget has increased by over 400 percent over the course of the decade. Yet the gap between assessed need and the ability of the traditional humanitarian system to respond has widened nearly every year since 2007. Furthermore, the majority of the 135 million people assessed as in need in 2018 also live in a state of protracted crisis— "short-term" and "emergency" are no longer synonymous with "humanitarian."[1]

The operating environment has also become more complex. Today, most people displaced by conflict and disaster are no longer in camps, but in urban environments—thus challenging long-standing response protocols. Changes in the nature of armed conflict, particularly in light of the Global War on Terror and the greater association of traditional humanitarian actors with donor-government foreign policy, have tightened restrictions on Western actors working to gain humanitarian access and have led to deteriorating conditions in staff safety and security requiring the rise of remote management and new operational protocols—but also bringing greater attention to local actors. The nature of response has shifted away from in-kind material assistance to market-based programs, protection has become a more urgent priority, and enormous efforts have been made to make programs and policy more accountable and driven by evidence.

Finally, the humanitarian world is now recognized as comprising more than the traditional formal system of actors, activities, and policies established in the aftermath of World War II. It encompasses a much wider set of actors and changing policies and humanitarian practices, some of which may not be exclusively or even primarily humanitarian. All these factors have significantly changed the content and challenged old assumptions about humanitarian action, and have led to major reforms and innovations. But many familiar challenges remain, and more have been added. Perhaps the greatest challenges facing the humanitarian world are to learn from its own mistakes and successes and to adapt to an operating environment and policy context that is constantly in flux.

Understanding the Humanitarian World is our attempt to come to grips with the changes in what constitutes the humanitarian system. But it is also our belief that the reality of the "humanitarian world" is a complex set of institutions and may always be in flux. Indicative of this is that throughout the book, we have decided to use the term "humanitarian actor" or "humanitarian action" without narrow definition. We recognize that much of the complexity in understanding today's humanitarian world is compounded by the fact that there is no single accepted definition of what "humanitarian" means or what constitutes "humanitarian action." To some, it simply means a "concern for the person in need."[2] To some, it implies the notion of working in a conflict- or disaster-affected context. To others, it implies operating under the auspices of International Humanitarian Law and the core humanitarian principles of neutrality, impartiality, and independence, or adherence to accountability practices and contemporary minimum standards. To still others, it implies an ethos not only of assistance, but also of solidarity, of witness, and of advocacy for rights. To us, it is all these things, but it is also constantly evolving and difficult to pin down in a single, right definition. Understanding the humanitarian world requires a wide analysis.

In this book we first review some of the critical historical case studies that contextualize the origins of global humanitarian action, and then provide a synopsis of the contemporary system of humanitarian actors, architecture, and action. Finally, we outline the major operational and policy changes happening in today's crisis response contexts.

This book is not a comprehensive history of humanitarianism, a training manual, or an in-depth analysis of all of policy issues currently being debated; rather, it is a nuanced portrait of the trends affecting humanitarian action today that must be understood to continue to drive change and make improvements.

Both of us are teachers and researchers. But, first and foremost, we are also both practitioners. So our objective in this book is to provide an introduction to the humanitarian world—mostly for students, but also for new humanitarian aid workers or even experienced field workers who have never had the opportunity to step back and consider the overall humanitarian endeavor. We believe that humanitarian action has to be understood as a phenomenon in its own right, but ultimately it is a practice that urgently needs to be reformed and improved to meet the growing demands made on it every day.

We hope that readers—whether scholars, practitioners, or students, both formal and informal—will gain a more nuanced understanding of humanitarianism from this book. As such, readers will be able to see beyond daily news headlines from crisis zones to become more critical consumers, thoughtful donors, and engaged citizens helping to improve the global humanitarian system.

The Authors
September 2018

Notes

1 Many terms are used to describe the context of humanitarian action. These terms are often used interchangeably; sometimes they connote a hierarchy of severity and frequently simply remain ill defined. In this book, we use the term "crisis" as the over-arching term. Crises can be driven either by natural hazards (in which case we refer to them here as "disasters") or by conflict. Frequently of course, crises are driven by multiple factors, in which case we just refer to them as crises. The term "emergency" is used only in reference to relatively short-term, acute crises; in today's context, most crises are long lasting or "protracted"—although they still exhibit "acute" symptoms. (Particularly in the Integrated Food Security Phase Classification or IPC framework, "crisis," "emergency," and "catastrophe" are presumed to have a hierarchical relationship, with each successive term implying greater levels of severity. We imply no such hierarchy here. Rather these terms mean qualitatively different things.)
2 Tony Vaux, *The Selfish Altruist: Relief Work in Famine and War* (London: Earthscan, 2001).

Acknowledgements

Many people have contributed to this book and the ideas or debates that are addressed here. The most important acknowledgement is to the millions of people caught in crisis, helping their neighbors, and recovering from human tragedies happening around the world. The unspeakable misfortunes and the unrecorded triumphs of those who have been devastated by, but survived and overcame crisis are, and continue to be, an inspiration.

This book would not have been written without the incredible research assistance of several students and former students whom we have been lucky enough to teach, mentor, and learn from. They include Peter Hawes, Lauren Jackson, Makayla Palazzo, Maria Wrabel, Allison Hawkins, and Janet Kim. We would especially like to thank our editors Thomas Weiss and Rorden Wilkinson, who oversee the Global Institutions Series, for their detailed review of the draft manuscript; and Ella Halstead, Nicola Parkin and Robert Sorsby at Routledge for their support throughout the process. We are particularly grateful to the co-author with Dan of *Shaping the Humanitarian World*, Dr. Peter Walker, for permitting the reuse of some of the historical material from that book. We would like to thank Joyce Maxwell for her careful copy editing of the draft manuscript. We would also like to thank all of the readers of drafts, as well as all the researchers and practitioners whose work we have cited throughout this book.

We would very much like to acknowledge many colleagues and mentors who have encouraged us over the years and whose views and contributions have profoundly shaped our own understanding of the humanitarian world. These include (for Kirsten) Sue Lautze, Patrick Webb, Joanne Sandler, Hansjoerg Strohmeyer, Norah Niland, Ahunna Eziakonwa, Oliver Lacey-Hall, Christina Bennett, Allan Stam, Craig Volden and David Leblang; and (for Dan) Fikre Nigussie, Dawelbait Mohamed, Geoffrey Chege, Afurika Juvenal, Jon Mitchell, James

Darcy, David Rieff, Joanna Macrae, Antonio Donini and Margie Buchanan-Smith.

We also of course thank our spouses and families: (for Kirsten), Mark, Cash and Sabina, you are my greatest source optimism and love; (for Dan) Joyce, Patrick and Clare, likewise! We also thank you for putting up with a project like writing this book, which always requires some sacrifices in time and attention.

Finally, this book was motivated by the ambitions and potential of the students who enrolled in our humanitarian action classes. These students inspire us and give us hope that some of the challenges outlined here may be better addressed by the next generation. We thank you.

Daniel Maxwell and Kirsten Heidi Gelsdorf
September 2018

List of abbreviations

AAP	Accountability to Affected Populations
AHA	ASEAN Coordinating Centre for Humanitarian Assistance
ALNAP	Action Learning Network for Accountability and Performance
ARA	America Relief Administration
ARC	American Red Cross
ASEAN	Association of East Asian Nations
AU	African Union
CaLP	Cash Learning Partnership
CAP	Consolidated Appeals Process
CARE	Cooperative for American Remittances to Europe (original name)
CBO	community-based organization
CBPF	country-based pooled funds
CCCM	Camp Coordination and Camp Management
CDAC	Communicating with Disaster Affected Communities
CERF	Central Emergency Response Fund
CERP	United States Commander's Emergency Response Program
CHS	Core Humanitarian Standard
CPA	Comprehensive Peace Agreement
CTP	cash transfer programming
DART	Disaster Assistance Response Teams
DEC	Disasters Emergency Committee
DFID	United Kingdom Department for International Development
DPA	Darfur Peace Agreement
ECB	Emergency Capacity-Building
ECHO	European Civil Protection and Humanitarian Aid Operations

ELRHA	Enhancing Learning and Research for Humanitarian Assistance
ERC	Emergency Relief Coordinator
EU	European Union
FAO	Food and Agriculture Organization of the United Nations
FAR	Forces Armée Rwandaise
FEWS NET	Famine Early Warning Systems Network
FFP	Office of Food for Peace (USAID)
FSNAU	Somalia Food Security and Nutrition Analysis Unit
FTS	Financial Tracking Service
GAHI	Global Alliance for Humanitarian Innovation
GDP	gross domestic product
GWOT	Global War on Terrorism
HAP	Humanitarian Accountability Partnership
HC	Humanitarian Coordinator
HCT	Humanitarian Country Team
HDX	Humanitarian Data Exchange
HIF	Humanitarian Innovation Fund
HNO	Humanitarian Needs Overview
HRP	Humanitarian Response Plans
HRR	Humanitarian Response Review
IASC	Inter-Agency Standing Committee for Humanitarian Response
ICRC	International Committee of the Red Cross
ICT	information and communications technology
ICVA	International Council of Voluntary Agencies
IDMC	Internal Displacement Monitoring Centre
IDP	internally displaced person
IFI	international financial institution
IFRC	International Federation of Red Cross and Red Crescent Societies
IGAD	Intergovernmental Authority on Development
IHL	International Humanitarian Law
INGO	international non-governmental organization
IOM	International Organization for Migration
IRC	International Rescue Committee
ISIS	Islamic State in Iraq and Syria
JCA	Joint Church Aid
JEEAR	Joint Evaluation of Emergency Assistance to Rwanda
JEM	Justice and Equality Movement
KSC	King Salman Center for Humanitarian Aid
M&E	monitoring and evaluation

MONUC	United Nations Mission in the Democratic Republic of the Congo
MSF	Médecins sans Frontières
MYP	multi-year planning
NATO	North Atlantic Treaty Organization
NEAR	Network for Empowered Aid Response
NGO	non-governmental organization
NNGO	national non-governmental organization
OCHA	United Nations Office for the Coordination of Humanitarian Affairs
ODA	official development assistance
ODI	Overseas Development Institute
OECD	Organization for Economic Cooperation and Development
OFDA	Office of United States Foreign Disaster Assistance
OIC	Organization for Islamic Cooperation
OLS	Operation Lifeline Sudan
R2P	Responsibility to Protect
RC	Resident Coordinator
ROHAN	Regional Organisations Humanitarian Action Network
RPF	Rwandese Patriotic Front
SARC	Syrian Arab Red Crescent
SCF	Save the Children Fund
SCHR	Steering Committee for Humanitarian Response
SDF	Syrian Democratic Forces
SDGs	Sustainable Development Goals
SLM/A	Sudanese Liberation Movement/Army
SPLA/M	Sudan People's Liberation Movement/Army
SPLM-IO	Sudan People's Liberation Movement-In Opposition
TFG	Somali Transitional Federal Government
TIKA	Turkish International Cooperation and Development Agency
TPLF	Tigrayan People's Liberation Front
UAV	unmanned aerial vehicle
UK	United Kingdom
UN	United Nations
UNAMID	United Nations Africa Mission to Darfur
UNAMIR	United Nations Assistance Mission to Rwanda
UNDP	United Nations Development Programme
UNFPA	United Nations Population Fund
UNHCR	United Nations High Commissioner for Refugees
UNICEF	United Nations Children's Fund

UNIDO	Universal Intervention and Development Organisation
UNMISS	United Nations Mission to South Sudan
UNPROFOR	United Nations Protection Force
UN Women	United Nations Entity for Gender Equality and Empowerment of Women
UOSSM	Union of Syrian Doctors
USA	United States of America
USAID	United States Agency for International Development
VOICE	Voluntary Organizations in Cooperation in Emergencies
WASH	water, sanitation, and hygiene
WFP	World Food Programme
WHO	World Health Organization
WVI	World Vision International
WWI	World War I
WWII	World War II

Introduction

- The world of crisis
- What is the "humanitarian world"?
- Overlapping agendas
- Humanitarian foundations
- Conclusion: Overview of the book

In 2011, a terrible famine struck Somalia caused by a triple whammy of back-to-back failures of seasonal rains, a global spike in the price of food that hit food importing countries like Somalia very hard, and intensified conflict between Al-Shabaab—an Islamist armed group—and the African Union forces propping up the Somali Transitional Federal Government (TFG). Later, a man from Baidoa district recalled the worst of it:

> Our family kept cattle, some camels, and we farm. Before the [crisis] of 2011, livestock numbers increased … but reduced to almost zero because of the drought, especially for cattle. I had invested to buy ten good-looking cows [and] we had a relatively good amount of sorghum reserves. Things were well and in order. Unfortunately the 2010–11 [short rains] failed. From February to April 2011, there was a very hot [dry season]. The cattle we had and the goats had nothing to feed on. We had to give part of the sorghum we had and share it between people and livestock. When the sorghum was out of stock we started giving the livestock the grass roof that was on our huts.

But things only got worse.

> Cattle started dying by February 2011 and by the end of April almost all were finished. By May people started getting displaced,

moving to different places. For our case, we divided the family in three groups: One group went to Dollo Ethiopia refugee camp, one group went to Baidoa, especially the weaker ones, and one group stayed or moved with the camels and few goats. I went to some clan members in Baidoa to assist me and save my family. All my family members are in Baidoa District and I don't have any family members in other countries that can [help], there are some clan members in Baidoa town that I can cry to for some assistance.[1]

Nearly 260,000 people died in the famine in Somalia in 2011 (see Chapter 3). But so much of what happened in that crisis is captured by this one story: the worsening crisis, the desperate attempts people made to protect themselves and their assets (livestock in this case) in the face of multiple threats, the displacement, the splitting of families, and the search for some kind of employment or assistance. As in so many cases today, humanitarian actors faced extreme constraints in reaching affected populations caught in areas controlled by armed groups like Al-Shabaab, and as a result, people relied first and foremost on their own resources and those of their neighbors, their kin, and local actors. International assistance eventually arrived, but too late to save many people. Access had been blocked both by armed groups and by donor-government policies. Much of the international aid effort had to be managed remotely and implemented on the ground by local Somali organizations. Humanitarian action had to adapt to changed circumstances, and local communities caught in the crisis had to look out for each other.

Conflict and disaster have been part of human history for as long as it has been recorded. Those who survive have had to deal with the consequences, pick up the pieces, and move on. Over time, more mechanisms for responding to crises have developed and become more systematized. Today a large and complex "global humanitarian response system" comprised of a multitude of local, national and international actors carries out a wide variety of responses. Formalized frameworks and normative structures aim to define action—like humanitarian principles, International Humanitarian Law (IHL), and the Core Humanitarian Standard (CHS). Organizations may have strict mandates that focus on food assistance or refugee protection. But as the story above notes, individuals and local communities still help each other, and wider networks of responders ranging from volunteer efforts to local organizations to government-led initiatives continue to aim to not only meet humanitarian needs but also to put an end to these needs.

Understanding the complex "global humanitarian system" that has developed over time, and the forces that shape it, are the focus of this book. The humanitarian system is not a logical construct. It grew by accretion—no one "designed" it. It serves many purposes and continuously has to adapt to changing contexts, different drivers of crisis, inconsistent resources, and new modes of response. Some of these changes may be driven by national interest and the projection of soft power, some by ideological interest, and some by a genuine concern for human suffering in the context of wars and disasters.

The world of crisis

Taking a global snapshot of the scale and scope of this human suffering is bleak. In many countries, brutal conflicts span decades; violent extremism, terrorism, and transnational crime exacerbate the effects. Entire generations live only with devastation and loss. The destruction doesn't stop with the loss of life or livelihoods or schooling but with violations of the worst kind that include chemical attacks and bombing campaigns in populated cities. Natural hazards and climate-induced disasters are becoming more frequent and intense. Pandemics, epidemics, and other global health threats emerge more frequently. The widening gap between the rich and the poor is further marginalizing the most vulnerable people, undermining resilience and recovery. All of these shocks leave millions of people in life-threatening conditions. People driven from their homes by violence or disasters are in search of safety or opportunity—and the willingness of neighboring countries to accept or assist these people is decreasing. In 2017, the number of people forcibly displaced by violence worldwide reached a record high of 12 million people in one year, almost double the number displaced the year before. And in over 135 countries, disasters—mostly floods and tropical storms—caused another 18.8 million people to leave their homes.[2]

Over 136 million people, predominantly women and children, were formally assessed in 2018 to be in need of humanitarian assistance (many more were not counted but are suffering). Local communities, national institutions, and even regional and international actors are forced to make triage-like decisions on who gets assistance and who does not. And not enough is done to find—and act on—solutions that can prevent such an affront to global humanity. And sadly these trends—and the issues they raise—have existed for years.

Table I.1 shows that the number of people formally assessed to be in need of humanitarian action—from protection to material assistance—has grown exponentially in the past decade. From 2007 to 2017, the

Table I.1 UN Consolidated Appeals Process (CAP)* appeals: People in need, funding requests, and gaps[3]

Category	2007	2008	2009	2010	2011	2012	2013	2014	2015	2016	2017
People in assessed need (millions)	26.0	28.0	43.0	53.0	65.0	62.0	73.0	76.0	82.5	125.0	128.0
Total CAP appeal ($ billions)	5.5	8.1	10.0	12.9	9.5	10.5	13.2	19.5	19.9	19.7	22.2
Total CAP funded ($ billions)	4.0	5.5	7.1	8.0	5.8	6.2	8.5	12.0	9.7	10.1	11.9
Budgetary gap ($ billions)	1.5	2.6	2.9	4.9	3.7	4.3	4.7	7.5	10.2	9.6	10.3
Assessed needs funded	72%	68%	71%	62%	61%	59%	64%	61%	49%	51%	53%

Note: * Now renamed UN Humanitarian Needs Overviews.

number of conflict- or disaster-affected people increased fivefold, from 26 million to 128 million. The formal request for funds by the United Nations (UN) and other international actors increased fourfold, from $5.5 billion to nearly $22 billion, while actual funding rose from about $4 billion to just under $12 billion.

Of concern in this picture is that the funding gap is growing, preventing formally designated humanitarian actors from assisting all of the people around the world in need. These trends and others are pushing systems to make "working differently" a priority, foreshadowing that over the next decade, the needs of vulnerable populations—and humanitarians' scramble to respond—will continue to change.

What is the "humanitarian world"?

There is no simple definition for humanitarianism, humanitarian action, or the humanitarian system. These terms are often used interchangeably but actually imply different things: a philosophy or belief system (-ism), an activity (action) or an institution, of sorts (system). These are made up of so many different actors, with diverse motivations, a range of resources, and differing perspectives that recently scholars and practitioners have begun referring to a humanitarian "eco-system" or wider network of humanitarian actors to capture the notion of interactive diversity as opposed to an organized construct.[4] Nonetheless, a generally shared understanding of humanitarian action is activities that save lives, protect livelihoods, alleviate suffering, and maintain human dignity during and in the aftermath of crisis, as well as prevent and strengthen preparedness for the occurrence of such situations.

No doubt when members of the current generation think of the "humanitarian system," they think of a UN-led process, funded by donors from Western countries, staffed by earnest-looking young (and probably fair-skinned) aid workers clad in multi-pocketed vests and t-shirts festooned with agency logos, transported in the ubiquitous white Toyota Land Cruisers (also adorned with logos), and helpless-looking and often visibly malnourished "victims," displaced from their homes and livelihoods—and with the international media capturing and packaging the whole spectacle for television consumption that is, of course, linked directly to fundraising efforts. That may have been a *partially* accurate portrayal of the formal humanitarian system in the 1990s, but who and what comprises the system, or "eco-system," has evolved rapidly since then and, in any case, the caricature above represented only the visible tip of the iceberg even decades ago.

Humanitarian action then and now may equally be represented by another (and often neglected) perspective of neighbors helping each other in the aftermath of an earthquake, keeping each other safe in the face of conflict and predatory armed groups, or helping each other find some kind of employment when livelihoods have been crushed by famine or war.[5] Or it may be represented by broader social networks, linking people outside of a crisis to those affected by it. These may be linkages of kinship and lineage, religious bonds, or other forms of solidarity shown through partnerships or, in some cases, simply transfers of funds via one cellphone to another. In many instances, these forms of assistance or protection actually comprise the majority of aid. Even in large-scale and well-funded emergency responses, the organized formal "system" may be late to arrive, may be harassed or prevented from gaining access, or may be severely constrained by authorities or armed groups. Despite the traditional view of the established humanitarian system as a pre-dominantly Western construct, in today's world, the agencies—and certainly the actual humanitarian aid workers—are much more likely to be from the affected country or from somewhere in the Global South. In addition, many other actors are engaged in humanitarian response, such as militaries (including armed non-state actors), the private sector, and traditional development actors like the World Bank. Many of these actors do not have traditional humanitarian mandates or objectives but are now involved in some part of global humanitarian action.

One important reality is that the world of crisis is larger than the world of humanitarian response. Figure I.1 represents a simplistic view of this. Risk and hazards like earthquakes, drought, and even conflict are ever-present, but only sometimes do these amount to shocks that affect vulnerable people enough that their needs outstrip their coping capacities—putting them in need of humanitarian assistance. While governments have the main responsibility for addressing these needs, in many contexts they are either unwilling or unable (and sometimes are even the ones driving the need). In these cases, it is often the global humanitarian response system that takes action. This book is mainly about that system (the right side of the figure). It includes humanitar-ian actors of all stripes (from local actors to UN organizations), the actions they take to protect the lives and dignity of affected popula-tions, the outcomes they seek to achieve, and how those outcomes affect populations and the risks they face. All this is done in the con-text of an "enabling environment": the policies of governments and organizations, the politics of crisis, IHL as well as principles and

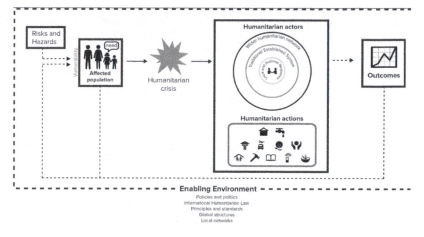

Figure I.1 The humanitarian world

standards, global funding and coordinating mechanisms, and local networks of response and mutual aid.

Overlapping agendas

Humanitarian action is always situated in a context of global agendas, and it is often unclear where humanitarian action ends and some other kind of action begins—whether that action is more explicitly political, developmental, economic, or human rights-oriented. This question also tugs at the very meaning of "humanitarian"—and is by no means resolved. Figure I.2 depicts where humanitarian action overlaps with other agendas.

Today's understanding of what constitutes "humanitarian" action emerged from a 1990s vision that expanded the definition from a "life-saving" emergency agenda to one that is more encompassing.[6] This definition sought not only to deal with the symptoms or outcomes of crises, but also with their causes; not only with human needs, but also with human rights; and, perhaps most controversially, to engage directly with other forms of action (political, economic, even military) so as to bring all resources to bear on the problems at hand. And it acknowledged that all this meant being more unequivocally political than humanitarians classically had been. For example, the new definition includes the whole element of disaster risk reduction—of intervening to make populations less vulnerable or preventing hazards from actually resulting in humanitarian crises.

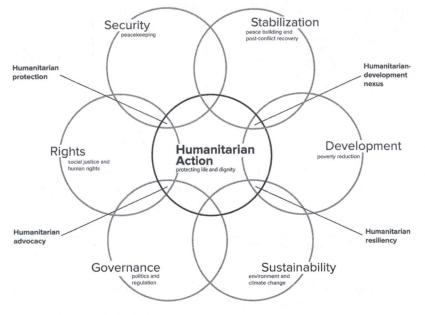

Figure I.2 Fuzzy boundaries

This expanded definition of humanitarianism faded from popularity a bit in the aftermath of the attacks of 11 September 2001 and the advent of the Global War on Terrorism, when it became clear that humanitarian action could be coopted to embrace security outcomes as well as to serve humanitarian objectives. But in many ways, this broader definition of humanitarian action re-emerged with the contemporary focus on resilience and attempts to determine how the development and humanitarian communities can work together in the age of the Sustainable Development Goals (SDGs). So while the core mission of humanitarian action remains the protection of human life and dignity, in many cases humanitarian action overlaps with myriad other agendas, from poverty reduction and good governance to peace building and human rights. But protecting human life and human dignity endure as humanitarian action's core focus.

Ultimately, different actors see the boundaries of humanitarian action in diverse ways, and policy agendas still struggle to gain consensus. For some, maintaining that central focus and keeping humanitarian action deliberately separate from other agendas is important; for many, the "ring fence" no longer exists around the core of humanitarian action in today's operational context. And for all, a larger question remains as to the power of the foundational concepts

and norms that originally defined humanitarian action. The next
section reviews these.

Humanitarian foundations

Four core principles form the ethical framework of much of contemporary humanitarian action: *humanity, impartiality, neutrality,* and
independence. Though Western in origin (and indeed rather Swiss,
given their close connection to the Red Cross movement) these principles are subscribed to by most contemporary humanitarian actors, who
attempt to use them to guide their actions on the ground. With the
changing nature of contemporary conflict and humanitarian actors on
the ground, these "classic" principles are by no means any longer the
sole ethical underpinning of humanitarian action. Nevertheless, most if
not all humanitarian actors embrace some semblance of these principles, at least in theory—they are exceedingly difficult to adhere to
completely in all circumstances.

At the core, the over-arching principle is *humanity*—sometimes
referred to as the *humanitarian imperative*: the fundamental inviol-
ability of human life, and the basic human impulse to protect the life of
a fellow human being who is suffering or caught up in crisis. Some
refer to this principle as the imperative to give and the right to receive
assistance, an expression of the universal value of solidarity between
people and a moral imperative. But the humanitarian imperative
always comes with caveats in a world of finite resources and contradictory agendas. All suffering everywhere cannot be addressed
instantly.

The second core principle is *impartiality*, which evolved specifically
to address this problem. Impartiality, as used in the humanitarian
context, encapsulates two concepts. First, suffering is addressed without discrimination: nationality, race, religious beliefs, class, or political
opinions make no difference. But second, because resources are finite,
priority is given solely on the basis of need. Humanity and impartiality
are considered the two fundamental principles of humanitarian action.

To protect humanity and impartiality, two operating principles have
evolved—the notions of *neutrality* and *independence*. To alleviate suffering, humanitarian actors must have access to those in need (or con-
versely, people in need must have access to assistance). This often
means reaching people in the midst of a conflict, war, or politically
fraught situation. Belligerent parties waging war or driving a political
agenda need to be confident that humanitarians are motivated only by
a desire to alleviate suffering and are not going to "interfere" in the

conflict or political competition. This is the principle of *neutrality*. It is a means to an end, a way to bolster impartiality and maximize the possibility of reaching those who are suffering. However, it comes at a price: Access to one "side" may explicitly preclude access to other "sides"—especially if one is a powerful state. And of course, neutrality in the face of mass atrocities can be morally indefensible even if it allows access. Working through such dilemmas is an increasingly demanding agenda for humanitarians.

The notion of *independence* seeks to support both impartiality and neutrality by ensuring that humanitarian action is free from the coercion of states and political actors. Like neutrality, this is increasingly difficult to put into practice. If humanitarian action is funded by government donors, can it be independent? If the majority of humanitarians are of one nationality, religion, or political persuasion, are they still independent?

These four core principles[7] have been the source of considerable debate and controversy since their adoption by the International Committee of the Red Cross (ICRC) in 1965. While the principle of humanity is generally considered above reproach as a principle (even though it is frequently totally undermined in practice on the ground), independence and neutrality are routinely criticized, both from within and outside the humanitarian community. External critics even attack impartiality—which at face value would seem above reproach as well.[8] The following chapters delve into the challenges of the principles of humanitarian action in many different cases.

The other main foundational piece is International Humanitarian Law (IHL)—the codified "laws of war" specifically restricted to violent conflicts, whether between states, civil wars, or insurgencies within a given state. IHL is an entire subject in its own right. Some of IHL is about restrictions on weapons and their use. Much of the concern here is about the Geneva Conventions, which govern who is and who is not a legitimate target in warfare, and the specific protections afforded to some categories of people. The first three Geneva Conventions focus on wounded soldiers, shipwrecked sailors and prisoners of war—in the context of international armed conflicts. The Fourth Geneva Convention focuses on civilians and other protected categories of people, and the Additional Protocols to the Fourth Convention extend IHL to non-international armed conflicts—the civil wars or armed rebellions that characterize most of contemporary armed conflict. As with the principles, IHL often has to be interpreted in many contemporary contexts that are very different from those for which it was invented.

Other treaties or international law address other elements of humanitarian action: The 1951 Refugee Convention defines who is a refugee (a person who is outside if his or her home country in fear of persecution or being killed because of who they are or what they believe), what their rights are, and the obligations of states to protect those rights. No international treaty specifies the rights of internally displaced people, who now significantly outnumber refugees worldwide. But the Guiding Principles on Internal Displacement, written in the late 1990s, established a normative framework for protection of people displaced in their own countries. The Refugee Convention is now considered part of "customary" IHL.

Finally, in the past two decades, a series of minimum standards and accountability practices to improve the quality and effectiveness of humanitarian assistance have been developed. They include efforts to increase accountability, defined as "the process of using power responsibly, taking account of, and being held accountable by, different stakeholders, and primarily those who are affected by the exercise of such power."[9]

Although controversial, IHL and the four principles have consistently been re-enshrined as the core ethos of humanitarianism and humanitarian action by nearly every major humanitarian initiative in recent history, including the World Humanitarian Summit of 2016 (see Chapter 6) that was attended by humanitarians of nearly all backgrounds and perspectives.[10] Accountability standards, while not codified, are increasingly important and viewed as critical. All of these foundational concepts are deeply rooted in the history of what humanitarians have actually done, the problems and issues they confronted, and how they sought to address these challenges. However, many in the humanitarian world do not necessarily subscribe to them, and some may have never heard of them.

Conclusion: Overview of the book

So, understanding the humanitarian world is clearly a complex topic. The next three chapters provide historical case studies that highlight the origins and growth of, and specific challenges to, humanitarian action. They set the stage for understanding why the contemporary system functions the way it does. Chapter 1 returns to the very origins of humanitarian action and traces its development through the end of World War II (WWII) and its immediate aftermath. Through these developments, the core "agendas" of contemporary humanitarian action emerge.

Chapter 2 traces humanitarian action through the Cold War and into the 1990s. Although some recall this as the "golden era" of humanitarianism, a close look at historical events strongly challenges that perspective. With a focus on seminal case studies from Biafra, the Balkan wars of the 1990s, and the Rwanda genocide and its aftermath, this chapter notes the ways that the humanitarian world has sought to learn from its mistakes and build mechanisms to prevent politicization and ensure accountability.

Chapter 3 picks up the storyline after the attacks of 11 September 2001, and examines some of the crises that have shaped the current context. These include not only the "Global War on Terror" and its humanitarian ramifications, but also the Darfur crisis, Somalia and the re-emergence of famine in the twenty-first century, the horror of Syria, and the Mediterranean displacement crisis.

The book then shifts to provide an overview of the contemporary humanitarian system. Chapter 4 outlines the main actors and the world in which they operate. Referring back to Figure I.1 above, this refers to the local communities ("responders of first resort"); governing authorities; the "traditional humanitarian system," including the main donors and agencies (the Red Cross, UN, and non-governmental organizations (NGOs)); and the wider cast of actors engaging with the humanitarian system.

What these actors actually *do* comprises the core of humanitarian action. Chapter 5 describes how these actors are organized and examines what humanitarian action looks like. What are the coordination structures that govern formal humanitarian action? What are the actions being carried out by the local, national, and global community to support the needs of people affected by crisis around the world? How do humanitarian actors plan and carry out their operations? What in concrete terms is humanitarian aid?

Chapter 6 then examines some of the most critical policy and operational adaptations in the past decade that are defining humanitarian action and the enabling environment today. This chapter gives the reader a working knowledge of at least the major contemporary debates and controversies in the humanitarian system.

Chapter 7 concludes the book with an analysis of some of the unresolved challenges in humanitarian aid, and outlines reasons why the humanitarian system and the actions undertaken in its name remain the subject of so much controversy and debate. It also sketches some of the likely directions of humanitarian change in the foreseeable future.

Together these chapters provide the reader a more nuanced understanding of the way humanitarian action operates in the twenty-first
century.

Notes

1 Nisar Majid, Guhad Adan, Khalif Abdirahman, Jeeyon Janet Kim, and
Daniel Maxwell, *Narratives of Famine: Somalia 2011* (Medford, Mass.:
Feinstein International Center, 2016), http://fic.tufts.edu/assets/Somalia
-Famine-Narratives-Maxwell-FINAL-2-1-20161.pdf.

2 IDMC, *Quarterly Update: April–June 2018* (Geneva: Internal Displacement Monitoring Centre, 2018), www.internal-displacement.org/sites/defa
ult/files/publications/documents/IDMC-quarterly-update_2018-QU2.pdf.

3 Development Initiatives, *Global Humanitarian Assistance Report 2015*
(Development Initiatives, 2015), http://devinit.org/wp-content/uploads/
2015/06/GHA-Report-2015_-Interactive_Online-1.pdf; ALNAP, *The State
of the Humanitarian System 2015* (London: ALNAP/ODI, 2015), https://
www.alnap.org/system/files/content/resource/files/main/alnap-sohs-2015-web
.pdf; FTS, "Total Reported Funding 2016," (Financial Tracking Service
(FTS), 2016), https://fts.unocha.org/global-funding/overview/2016; FTS,
"Total Reported Funding 2017," (Financial Tracking Service (FTS), 2017),
https://fts.unocha.org/global-funding/overview/2017; FTS, "Total Reported
Funding 2018," (Financial Tracking Service (FTS), 2018), https://fts.unocha.
org/global-funding/overview/2018.

4 Development Initiatives, *Global Humanitarian Assistance Report 2014*
(Development Initiatives, 2014), http://devinit.org/wp-content/uploads/
2014/09/Global-Humanitarian-Assistance-Report-2014.pdf.

5 Rebecca Solnit, *A Paradise Built in Hell: The Extraordinary Communities
That Arise in Disaster* (New York: Viking, 2009).

6 Clare Short, "Principles for a New Humanitarianism" (7 April 1998), http
s://publications.parliament.uk/pa/cm199798/cmselect/cmintdev/711/8042808
.htm.

7 These four—humanity, impartiality, neutrality and independence—are
considered the core principles. The International Committee of the Red
Cross embraces seven "humanitarian principles"—the other three being
universality, unity (of the Red Cross movement) and voluntary action.

8 Philip Gourevitch, "The Alms Dealers," *The New Yorker*. A Critic at
Large (11 October 2010). https://www.newyorker.com/magazine/2010/10/
11/alms-dealers.

9 CHS Alliance, Group URD, and The Sphere Project, "Core Humanitarian
Standard on Quality and Accountability" (CHS Alliance; Group URD;
The Sphere Project, 2014), https://corehumanitarianstandard.org/files/files/
Core%20Humanitarian%20Standard%20-%20English.pdf.

10 Ban Ki-moon, *One Humanity: Shared Responsibility (Report of the Secretary-
General for the World Humanitarian Summit)* (New York: United Nations,
2016), https://reliefweb.int/sites/reliefweb.int/files/resources/Secretary-Gener
al%27s%20Report%20for%20WHS%202016%20%28Advance%20Unedited
%20Draft%29.pdf.

1 The origins of contemporary humanitarian action

From the early beginnings to World War II

- Religious charity as humanitarian precursor
- The beginning of a global humanitarian system
- World War I and the birth of NGOs
- The birth of global humanitarian action
- Conclusion: the multiple agendas of humanitarianism

There is no simple history of humanitarianism or the humanitarian system.[1] Many strands were formed that are now woven together to form a recognizable system. Understanding the history of humanitarian action is critical to understanding why the system—or "ecosystem"—of humanitarian action is the way it is today. And understanding history helps to identify the ways it can—or should—change in the future. One recent analysis noted the different forms that the humanitarian imperative can take, even while there is a consistency about the meaning of humanity and compassion across different contexts: "What is also striking are the many different forms that such compassion can take, in its underlying ethos and the practical expression of care, and in the ways in which such differences have shaped state and civilian perceptions of and behavior in humanitarian action today."[2]

Understanding history reveals previously invisible constructs and allows them to be challenged. History demonstrates that original founding ideals can become distorted as organizations develop. It demonstrates that apparently inseparable alliances are in reality temporary conveniences, and it shows that, particularly in the case of humanitarian action, individuals can make a difference. The next three chapters recount the history of humanitarian action in a very encapsulated manner, drawing on specific examples to make particular points or highlight specific challenges. But this is by no means a comprehensive history.

This chapter highlights the early history of humanitarianism and some of its precursors, including charitable imperatives and actions in the major religions and histories that have helped shape today's humanitarian system. Then it presents a quick overview of humanitarian developments in the nineteenth century and the first half of the twentieth century. The chapter concludes with some over-arching historical themes still critical to understanding the humanitarian world of today.

Religious charity as humanitarian precursor

The earliest known precursors of humanitarianism stretch back millennia. Its early influences were mainly rooted in the traditions of Christianity and Islam, as well as the political and social circumstances of the times. The gradual development of charitable giving, between the beginning of recorded history and roughly the fifteenth century, laid the initial groundwork for the emergence of more clearly "humanitarian" actions that followed in later centuries.

In the ancient Greek and Roman empires, food scarcity, sometimes verging on famine, was a regular feature of urban life. Between 330 and 320 BCE, the state of Cyrene sent grain supplies north to 41 communities in Greece to alleviate famine there. In CE 6 during the reign of Emperor Augustus, and again in CE 12 and CE 32 during the reign of Tiberius, Rome was threatened with famine—the crisis of CE 6 being by far the most serious. Augustus reacted to the threat of famine with a series of measures that would seem strangely familiar today: He expelled "extraneous" personnel from Rome, including most foreigners; he introduced grain rationing; and he appointed a senior senator to manage the overall supply of both grain and bread across the city. He doubled grain handouts to the destitute. Looked at from a historical perspective, did his actions represent charitable action or self-interested defense of the state? Both interpretations seem possible. Over time, such charitable action became intimately tied up with the evolution of religious thought. Among the major religions, the Judeo-Christian and Islamic traditions have very likely contributed most directly to the development of today's humanitarian system. Notions of charity are central to all.

The Judeo-Christian tradition

After CE 325, the Roman emperor Constantine effectively co-opted Christianity as a state religion, shifting the responsibility for providing charity onto the church and thereby saving money for the Roman state. Acts of charity were considered the business of the ordinary individual (as in the parable of the Good Samaritan) or the ruling elite (as in Paul's first letter to the Corinthians) but not necessarily the government *per se*. These circumstances established the norm for well over a thousand years of Catholic Church predominance in organized charity.

In the 1340s, the church's role diminished. The Black Death (bubonic plague) killed between a third and half of Europe's population. This led to major changes in demographics and established the unequal relationship between the landed elite and the working farmer. The preeminence of the church as spiritual guide and charitable giver was decimated. Mandated with providing cures, treatments, and explanations, it proved unable to provide any of these.[3] These social upheavals laid the foundation for the discontent that gave birth to the reformation. In 1517, Martin Luther in Germany crystallized the discontent of the old world order and paved the way for the creation of Christianity's Protestant denominations. Under Protestantism, charity and social order were more firmly linked. For the wealthy elite of the newly reformed Protestant states, poverty was not the enemy but rather the unacceptable social face of destitution.

Many contemporary Western humanitarian NGOs—whether faith-based or not—trace their origins to this Protestant ethic of charity. But the state-sanctioned churches founded during the Reformation era established the basis for organizing charity as a state responsibility. The Peace of Westphalia that ended the Thirty Years War a century later established the state—not the church—as the ultimate arbiter of sovereignty, with the understanding that states would be responsible for their own citizenry—and not interfere in the internal matters of other states, a state of affairs that went largely unchallenged for 350 years.[4]

The Islamic tradition

Islam was founded in the early seventh century by the prophet Muhammad in what is now Saudi Arabia. Like Judaism, it embodied a notion of charity as a duty. The notion of *zakat*, or dutiful charitable giving, is derived directly from the Quran. In contemporary Muslim societies, the application of *zakat* takes many forms, from individual acts of charity to institutions fully incorporated in the state and tantamount to a national tax-welfare system.[5] Some Islamic scholars have held that *zakat* is fundamentally different from the Christian concept of charity, being based on the premise that both individual need and class distinctions run counter to Islam and the good of society. They assert that the doctrine of *zakat*, where it was incorporated into state institutions, represented the first formal social security system.[6] A closely related notion in Islam is *sadaqa*—a voluntary action to be done without fanfare. *Sadaqa* and *zakat* are often used interchangeably but, in their original meanings, *zakat* was an obligation while *sadaqa* was voluntary.[7]

The other Islamic tradition of importance is that of *waqf,* the Islamic equivalent of a charitable foundation which dates back almost to the foundations of Islam. It is often used to set up an endowment to fund the purchase of land for the construction of a building that will be used for Islamic purposes—a mosque or a school. At the start of the nineteenth century, at least half of the lands of the sprawling Ottoman Empire were administered under *waqf.*[8] Between the fourteenth and nineteenth centuries, a vast system of public feeding programs was established across the empire to hand out free food to the needy.[9]

Hence the ideals of charity, the obligation to alleviate the suffering of others, and the formation of organized bodies to carry out these acts are not solely the prerogative of the state or of any one religious or philosophical tradition. The present humanitarian system, historically dominated as it is by the patronage of the powerful states of nineteenth- and twentieth-century Europe, reflects a predominantly Christian, and Protestant, philosophical heritage. But, the philosophy that underlies contemporary humanitarian action has its roots in a universal altruistic human ethic. It is expressed and practiced in all major world religions and philosophies.

The emergence of humanitarian activity in Europe

The modern notion of humanitarianism began to emerge between the sixteenth and eighteenth centuries. In response to specific disasters, states and other actors mobilized to support populations affected by crisis—though often in ways that would seem problematic today.

During the reign of Queen Elizabeth I at the end of the sixteenth century, some 50,000 French and Walloon Protestants fled Catholic Europe to seek refuge in Protestant England. This was the first recorded instance of a major movement of people fleeing religious persecution rather than economic deprivation. It was also the first known time that a state deliberately sought to assist with the mass movement of a population and its subsequent support in the country of refuge.[10] The analogy between modern refugee action and that of Elizabethan England is limited: No attempt was made to be impartial—England did not assist the equally persecuted Jews, or indeed other Protestant sects less popular in England. England's actions were politically motivated and its treatment of the arriving refugees, although better than the norm for previous foreigners (that is, hostility), was at heart, self-serving.

The first recorded instance in modern history of a comprehensive disaster-response strategy—and international relief action following a disaster—was the earthquake that destroyed the Portuguese capital Lisbon in 1755. Portugal's first minister, the Marques de Pombal, is credited with ordering the burial of the dead the day after the quake and the distribution of food the next day, along with a freezing of grain prices, the placement of troops to keep the peace, and the planning for the city's reconstruction within a week of the quake—a response plan and operation that puts that of many modern cities to shame.[11] Both the Spanish Crown and the British Parliament, upon hearing of the disasters, sent aid. Writing three years after the event, Emmerich Vattel notes that "the calamities of Portugal have given England an opportunity of fulfilling the duties of humanity." Vattel went on to lay down what he saw as one of the precepts of good nationhood: "If a nation is afflicted with famine, all those who have provisions to spare aught to relieve her distress without, however, exposing themselves to want."[12] Vattel was essentially postulating humanitarian action as an intrinsic property of sovereignty.

The beginning of a global humanitarian system

Several events in the middle of the nineteenth century transformed humanitarian action from a disconnected collection of activities into a more organized global system. This era also marks the first true period of globalization. Under the European and Ottoman empires, the world was connected like never before. The railways and telegraph revolutions had bolstered trading routes and eased travel across the world.[13] For the first time, the enlightened, the philanthropic, and the politically ambitious had a global stage to play on.

Over this period, suffering on the other side of the world was no longer "far away", remote, and reported only many weeks after the event. It was close to home and reported almost immediately by the telegraph and mass-circulation newspapers. The names of affected countries—often those that supplied tea, coffee, and the raw materials of empire—were familiar. This early manifestation of a "global village" provided the grounds on which notions of international humanitarian action could take seed.

Humanitarian action against famine

The famine of 1837–38 in India marked the first time that modern principles of relief emerged in the history of humanitarian action. Organized public works, providing food or cash in return for labor, coupled with free food distribution for the most destitute, were first experimented with in northern India, despite the British rulers' formal adherence to an unfettered free-market economy. The fear of public disorder, a sense of humanitarian responsibility, and simple pragmatic concerns over maintaining a governable nation all pushed the British administration to act. The language used to describe those seeking assistance in the face of famine at that time is instructive. They were referred to as "destitute," "paupers," "vagrants," and the "laboring poor"—all terms that essentially set them up as a threat to law and order. Relief works not only sought to put the laboring poor back to work but were seen as opportunities to encourage discipline and obedience to authority within the confines of the controlled relief camps.[14] The colonial rulers sought to maintain the status quo and ensure famine did not lead to revolution. The famished peasantry sought to survive and challenge a system that slotted them into preordained subservience. This experiment—with relief following strict economic principles and steeped in the political dogma of the day—was carried over from India to Ireland a short seven years later.

The Great Irish Famine spanned 1845 to 1849 in a country that had been formally part of the greatest economic power on earth—the United Kingdom—for two generations. The proximate cause of the famine was the potato fungus that caused almost the entire subsistence crop of the Irish to rot, the subsequent death by starvation of 1.5 million people, and the flight as economic migrants of a further 2 million people. However, the real causes lay in the political and economic relationship between Ireland, the conquered state, and Britain, the conqueror.[15] Under British rule, potatoes became the crop of choice because they could grow on poor land and could withstand the annual trampling by marauding armies. Thus, when the potato crop rotted in 1845–47, a politically marginalized and impoverished population was robbed of the one crop they could grow in their gardens that would provide enough food to survive.

The state's reaction was initially to open up public works modeled on the Indian example, but the subsistence wages were never enough to compete with the inflated price of what little food was still available and certainly not enough to encourage the commercial importation of food. Indeed, at the time Ireland was still exporting grain and did not become a net importer of grain until two years into the famine.[16] The public works, where they were completed, benefited absentee landowners and businesses, not the peasantry. At their peak in March 1847, 750,000 people were employed by such schemes. By the summer of that year, all the works were closed down as it became clear that local funding was never going to provide even a fraction of the cost of running them. Direct aid in the form of soup kitchens was introduced in the spring of 1847. By July, 3 million "meals" a day of watery soup were being served. By September, the kitchens had closed down as funding from local authorities and charities dried up. The following winter saw massive death by starvation—and large-scale migration to America.[17]

The course of the Irish famine also demonstrates the two prevailing political views of humanitarian action. According to one view, only the massive and unimpeded importation of food and its distribution would alleviate the famine. The other was that any major attempt to prevent famine would bankrupt landowners and industry, destroy self-reliance, and ultimately slow down economic growth. Famine relief, when it finally came, was only in the self-interest of preserving British power in the face of a potential outright rebellion by the Irish peasantry. The Irish experience, coming as it did on the heels of the earlier Indian famines, demonstrated the necessity of addressing a major calamity (whether for humanitarian reasons or more pragmatic ones) coupled with the difficulty of mounting and controlling such large, external interventions.[18]

The first real attempt to systematically deal with this dilemma came later in India. Following the Orissa famine of 1866, the first thorough study of the cause of famine and its possible relief was carried out by the government-appointed Famine Commission. The commission looked not just at food supplies, but at markets, transport networks, and land tenure issues. It proposed a complex web of interventions to both control and supplement local market forces in preventing famine. Out of this and subsequent commissions, reflecting a succession of famines and relief efforts over the next few years, the Famine Codes of India were published in 1883. The Famine Codes identified early indicators of impending famine in the form of rapidly changing market prices and the mass movement of landless laborers. They advocated the trial opening of relief works to test if times were sufficiently dire to force the working peasantry to be willing to labor on public works for near-subsistence wages, and they recognized the pivotal role of an integrated food market in allowing the state to intervene, to alleviate the worst suffering.[19]

When famine broke out in British-administered Sudan in the 1920s, the Famine Codes from India were re-enacted as the basis for famine relief. Sudan, however, was not India. In India, famine victims were largely the landless laborers, who showed up among the famine-affected as soon as food prices rose or laboring opportunities dropped. In Sudan, as in most of Africa, famine victims were small-scale farmers who went through a whole host of coping measures—selling off farm implements, eating seed grain, and selling cattle and land—before becoming destitute. Thus destitution in Africa was a late, not an early, sign of famine and one that called for the reestablishment of the asset base of the farmer, not just the filling of the belly of the laborer. Sudan had neither India's armies of bureaucrats, nor a well-developed transport system to administer relief and move food.

In Sudan, and throughout colonial Africa, politics dictated relief. With fewer resources available, relief was focused on the urban environment where fear of political discontent was as much the stimulus to action as was empathy with the hungry.[20] Thus throughout the nineteenth century, state and colonial authorities sought to control the impact of famines—mostly in order to protect the existing political order. While sometimes problematic and often unsuccessful, they established the precedent for famine response in the future.

Limiting the atrocities of war

One branch of the early history of the humanitarian system was rooted in responding to famine and to disasters with natural causes, such as earthquakes. The other early form of humanitarian action was in response to the suffering brought about by war.

A Swiss businessman, Henri Dunant, is commonly credited with being the founder of the modern notion and construct of humanitarian action. From his work emerged the International Committee for the Red Cross (ICRC), the Red Cross and Red Crescent Societies around the world, the principles of impartiality, independence and neutrality in humanitarian action, and the codification of military behavior in times of war now known as International Humanitarian Law (IHL).

On 24 June 1859, Dunant, then 31 years of age, was on a business trip in northern Italy in the town of Solferino. He arrived in time to witness the aftermath of a battle between the French and Austrian armies: a battlefield and nearby town crowded with some 40,000 wounded and dying soldiers left to fend for themselves. Dunant (crucially being neither French nor Austrian), urged the battlefield commanders to allow him to organize relief for all the soldiers left on the battlefield.

He persuaded the women of Solferino (being Italian, not French or Austrian) and the surrounding villages to volunteer and come with him onto the battlefield to provide relief. In his actions, Dunant established some of the fundamental ideals and methodologies of modern humanitarian action. He negotiated access, chose to act impartially assisting the most needy first, used his position as a neutral body, and organized civil society in a voluntary fashion.

In *A Memory of Solferino*, Dunant articulated many of the ideas that would later underpin the Red Cross and Red Crescent Movement (see Chapter 4).[21] He called for local voluntary relief committees to be set up to aid the authorities in times of war and for these volunteers to be protected by law when they were about their business. By 1863, the Geneva Society for Public Welfare had set up a five-person committee to consider how his ideas could be put into practice. Called the International Committee for the Relief of the Wounded, it organized an international conference in October of that year attended by 13 nations. There the ICRC was born, with the Red Cross emblem as its symbol (the symbol was the reverse of the white cross on a red background of the Swiss flag—it was not intended to symbolize anything specifically Christian, though it has often been interpreted that way). This led to the adoption of the "Geneva Convention for the Amelioration of the Condition of the Wounded in Armies in the Field"—in effect, the first treaty in what is now called IHL.

The newly established ICRC (comprised entirely of Swiss citizens) set about encouraging the organization of similar bodies in other countries, starting with those 12 that had attended the diplomatic conference. These were the first national Red Cross and later Red Crescent societies.

In parallel with these early attempts to codify humanitarian work, members of the early ICRC used the reputation of their committee, and of other Swiss citizens they employed, to negotiate access to the wounded on the battlefield. This initiated the relief and protection actions that are now the core mandate of the ICRC. And finally, they lobbied states to curtail the worst excesses of warfare through a series of treaties that form what came to be known as IHL.[22] In 1899, later revised in 1906–07, the Hague Conventions addressing the conduct of warfare were adopted as international treaties. In 1901, nine years before his death, Henry Dunant was awarded the first ever Nobel Peace Prize.

World War I and the birth of NGOs

With the outbreak of World War I in 1914, much of the Western world was thrown into unprecedented upheaval. The war ended in 1918 with

8.5 million battlefield deaths. But not all hostilities ended with the WWI cease-fire declaration in 1918. The Allies continued a blockade against Germany and Austria-Hungary, causing near-famine conditions for the civilian population. Along with the upheaval of the war, these continued humanitarian needs changed the face of humanitarian action and led to the birth of what still operate today as humanitarian NGOs.

One of the most-researched examples is the formation of the Save the Children Fund (SCF). Eglantyne and Dorothy Jebb, sisters born into a wealthy, well educated, and socially active English family, had been active throughout the war in charitable work. Eglantyne Jebb had traveled to Macedonia in 1913 on behalf of the Macedonian Relief Fund, returning just before war broke out. By 1919 a pressure group, "Fight the Famine Council," was set up, with Eglantyne and Dorothy as activists, to pressure the British government into lifting the blockade against the defeated powers. But it soon became clear that advocacy was not enough. Direct action was needed to address the hunger caused by the blockade. On 15 April 1919, Eglantyne Jebb and colleagues established the SCF to raise funds to send relief to the children behind the blockades. In the same year, activists in Sweden set up a similar organization, Radda Barnen, and a year later, they formed the Geneva-based International Save the Children Union.

As the Allied blockade came to an end, income to the fund rapidly dropped off but a change of tactic revived the organization. It began more targeted work, some of it among poverty-stricken children in the United Kingdom (UK), and crucially, they realized that the protection of a vulnerable group like children required laws to back up charitable action. Jebb drafted the Declaration of the Rights of the Child and lobbied for its successful adoption by the League of Nations in 1924. The declaration became, in effect, the mission statement of the organization. While it was never adopted by the League of Nations, the language of the declaration can be traced through history directly to the Convention on the Rights of the Child, adopted by the United Nations in 1989—more than half a century later.

SCF was thus the first true, recognizable, non-governmental organization. The Red Cross, although started outside of government, relied upon government recognition, funding, and law to operate. As an NGO, Save the Children engaged in direct fundraising, managed its own relief actions independently, and lobbied for international legislation to protect victims of abuse and crisis. In doing so, it created the model for independent, activist, and operational NGOs. The development of the NGO sector and the plethora of NGO actors in the humanitarian world today are explored in greater detail in Chapter 4.

The birth of global humanitarian action

Descriptions of post-war Europe note starvation in the cities, mass movements of millions of former troops making their way home of their own volition and often through openly hostile territory, and economic and social collapse. The Ottoman Empire dissolved into numerous nation-states, creating the Balkans as they are known today. The Armenian genocide devastated the Caucasus.[23] Two million Poles were on the move back to freed Poland, and as many as 1 million Germans were moving home from across the old Austrian-Hungarian empire. Everywhere, destitute people were on the move.[24] Again, the coalescing movement of humanitarian actors had to adapt to rapidly evolving circumstances.

The United States (US) was perhaps the only country that survived the war with the financial, manpower, and organizational wherewithal to even begin to address this challenge. Even as the war began, America had been prominent in organizing relief to occupied Europe. The Commission for Relief to Belgium, formed in 1914 and headed by Herbert Hoover, later to be president of the USA, raised over $20 million to provide famine relief there. As the war drew to an end, that commission metamorphosed into the America Relief Administration (ARA), still headed by Hoover and providing relief across Europe but with a particular eye on Russia. The Bolshevik revolution had ushered in a new Russia, which now had 3 million troops spread out across Europe with no formal mechanism for returning home. As early as 1917, the ICRC began to highlight the growing problem of troop repatriations.[25] By the winter of 1920, famine was stalking Russia. The effects of war, the revolution, the breakdown of transportation systems, and a run of bad rainfall all combined to cause three years of famine that would eventually kill an estimated 5.1 million people.[26] Earlier in the year, the Norwegian explorer Dr. Fridtjof Nansen had been appointed by the League of Nations as its first "high commissioner for refugees" (though with the very limited mandate of only administering assistance to Russian refugees[27]). The League of Red Cross Societies and the International Save the Children Union were also key actors but, in reality, the ARA and Herbert Hoover drove the operation. At its height, the ARA was feeding over 10.5 million people a day and had more than 120,000 employees in Russia.

The standoff between the ARA led by Hoover and the new Russian revolutionary government led by Vladimir Lenin was in many ways a taste of things to come. The ARA demanded a full say over the use of Russia's railway system to distribute food; Lenin refused, seeing this as interference in the internal affairs of the new Soviet state. The standoff in many ways sowed the seeds of the US–Soviet relationship which would dominate history for the next 70 years.[28]

The American Red Cross (ARC) had been active throughout the United States' involvement in the war, supporting US troops. As early as May 1917 when America's President Woodrow Wilson appointed Henry Davidson to chair the American Red Cross War Council, it was clear that Davidson was already thinking about harnessing US resources to reconstruct Europe via what he termed a "real International Red Cross." Davidson saw the potential for a humanitarian version of the newly established League of Nations, and one with the ARC firmly in the driving seat. During 1917 and 1918, Davidson and his colleagues corresponded back and forth with President Wilson and with a small group of like-minded Red Cross Societies about setting up a League of Red Cross Societies, independent from the old Swiss ICRC.

The league not only challenged the role and authority of the old ICRC, it also implicitly challenged its perception of neutrality, so tied up then with notions of Swiss neutrality. In early 1919, less than six months after Davidson had first raised the idea of the league with Wilson, the nascent institution was formed with five founding member societies: Britain, France, Italy, Japan, and the United States. Its focus was unashamedly public health and disaster relief, eager to spread the civilizing process of Red Cross activism.

Unlike its namesake, the League of Nations, the League of Red Cross Societies survived the lead-up to and carnage of World War II. In 1991 it renamed itself the International Federation of Red Cross and Red Crescent Societies (IFRC) and by 2007 has grown to 181 members, making it today one of the largest global humanitarian organizations (see Chapter 4 for more on the Red Cross movement in today's humanitarian world).

Wilson's vision of a world order created through open dialogue facilitated by the League of Nations, firmly led and underwritten by the United States, was one that sat increasingly uneasily with the American people. When Franklin D. Roosevelt came to power in 1933, his inclination was to seek re-engagement in the world but his priority was to stop the near-fatal hemorrhaging of the US economy. The depression had caused massive unemployment across the states. Internally displaced people built shantytowns in New York's Central Park. Women and children scavenged through the garbage of the great cities and soup kitchens with lines of people stretching block after block became the norm. Up to this point in America's history, dealing with such issues had been a state affair, not a federal one. Roosevelt changed all this. In proposing his "New Deal," he envisaged a welfare and facilitating role for the federal government—a role it had never undertaken before. Federal public works schemes were opened across the country in an attempt to rebuild the economy that gradually, through the late 1930s, lifted the United States out of the Great Depression.[29]

Aftermath of World War II

In essence, much of the international apparatus that today makes up the global humanitarian system was born out of the consequences of World War II and, in particular, the consequences of the Cold War, which in many ways started during the final phases of WWII and ended with the demise of the Soviet Union in the early 1990s.

WWII and its aftermath fundamentally shaped the formal humanitarian community of today. The United Nations and its agencies were born. The Bretton Woods institutions (the World Bank and the International Monetary Fund) were created, IHL was expanded, and a whole new family of NGOs was created to work alongside, comfortably or not, the old ICRC, the League and the older NGOs (the topic of Chapter 4). Post-war Europe morphed into the Cold War (the topic of Chapter 2). But to complete the picture of WWII and its aftermath, understanding the European Recovery Program is critical, as it became the means by which the United States sought to stabilize post-war Europe.

The severe winter of 1946–47, coming on top of wartime devastation and major refugee movements, brought real starvation to parts of northern Europe. Original hopes that Europe's economy could be rebuilt by the UK and France off the backs of their colonial empires proved short lived. Europe was not recovering from the war, its people still lived under wartime austerity, and the only country with the wherewithal to inject capital was the United States. Its economy had boomed during the war and its infrastructure had remained intact. In the summer of 1947, Secretary of State Marshall, arguing more on grounds of national security interest than out of humanitarian concern, convinced President Harry Truman of the need to rebuild the economy of Europe, a much needed trading partner, and to head off the allure of communism. The European Recovery Program—quickly dubbed the Marshall Plan—was signed into law in April 1948 and in the same year the participating countries, essentially Western Europe, Turkey, and the United States, created the Organization for European Economic Cooperation to coordinate aid efforts. In 1961 the organization was renamed the Organization for Economic Cooperation and Development (OECD).

The Berlin blockade—and the Berlin airlift—in many ways captured both the competition for post-war Europe and the determination of the Americans. West Berlin—the area of the German capital occupied by French, British, and US troops at the end of the war—was blockaded by the Soviet Union on 24 June 1948, in an attempt to stop the introduction of the new West German mark in Berlin. Two days later, the Western allies—primarily the United States and the United Kingdom—launched an airlift to West Berlin in an operation that continued for nearly a year to provide all food, fuel, and other necessary supplies. While this was strictly a military operation in terms of logistics, the airlift was forever associated with the iconic "CARE Package"—packed and provided by voluntary contributors in the United States and distributed in Europe by the newly formed agency CARE (which initially stood for Cooperative for American Remittances to Europe). Over the course of the airlift, some 500,000 of these packages were delivered to West Berlin.[30]

Over the four years of the Marshall Plan, $12.4 billion in aid was disbursed. The funds were not grants, but loans, repaid in local currency, held by each local government in special funds to be plowed back into economic development. Initially used for staple food supplies; then for urban, agricultural, and industrial rehabilitation; and finally the rehabilitation of the European military, the plan and the use Europe put it to helped raise industrial production by 35 percent over its lifetime. Thus, the Marshall Plan went well beyond just the provision of short-term, life-saving assistance, and embraced the long struggle for post-war reconstruction, while providing support to a civilian population in need.

Equally importantly, the plan allowed European governments to relax wartime austerity programs, reducing civil discontent. Historians argue over whether the Marshall Plan represented American generosity or hard-nosed pragmatism, securing Europe's dependency on American goods and services and building political, military, and economic clientelism as the West faced off with the East. Whatever the analysis, European rehabilitation depended on being driven and planned, if not fueled, by the governments of affected countries and not by an external, multilateral, or unilateral power—a lesson that should not be lost today.

Conclusion: the multiple agendas of humanitarianism

Throughout this period, the makings of a contemporary humanitarian system were shaped by a set of constantly competing agendas. First was the agenda of *compassion*, reflected in private acts of charity and state acts to alleviate acute suffering, where the end of suffering and the means to prevent it are wrapped up in the same set of activities. The manifestations of this agenda are best captured historically by the formation of the Red Cross.

Second was the agenda of *containment*, where humanitarian action intended primarily to maintain the status quo, prevent rebellion, and promote security and stability—and thus humanitarian action was primarily a means to a very different end. This was manifest histori-cally in the development of the Indian Famine Codes and the response to the Irish famine, but in numerous other cases as well.

Third was the agenda of political *change*, demonstrated in advocacy against "collective crimes" in colonial India or the call to reform the Poor Laws back in the British homeland. This is best seen historically in the formation of Save the Children Fund. SCF rapidly became an operational—as well as an advocacy—kind of organization. This highlights the sometimes-fraught relationship between advocacy as the means to the end of human suffering and direct action to at least mitigate it, with direct action often viewed as a poor second choice.

Finally, while much of the early work in humanitarian action was to provide relief in acute, short-term emergencies, the experience of the Great Depression and the post-war reconstruction in Europe raises the fourth (and sometimes ill-fitting) agenda, the provision of *continuous support*. Although "humanitarian action" is still often referred to as synonymous with "emergency response", humanitarians have often found themselves providing long-term support in contexts that can hardly be described as "emergencies". This role is sometimes more akin to recovery or reconstruction, but is more frequently similar to the provi-sion of social safety nets or to the contemporary agenda of social protection—but in the context of conflict or post-conflict situations.

These (sometimes) competing agendas—compassion, containment, change, and continuous support—have all been debated throughout the recent history of humanitarian action (the topic of Chapter 3). They have shaped the structure of the contemporary humanitarian system (Chapters 4 and 5) and, looking to the future, compete to determine just what the role of the humanitarian system will be in the twenty-first century (Chapters 6 and 7).

Notes

1 This chapter reuses edited segments from the original book, *Shaping the Humanitarian World*, with permission from the authors of that book (Walker and Maxwell).

2 Randolph Kent, Christina Bennett, Antonio Donini, and Daniel Maxwell, *Planning from the Future: Is the Humanitarian System Fit for Purpose?* (London; Medford, Mass.: Humanitarian Policy Group at the Overseas Development Institute; Feinstein International Center at Tufts University; the Policy Institute at King's College London, 2016), www.planningfromthefuture.org/uploads/4/5/6/0/45605399/pff_report_uk.pdf.

3 Norman F. Cantor, *In the Wake of the Plague: The Black Death and the World It Made* (New York: Free Press, 2001).

4 Henry Kissinger, *World Order: Reflections on the Character of Nations and the Course of History* (Penguin Books, 2014).

5 Jonathan Benthall and Jérôme Bellion-Jourdan, *The Charitable Crescent: Politics of Aid in the Muslim World* (London; New York: I. B. Tauris, 2003). See in particular chapter 1, "Financial Worship," and chapter 2, "Qaqf and Islamic Finance: Two Resources for Charity".

6 For a good discussion of this early history, see Michael Bonner, "Poverty and Economics in the Qur'an," *Journal of Interdisciplinary History* XXXV, no. 3 (1 January 2005): 391–406.

7 Barbara Ibrahim and Dina H. Sherif, *From Charity to Social Change: Trends in Arab Philanthropy* (Cairo: American University in Cairo Press, 2008), http://site.ebrary.com/id/10413282.

8 John Robert Barnes, *An Introduction to Religious Foundations in the Ottoman Empire* (Brill, 1987), 83.

9 Amy Singer, "Serving Up Charity: The Ottoman Public Kitchen," *Journal of Interdisciplinary History* 35, no. 3 (2005): 481–500, https://doi.org/10.1162/0022195052564252.

10 Andrea Paras, "Once Upon a Time: Huguenots, Humanitarianism, and International Society" (Annual Meeting of the International Studies Association, Chicago, 2007), 36.

11 Adam N. Khedouri, "'Bury the Dead and Feed the Living.' Lessons from Lisbon: An Opinion" (ReVista: Harvard Review of Latin America), https://revista.drclas.harvard.edu/book/bury-dead-and-feed-living.

12 Emer de Vattel, *The Law of Nations: Or, Principles of the Law of Nature: Applied to the Conduct and Affairs of Nations and Sovereigns*, Early American Imprints. First Series No. 45185 (Philadelphia, Pa.: P. H. Nicklin & T. Johnson, 1935), 136.

13 Niall Ferguson, "Empires and Races," in *The War of the World: Twentieth-Century Conflict and the Descent of the West*, First American edition (New York: The Penguin Press, 2006), 3–42.

14 Mohiuddin Alamgir, *Famine in South Asia: Political Economy of Mass Starvation* (Oelgeschlager, Gunn & Hain, 1980), 68.

15 Cormac Ó Gráda, *The Great Irish Famine*, Studies in Economic and Social History (Basingstoke, Hampshire: Macmillan, 1989).

16 Cormac Ó Gráda, *Ireland Before and After the Famine: Explorations in Economic History, 1800–1925*, 2nd ed. (New York: St. Martin's Press, 1988), 109.

17 Christine Kinealy, *This Great Calamity: The Irish Famine, 1845–52* (Boulder, Colo.: Gill & Macmillan, 1994), 71–86.

18 Ibid.

19 Alex de Waal, *Famine Crimes: Politics and The Disaster Relief Industry in Africa*, African Issues (London: African Rights & The International

African Institute, 1997). See in particular chapter 1, "Rights and Entitlements: The Conquest of Famine in South Asia."

20 de Waal, *Famine Crimes*. See in particular chapter 2, "Africa 1900–85: A Fragile Obligation to Famine Relief."

21 An English translation of the original 1863 publication can be found at Henry Dunant, "A Memory of Solferino" (Geneva: International Committee of the Red Cross, 1939), https://www.icrc.org/eng/assets/files/publications/icrc-002-0361.pdf.

22 For a succinct history of the early years of the Red Cross, see International Committee of the Red Cross, *Discover the ICRC* (Geneva: International Committee of the Red Cross, 2005), https://www.icrc.org/eng/assets/files/other/icrc_002_0790.pdf.

23 Samantha Power, *A Problem from Hell: America and the Age of Genocide* (New York: Basic Books, 2002). See in particular chapter 1, "Race Murder."

24 Michael Robert Marrus, *The Unwanted: European Refugees in the Twentieth Century* (New York: Oxford University Press, 1985).

25 Caroline Moorehead, *Dunant's Dream: War, Switzerland, and the History of the Red Cross* (New York: Carroll & Graf, 1999).

26 Benjamin M. Weissman, *Herbert Hoover and Famine Relief to Soviet Russia, 1921–1923*, Hoover Institution Publication, 134 (Stanford, Calif.: Hoover Institution Press, 1974).

27 Sir John Hope Simpson, *Refugees: Preliminary Report of a Survey* (Oxford: Oxford University Press, 1938).

28 Bertrand M. Patenaude, *The Big Show in Bololand: The American Relief Expedition to Soviet Russia in the Famine of 1921* (Stanford, Calif.: Stanford University Press, 2002).

29 Robert S. McElvaine, *The Great Depression: America, 1929–1941*, reprint (New York: Times Books, 1993).

30 CARE, Annual Report of CARE Canada (Ottawa, 1999).

2 Humanitarian action in the Cold War and its aftermath

- The rise of independent humanitarianism: Biafra 1968–70
- A more politically engaged humanitarianism?
- Famine in the Sahel: 1972–74
- Famine, regime change, and global intervention: Ethiopia 1984–85
- The Balkans wars: 1991–99
- The Rwandan genocide and its aftermath: 1994–96
- Conclusion: crisis and reform—learning and change as one impact of crisis

The immediate post-World War II era to the 1960s was relatively quiet for humanitarian action.[1] Characterized by greater involvement of the United States in world affairs and by the euphoria of the end of colonial rule in Asia and Africa, global action in this era was focused much more on development and nation-building than on humanitarian engagement—even in situations that might have demanded it. The two major wars of the era, in Korea and Vietnam, provoked great turmoil, but relatively little in terms of humanitarian intervention. What humanitarian engagement emerged in Vietnam tended to be more of a political statement made on humanitarian turf.[2]

The 1970s and 1980s saw relatively more humanitarian action, and in this period NGOs—though founded decades earlier—came into their own as significant humanitarian actors. Several key events during this era contributed strongly to the shape of the contemporary humanitarian world. Principally, these included the Nigerian civil war (or the Biafra war, depending on one's perspective), the Sahelian famines of the early to mid-1970s (which in fact stretched across the African continent from the Atlantic to the Red Sea in the areas just south of the Sahara desert), and the catastrophic famine in the Horn of Africa in 1983–85. With the independence of Portuguese colonies in Africa in the mid-1970s, two wars of national liberation were soon transformed into protracted civil conflicts in Angola and Mozambique. These conflict emergencies, first fought in the context of the Cold War and the regional politics of white minority rule and subsequently on more local grievances, became what the humanitarian world would call "complex political emergencies": conflict-related crises, but with multiple causal factors and extensive civilian suffering, often far from the attention of either the media or the international community.

The period from WWII to the end of the Cold War is widely recalled (incorrectly) as a "golden era" for humanitarian action. Humanitarians were viewed as "angels of mercy" and as gadflies—well-meaning "do-gooders"—but for the most part, political lightweights. But all these perceptions would change, and in retrospect, clearly there never was a golden era of humanitarian action.[3] By the end of the 1980s, not only was there a much broader public appreciation for—and involvement in—humanitarian action, there was also a core group of humanitarian workers who would lead the endeavor for much of the ensuing generation. This chapter reviews the war in Biafra, famine in the Sahel and Ethiopia, the wars in the Balkans, and the Rwanda genocide and the subsequent refugee crisis in Zaire. Many of the debates and controversies that characterize this era continue unresolved today, but hard lessons learned from many of these experiences formed the core of the reforms that shape today's humanitarian world.

The rise of independent humanitarianism: Biafra 1968–70

War gave rise to the first formal humanitarian organizations in the nineteenth century. In the late 1960s, the Nigerian civil war marked a turning point for twentieth-century humanitarianism. The self-declared "Republic of Biafra"—the southeastern quarter of the Federal Republic of Nigeria—split off from the rest of Nigeria in May 1967. Although diverse, Biafra was largely thought of as an ethnic Igbo nation covering most of the oil-rich Niger delta region. The split was caused by many factors: colonialism and its reliance on "native rule," ethnic competition, and the massacre of some 30,000 Igbo people living in the north in late 1966 that resulted in the return of nearly a million people of Igbo origin to the southeast and the expulsion by local government of non-locals. Given the Cold War's political constraints of the time, the UN did not intervene in either a political or a humanitarian role when Biafra seceded from Nigeria. There was little support for the secession or the creation of a new fledgling state in Africa from either East or West—indeed both the UK and the Soviet Union aided the Nigerian federal government in the war. Only a handful of countries ever officially recognized Biafra.

The military strategy of the federal government was to cut off not only Biafra's source of revenue (the oil) but also its overland supply lines. As a military strategy, this worked very effectively: Biafra was militarily defeated in January 1970, and its leaders fled into exile. The humanitarian consequences of this strategy, however, were profound, leading to widespread malnutrition and mortality. Though there never was an official count, estimates are that several hundred thousand to as many as two million Biafrans died during the famine caused by the blockade.[4]

In 1969, fearing that military assistance was being disguised as humanitarian aid, the Nigerian government banned the ICRC from delivering supplies to Biafra except on planes that flew during daylight hours from Nigerian airfields and that were inspected prior to departure. In return, the Biafran authorities denied permission for daytime flights to land. In the summer of 1969 an ICRC plane was shot down, and, following well-established procedures, they withdrew from the operation while continuing to quietly lobby the federal government to reconsider and grant it access. That left Joint Church Aid (JCA)—a coalition of Catholic and Protestant churches as well as a handful of secular NGOs—in charge of the airlift, an operation that rivaled the 1948 Berlin airlift both in the volume of relief ferried and for sheer audacity in the face of authorities. Federal air raids indiscriminately hit humanitarian as well as military targets at Uli—the only functioning airfield in what remained of Biafra by 1969. The JCA airlift provided relief to starving Biafrans but, because of both the material assistance it provided and the link it created to the outside world, it is also credited by many analysts with prolonging the war—as well as the suffering.[5]

A more politically engaged humanitarianism?

Essentially, the independence struggle was lost by the time news of the humanitarian crisis emerged in the international media, but it spawned a propaganda campaign that extended both the life of Biafra as a political entity and the misery of its people. The classic humanitarian choice—whether to just do one's best to meet the needs of crisis-affected people or to speak out vocally about the causes of the man-made crisis—played out in Biafra with a previously unrivaled poignancy. A whole generation of humanitarian workers came of age in the crucible of Biafra, and several new humanitarian agencies were born out of the

Biafran experience—most notably Médecins sans Frontières (MSF) and Concern (humanitarian NGOs are described in more detail in Chapter 4). Though "Dunantist" in philosophy, this new kind of organization was motivated as much by a sense of solidarity with the victims of crisis as by traditional humanitarian principles—and was much more outspoken in its condemnation of the causes of man-made disasters. MSF, born in 1971, would in the following decades play a central role in both responding to crises and advocating for those caught in them—and would ultimately grow to become a humanitarian powerhouse and a strong advocate for independent, principled humanitarianism. The dynamics of the humanitarian movement were permanently changed.

The contentious issues faced by humanitarian workers in Biafra still echo in contemporary debates: questions of national sovereignty versus regional self-determination; the instrumental manipulation of humanitarian assistance for political purposes; the physical security of humanitarian workers; the maintenance of political neutrality vis-à-vis belligerents while expressing solidarity with humans caught in conflict; the objective measurement of evidence versus being forced to act in an extremely information-scarce (and, in retrospect, propaganda-rich) environment; and the imperative to assist acutely disaster-affected people, but without prolonging the suffering or contributing to its impact. As in later conflict emergencies, many humanitarian workers saw the Biafran people as an oppressed minority and identified as much with their political cause as with their human suffering. Ultimately, however, the predicted "bloodbath" that many feared would follow a federal military victory in Biafra never took place.

Famine in the Sahel: 1972–74

If Biafra was, for humanitarian actors, the forerunner of the conflict emergencies of a later era, the Sahelian famine[6] of the early 1970s forever put the term "slow-onset crisis" on the humanitarian map. The world had to confront, for the first time since the 1940s, the possibility that there might not be enough food to go around for everyone. The culmination of five years of drought, the large-scale famine developing on the southern fringes of the Sahara desert in Africa put millions at risk.

Though long supporting a human population, the Sahel receives barely enough rainfall in a normal year to permit crop production. Periodic drought in the region is common, but following an era of exceptionally good rainfall in the 1950s and 1960s, the period from

1968 onwards was characterized by less-than-average rains and then by outright drought. By 1972, it was sufficiently serious to warrant a request for emergency assistance. Only in 1973–74 was a major response mounted—predominantly by the World Food Programme (WFP) and the Food and Agriculture Organization (FAO) of the United Nations, as well as NGOs (all discussed in Chapter 4).

One critic noted that

> a massive response followed, in which across much of the Sahel relief aid was used ... for political purposes by African states, targeting of aid provision was amateurish, local grain markets were harmed, tens of thousands of Africans and their livestock perished, aid entrepreneurs enriched themselves, corruption was rampant, and scores of international NGOs planted permanent roots in countries in which they had never worked."[7]

The manner in which the crisis was understood, and the patterns set by the response, had repercussions for ensuing decades.

The scope of the crisis stretched from Mauritania and Senegal on the Atlantic coast to the Red Sea coast of Ethiopia, but the main impact was felt in Mali, Niger, Burkina Faso, and Chad. Estimates of mortality vary. The Centers for Disease Control put the death toll at 100,000[8] while others have put it much higher.[9] The causes of the crisis were blamed on ecological factors at the time,[10] while more-recent analyses have emphasized political factors.[11] But in all the discussion over causes and manifestations of the famine/drought, the humanitarian response itself has been largely overlooked. Much of the actual response to the famine came from international donors through national governments. Stephen Devereux notes three main reasons for the failure of timely humanitarian response: poor information, poor logistical capacity, and in some cases, callous disregard for the consequences of the crisis.[12]

The beginnings of famine early warning

But what captured the attention of policymakers at the time was the question of the availability of good information. As the Sahelian crisis unfolded, information about the drought and its impact was limited at best. The invention of famine early warning systems was the longest-lasting legacy of the Sahel crisis. Amartya Sen[13] would later demonstrate that the crisis faced by Sahelian farmers and pastoralists alike had less to do with an outright food shortage than with the inability of some groups to access what food was available. Though his work on famine would not come out until eight years later, his analysis helped to underpin the development of famine early warning systems, and though drought played a significant role in triggering the crisis, it was not characterized by an outright shortage of food. Indeed, surplus-producing regions existed immediately adjacent to the hardest-hit famine locations. People hit by these crises did not suffer an outright decline in the availability of food but rather a serious decline in their access to food, or an "entitlement failure" in Sen's terms. This was brought about by a variety of factors, including an inability to produce adequate food, but also a distinct repositioning of the value of labor, livestock, and other assets that represented both current and future income streams for the hardest-hit groups.

Though Sen's insight was primarily theoretical, the practical consequences were that if the *process* of entitlement failure could be mapped, it should be possible to predict actual famine *events* more accurately. Understanding the various means people use to cope with declining access to food combined with improved remote sensing gave birth to the science of famine early warning.

At the same time, the link between addressing humanitarian concerns in an acute crisis ("humanitarian assistance") and addressing the causes of the chronic problems that may result in such crises ("development assistance") became enshrined as the "relief-to-development continuum"—the notion that external intervention could and should shift quickly from addressing short-term manifestations of a crisis to longer-term causes.

The problem of "late response"

But with the founding of early warning has come the dilemma that, for a variety of reasons, has dogged the humanitarian endeavor ever since the time of the Sahelian crisis: Despite relatively good early warning information, the international community remains painfully slow to respond in crises where quick and early response should be a relatively straightforward task.

One recount of the crisis calls the humanitarian endeavor to counter famine in the Sahel an institutionalized "partial success."[14] Although hundreds of thousands of lives were no doubt saved, the response did not reach high gear before tens of thousands had already died. And despite more than three decades of subsequent experience, the speed and flexibility of humanitarian response in slow-onset crises has improved only incrementally. Another analysis notes that, frequently, donors do not trust the agencies on the ground, or they have competing objectives.[15] Recent work (not related to the Sahel famine) shows that good humanitarian information, and even media pressure, is often insufficient to elicit a humanitarian response from donors in the absence of a clear geo-political rationale.[16] But some accounts suggest that the early warning and response systems that were developed following the Sahel crisis addressed the needs of external interveners rather than those of the communities at risk or of African governments:

> At root, the role of the international early warning and response system was to inform African governments when they had a problem and to initiate the process through which officials back home in Washington, Ottawa, Brussels, or other European capitals made the political decisions to respond. As the 1980s ended, therefore, the international relief community had built a system founded on African incapacity, assuming African corruption, deeply tied to export markets in the North, focused on accounting for goods moved not good done, and one that constructed the problem as much larger than Africans could possibly handle on their own ... This produced debilitating gaps between those who diagnosed, those who decided, those who acted, and those whose sovereignty and human rights were at stake.[17]

Famine, regime change, and global intervention: Ethiopia 1984–85

The Ethiopian famine of the mid-1980s probably shaped people's view of humanitarian action more than any other single event during the Cold War. The world was dramatically re-awakened to African famine by Michael Buerk's famous BBC broadcast and the film footage by Kenyan photographer Mohamed Amin in the autumn of 1984 depicting thousands of people, displaced by famine, starving in a "famine camp" in Korem, in the Tigray region of Ethiopia:

> Dawn, and as the sun breaks through the piercing chill of the night on the plains outside Korem it lights up a biblical famine, now, in the 20th century. This place, say workers here, is the closest thing to hell on earth ... Death is all around.[18]

Ethiopia and other parts of the Horn of Africa had also been hit by the drought that affected the Sahel, first affecting the pastoral lowlands and later the more politically sensitive and chronically vulnerable central highlands areas of Wollo and Hararghe. Failure to recognize and deal swiftly with the consequences of a previous 1972–74 famine is widely believed to have been one of the factors leading to the overthrow of the feudal monarchy and Emperor Haile Selassie in 1974 by a group of young army officers in what came to be known as the Derg.[19] The impact of famine on the stability of the government in power was apparently lost on the leaders of the Derg themselves, but was duly noted by the internal opponents of the Derg and by donor governments around the world.

In the earlier 1972–74 famine, information clearly was suppressed, the extent of the crisis did not become clear until far too late, and the limited response from the government was mainly politically motivated. These factors were repeated in Ethiopia's 1984–85 crisis. And indeed many observers believe that the policies of the Derg in dealing with the 1984–85 crisis (both the role of the army in causing the crisis and the subsequent failure to control it) ultimately led to its overthrow at the hands of guerilla movements from Tigray and Eritrea, with whom the Derg was at war at the time of the crisis.

The famine had many complex elements: First, of course, was the abject humanitarian suffering, captured on television for the world to see. In the end, the best estimate is about 1 million deaths from the famine, with close to 8 million people affected—a quarter of the population of the country at the time. Second, this crisis unfolded directly around Cold War competition between spheres of Western and Soviet influence. The Derg transformed Ethiopia into a Soviet client state in relatively short order after the overthrow of Haile Selassie, collectivizing rural agriculture and clamping down on private business. But most of the humanitarian response came from the West. Third, like the earlier crises in the 1970s, this one was characterized by a dearth of accurate information—or more accurately, deliberately covered up information—until it was far too late.

Fourth, while the crisis of 1984–85 was *triggered* by a massive drought, the sum total was not caused just by drought. The famine was to some extent a starvation strategy in the on-going wars in Eritrea and Tigray provinces. The use of food as a weapon was a common tactic of the Ethiopian military.[20] Already by 1984, it had caused massive displacement of people both internally and across the border into Sudan and disrupted production in the affected areas.[21] The humanitarian agencies demurred from making such an accusation at the time. But aid was systematically diverted or manipulated by the Derg, who in turn were able to keep both donors and agencies from doing much about it—fearful as the agencies were of losing access to famine-affected populations were they to publicly highlight any diversion. De Waal[22] notes that a silent agreement existed between the agencies and the Derg whereby the agencies maintained a "hands-off" policy towards the war in return for relatively free access to famine-affected populations outside the war zone. Forced resettlement was another component of the war strategy. This not only was an abuse of human rights by its very nature; it also resettled people where there was no rural infrastructure in terms of health, education, or local governance.[23] When the crisis inevitably affected these areas too, neither local government nor kinship structures were in place for families to fall back on. However one looks at it, while no doubt drought played a factor, the Ethiopia famine of 1984–85 was not just a "natural disaster."

Fifth, and probably most importantly in terms of the humanitarian enterprise, was the massive international response that included actors beside the usual humanitarian agencies and actors. The Ethiopian famine became a cause célèbre worldwide· and led to unprecedented fundraising and awareness-raising by celebrities including, most famously, rock star Bob Geldof, who organized the Band Aid initiative by recording and selling a popular song about the famine[24] and went on to organize the Live Aid concert on 13 July 1985. Watched by a television audience of an estimated 1.5 billion people, Live Aid raised $140 million for both immediate famine relief and later recovery programs. Buerk's famous broadcast from Korem and Geldof's global rock concert both underlined the power of television to humanitarian action. And both brought a new level of awareness of humanitarian crises to global audiences.

But the perception of the famine as an "act of God" meant that politics were kept out of the reporting and the imagery. The "biblical" famine of Buerk's BBC report didn't mention (or record) the Derg's fighter-bombers as they flew overhead northward into Tigray to bomb not only Tigrayan People's Liberation Front (TPLF) targets, but also food markets and population centers; nor did Amin's cameras record the rocket launchers just outside the famine camps of Korem. Challenging the political causes *as well as* responding to humanitarian needs was the purpose for which MSF had been founded and, true to its calling, MSF-France did withdraw from its humanitarian work in Ethiopia in a dispute with the Derg. But the challenge of both speaking truth to power and providing assistance to those who need it arose yet again in 1984–85 and remains one of the unresolved challenges of humanitarian action.

Competing ideologies in an era of televised humanitarian action?

The ideology of famine response had been conditioned by the experience of the Sahelian drought in the 1970s—where the problem had been diagnosed at least to some extent as a failure of development—and the "developmentalist" school of thought reigned supreme among aid agencies by the mid-1980s. Humanitarian response had long been equated with the mythical "give-a-man-a-fish" narrative, but "teach a man to fish" had become the dominant ideology by the mid-1980s. Thus, agencies ignored real evidence of the famine because the aid response that was clearly necessary would put development programming on hold. *Humanitarianism* was about an old-fashioned kind of charity that viewed "beneficiaries" as helpless victims, whereas *development* was about a new kind of partnership in which "participants" took control of their own lives and improved them—"a hand up, not a hand-out" was the slogan of another agency during the era. But of course, if humanitarian action didn't fit the developmentalist ideology, neither did war—especially a predatory war by a state against its own people. Agencies "lived in a dream world from which the famine was a rude awakening."[25]

Hence, in many ways, the story of the Ethiopian famine was about everything and everybody—the politics, the excuses and finger-pointing, the late response, the politicians and rebel movements, the journalists, aid workers and celebrities who all weighed in. Perhaps the only missing "voice" on the famine—its causes and what the appropriate response should have been—was that of the people who suffered its effects.

The Balkans wars: 1991–99

The Bosnian war engraved the term "ethnic cleansing" into the humanitarian lexicon. A brief period of euphoria in international relations followed the fall of the Berlin Wall and the end of the Cold War, but it soon became clear that both the breakup of the former Yugoslavia and the inability of the rest of Europe to effectively prevent it was one of the consequences. Though preceded by important changes that increasingly regionalized Yugoslavia's economy, resurgent Serbian nationalism was widely believed to have led to the breakup of the country. The national army, which by then was a proxy for Serbian forces, moved into Croatia and Slovenia in the summer of 1991. The war quickly ended in Slovenia, resulting in its independence, but continued in Croatia, and by early 1992 had spread to the multi-ethnic region of Bosnia-Herzegovina.

Whole areas were cleared of non-Serb populations and Muslims in particular were forcibly displaced into cordoned-off zones. Large-scale displacement began in northern Bosnia in March of 1992. The provision of humanitarian assistance to the displaced began shortly thereafter. While the war initially pitted Bosnian Serbs against the Muslim majority, eventually fighting broke out involving Bosnia's Croat populations as well. Eventually the fighting displaced some 4 million people—all but a tiny fraction of whom remained in Bosnia, but in areas controlled by their own ethnic group. Even for those not displaced, the war caused extreme hardship, particularly during the harsh Balkans winters. The war lasted until the end of 1995 when, after heavy North Atlantic Treaty Organization (NATO) aerial bombardment, the Bosnian Serb Army suffered significant military setbacks and finally agreed to peace talks.

Several features stand out about the Bosnian war. It was the first actual military combat on the European continent since 1945 and had a significant chilling effect on the optimism that followed the end of the long Cold War. Unlike humanitarian crises elsewhere in the world, reporters and aid workers alike noted "profound similarities" between themselves and the people on whom they were reporting, or who they were meant to be aiding.[26] A resurgent Europe took it upon itself to manage the crisis, but found that there were distinctly different political allegiances and priorities, and ultimately there wasn't much of a coordinated European approach to the problem.

But more fundamentally, European countries agreed that if war—and its humanitarian consequences—was going to recur in Europe, it had to be contained within the former Yugoslavia and preferably within Bosnia itself. Thus the UN refugee agency, UNHCR (United Nations High Commissioner for Refugees), came to lead the humanitarian response to a crisis in which the vast majority of victims had not crossed any international boundary and, thus, were not covered under international refugee law. And indeed while UNCHR's mandate was the protection of the rights of refugees, in Bosnia the primary task was relegated to the provision of assistance. While Bosnia certainly underlined the need for more adequate civilian protection mechanisms in war, few were made available, and those that were available were feeble and misunderstood. So-called "safe areas" were established as designated places in eastern and central Bosnia, but often offered little in the way of real protection.

This reality was forever burned into international humanitarian consciousness when Serb forces massacred an estimated 8,000 Muslim men and boys inside the "safe area" of Srebrenica in 1995, even as the

UN protection force, UNPROFOR, stood helplessly by. UNPROFOR's mandate was to protect humanitarian assistance intended for people affected by the war, not to provide protection for the people themselves—underlining both the impotence of the international community to stop the war and its equal determination to contain the spill-over effects from the war within Bosnia itself. A regional refugee crisis was to be prevented at all costs—containment of the crisis, not its resolution, was the policy objective for several years of the war.[27]

Most observers agree that, even against that background and effectively without existing guidelines for how to deal with such a crisis, UNHCR did a good job in coordinating the humanitarian response. The Sarajevo airlift in particular kept the inhabitants of the city supplied with the minimal necessities of food and non-food items through the long siege. WFP delivered over a million tons of food aid. But in effect, humanitarian assistance was substituted for political action to stop the war in Bosnia.

The Bosnian war caused a deep re-thinking of the humanitarian principles of neutrality and impartiality. The Bosnian government complained bitterly during the war that the international community subjected it to the same arms embargo that it subjected the Serbs, even though the Serb army was re-supplied by Belgrade and was clearly the aggressor. Humanitarians too came to question their commitment to neutrality as either a basic operating principle or a necessary means to the end of maintaining access to affected populations. And UNHCR in effect had to be a passive participant in ethnic cleansing by helping Muslims to escape areas overrun by the Bosnian Serb Army—or else stand by and watch while people were murdered.[28] These realities politicized humanitarian aid workers like no crisis since perhaps Biafra—in the aftermath of the Bosnian war, the delivery of humanitarian aid was increasingly couched in the language of human rights, and humanitarian agencies increasingly devoted resources to advocacy as well as to on-the-ground operations.

The rise of "humanitarian warfare"

The Dayton Peace Accord of 1995 ended the fighting and essentially partitioned Bosnia into ethnic areas. But the breakup of the former Yugoslavia continued for many more years. By the time fighting broke out in the Muslim-dominated Serbian province of Kosovo in 1999, the language of "humanitarian warfare" (military invasion in the name of humanitarian—not military—objectives) was in full flower, and indeed NATO responded quickly and decisively to prevent a situation like

Bosnia from recurring in Kosovo. A short war with an acute refugee crisis ensued, but NATO air power relatively quickly ended that conflict. The Kosovo war not only put "humanitarian warfare" on the map, it also brought out in graphic terms the growing gap between what humanitarian donors were willing to pay for in a conflict in their own back yard (the Balkans) compared to their response to distant and untelevised places: The per capita spending for the response to the Kosovo war was the highest of any crisis on record up to that date. But above all, the Balkans wars highlighted the fact that contemporary humanitarian crises, and thus humanitarian action in crisis, are as much about protection as they are about the provision of material assistance. These wars foreshadowed the extended debate about the obligations of the international community to intervene—with military force if required—to protect civilians in conflict. This debate came together with the doctrine of the "Responsibility to Protect" (R2P) in 2001, and still echoes 20 years later—a theme further explored in Chapters 3, 6, and 7.

The Rwandan genocide and its aftermath: 1994–96

Of all the events that have shaped the contemporary humanitarian enterprise, none had a more powerful impact than the Rwandan genocide of 1994.[29] While one of the proximate causes of the genocide was the failure of peacekeeping and a vacuum of political action, humanitarian action was implicated in its aftermath, and even in its antecedents, in ways that demanded profound changes in organization and implementation.

Volumes have been written on the genocide, the events leading up to it, and the accounts of states, institutions, and individuals caught up in trying either to halt the genocide or to make excuses for their inaction. But the critical impacts on the humanitarian system resulted from both the humanitarian response to the genocide and the refugee crisis that it spawned.

From the time of its independence from Belgium in 1962 until the invasion by the Rwandan Tutsi rebel group the Rwandan Patriotic Front (RPF) from its base Uganda in October 1990, Rwanda had been considered a poster child for development orthodoxy. The country was considered stable, if not very wealthy, and its president, Juvenal Habyarimana, democratic (though he came to power in a coup d'état). Although the Hutu–Tutsi rivalry that partially drove the genocide was clearly evident in the country's history, the pogroms of the late 1950s that drove the Tutsis to Uganda in the first place were forgotten or ignored by the international community, as was the "semi-official racism" in the national political system. The country's economic data was reasonably impressive. Economic growth was constant if modest; child mortality was dropping; and the balance of payments, bolstered significantly by foreign aid, compared favorably to other nations in the region. That a "development success story" (if only a modest one) could descend into the nightmare of ethnic holocaust was simply unbelievable to many who knew the country well. But "development" in this sense was viewed as an entirely apolitical process. The belief by the international community in Rwanda as a success story contributed to a collective disbelief that genocide was actually taking place in 1994, and hence to the virtually non-existent international intervention.[30]

The RPF attacked northern Rwanda in late 1990, and after a brief flurry of activity, the war settled into a relatively low-grade conflict that simmered along for three years through several cease-fire agreements, the last of which in 1993 had international backing and a UN Security Council resolution and peacekeeping force (UNAMIR, the UN Assistance Mission to Rwanda). Generally, Rwanda was thought of as an "easy" case in terms of peacekeeping, in comparison with other conflicts of the time.[31] It is impossible to understand the international response to Rwanda without looking at concurrent crises, most notably Somalia. In the aftermath of the Cold War, the political and security arms of the UN experienced a resurgence as it was called upon to intervene in many crises between 1990 and 1993; the peacekeeping budget had doubled and then doubled again. The UN was having "a pretty good year" until the Somalia debacle (the real debacle for the UN had been the killing of 24 Pakistani peacekeeping troops by forces of the Somali National Alliance, though what most of the world remembers was the downing of two US helicopters and the image of an American corpse being dragged through the streets of Mogadishu).[32] In the aftermath of the Somalia fiasco, the international community—especially the United States—was deeply reluctant to engage in complex internal conflicts.

There were warnings of the potential for catastrophic inter-ethnic violence in Rwanda. The commander of the UN Peacekeeping Force (UNAMIR), Canadian Lieutenant General Romeo Dallaire, indicated as early as January 1994 that he had gathered intelligence indicating plans for Hutu *Interahamwe* militias to engage in the widespread killing of Tutsis—and members of his peacekeeping force—with the knowledge of the Rwandan government. But the information was not taken seriously by leaders in UN headquarters who were reluctant to step up what was supposed to be a relatively straightforward mission.

Violent attacks increased in February and March; then on 6 April, a plane carrying both President Habyarimana and his Burundian counterpart was shot down as it landed at Kigali airport. Hard-line Hutu militants seized power, over-riding the constitutional successor to the presidency—the prime minister—eventually killing her and her family. Ten Belgian peacekeepers assigned to protect the prime minister were also killed, which had the intended effect: Belgium withdrew from the UNAMIR force even as widespread and obvious massacres kicked into high gear. In response, the RPF pulled out of the ceasefire and began a concerted march towards Kigali as the only way to stop the killing of Tutsis. Two weeks later, the UN Security Council further *reduced* UNAMIR's strength.

Over the following three months, an estimated 800,000 Rwandans were killed, mostly Tutsis and any Hutus who were opposed to the killings, mostly with primitive weapons like machetes and mostly at the hands of their neighbors and acquaintances. The national army and the *Interahamwe* militias played a major role in the genocide, but much of it was inciting the masses to join in the killing. The international community debated and dithered, even as bodies literally floated down rivers into other countries and General Dallaire reported increasing numbers of killings inside Rwanda. In May, the Security Council finally agreed to increase UNAMIR's strength. The RPF meanwhile, had stepped up military pressure and by late May had captured Kigali airport. As the extremist government collapsed, the Security Council finally authorized "Operation Turquoise," led by the French, to create a "safe zone" in southern Rwanda. The RPF captured all of Kigali in early July, signaling the end of both the previous government and the genocide. In the following several weeks, some 2 million refugees, primarily of Hutu origin, fled to neighboring Tanzania or Zaire (now the Democratic Republic of Congo) fearing reprisals.[33]

Genocide, a refugee crisis, and humanitarian action

Humanitarian action during the genocide itself was minimal. The ICRC maintained its presence in Rwanda through the crisis, and the UN set up a small humanitarian unit. But the ICRC could only manage limited operations, and the UN effort was tiny in comparison to the scale of the slaughter—and largely powerless to do much about it. Most other agencies left the country when the genocide began in April and only returned in July and August.

The response to the refugee crisis, however, was quite different. Over a million refugees crossed into Zaire, the vast majority of them into the small border town of Goma at the northern end of Lake Kivu. This massive concentration of human beings, without adequate food, water, or sanitation, completely overwhelmed the infrastructure of the town and led almost immediately to a major cholera epidemic that killed an estimated 50,000 people in just over four weeks.[34] In contrast to the inaction of the international community during the genocide itself, donors were quick to respond to the refugee crisis, with UNHCR and some 100 agencies moving into camps in both eastern Zaire and northwestern Tanzania. Supported by a military airlift, the humanitarian operation contained the cholera epidemic and related problems over the ensuing months. But in the general lawlessness of eastern Zaire at the time, there was little to stop the former leaders of the genocide from using the refugee camps to regroup, re-arm, and effectively take control of refugee populations for use as a human shield. When this manipulation became apparent to the humanitarian community, and particularly when it became clear that neither the UN, nor the Zairean government (nor any other authority) was going to intervene, some of the agencies—most notably MSF and the International Rescue Committee (IRC)—pulled their operations out of eastern Zaire, but with little effect on the problem. The combination of idealistic but ill-informed agency staff, the inability of the UN, and the disinterest of the major powers about the role of the ex-Forces Armée Rwandaise (FAR) and the *Interahamwe* militias in the refugee camps led to "calamitous" consequences.[35] These consequences included the use of refugee camps to stage attacks against Rwanda, a mass forcible return of refugees in 1996 at the hands of the Rwandan army, and the extension of the Congolese civil war into a massive, multi-country conflict after Rwanda invaded the country. Civilian death rates were estimated to be higher in that crisis than during the Goma crisis. But whereas the Goma crisis took place in the full glare of the media, subsequent military action failed to attract much attention from either the media or the international community.[36] The overwhelming conclusion was that humanitarian aid had been subverted to support those who had caused the crisis in the first place.

Several conclusions can be drawn for the purposes of this discussion: First, humanitarian assistance, both on a small scale in Rwanda itself during the genocide, but more in neighboring countries—particularly in Goma—in the aftermath was at least partially used by the international community as an alternative to concerted political action.[37] Critics emphatically noted that in the context of genocide, humanitarian assistance by itself cannot contain the suffering, and it does not address the causes. Some observers caution against humanitarianism trying to take on the latter role.[38]

Second, both the international community generally and the humanitarian community in particular failed in their analysis of a given crisis at the point when critical decisions had to be made. Sometimes this stemmed from their refusal—in Rwanda as well as in previous examples—to see the likelihood of a humanitarian crisis when everyone is focused on what is conceived as a "development" problem. And, as happened in Rwanda, external analysis often seems to be more focused on the *last* crisis—its context, its failings, and its consequences—rather than on the details of the *current* crisis. So, many analysts looked at Rwanda and saw a benign but impoverished country but, once the genocide began, saw it as a "second Somalia"—a crisis in which Western public opinion and political interests would not support intervention.

Third, it is often unclear whether the impartiality of humanitarian action—responding to human needs rather than to political imperatives—is distinguishable from impartiality in other kinds of international engagement. Many times in the run-up to the crisis in Rwanda, UNAMIR asked for permission to take pre-emptive action that might have derailed or significantly mitigated the genocide. But it was instructed that its role was to remain "impartial"—which in this case had little to do with treating all parties fairly and had more to do with avoiding the messiness of engaging with local political realities.

Fourth, and probably the most damaging, was the realization that humanitarian action had in fact become the context in which the forces that had carried out the genocide regrouped and re-armed themselves. Humanitarian assistance had addressed some of the human suffering but had caused great harm in the process.

Conclusion: crisis and reform—learning and change as one impact of crisis

Throughout recent humanitarian history, major crises—and large-scale shortcomings in response—have been the cause for significant rethinking and reform of humanitarian policies and processes. The magnitude of the crisis and the size and problems of the response demanded a multi-agency evaluation of the response to the Rwanda genocide and the refugee crisis it spawned. In the aftermath of Rwanda, the Joint Evaluation of Emergency Assistance to Rwanda (JEEAR) was the first in a series of assessments that led to numerous reforms. Published in 1996, it involved five major donors (the Scandinavian countries as well as the United Kingdom and the United States) and resulted in five major studies including historical perspectives on the genocide, early warning and conflict management, humanitarian aid and its effects, post-genocide rebuilding, and a synthesis and principal recommendations.[39] Among the main issues that JEEAR identified, two had direct impacts on humanitarian action: enhancing performance within the humanitarian sector through better standards and self-regulation measures, and improving accountability in humanitarian assistance— particularly accountability to affected groups. The impact of JEEAR on humanitarian action over the ensuing ten years was profound.

Three different initiatives resulted from JEEAR's recommendations: the Sphere Humanitarian Charter and Minimum Standards for Disaster Response (Sphere Projects 2000 and 2004), the Action Learning Network for Accountability and Performance (ALNAP), and the imperative for greater accountability of humanitarians to the populations they serve, which eventually resulted in the Humanitarian Accountability Partnership-International (HAP-I) (see Chapter 6 for details). Although the efforts to work on industry-wide standards that eventually became the Sphere Minimum Standards had actually begun before the genocide, the Goma crisis and JEEAR provided the necessary focus and imperative to develop standards quickly. The Sphere Project was launched in 1997, and the first edition of the Minimum Standards was published in 2000 (and has been updated three times since).

ALNAP was also formed in 1997, hosted by the UK's Overseas Development Institute, to provide a mechanism for the humanitarian community to share knowledge and learning, identify common problems, and develop joint means of addressing these problems. ALNAP publishes key new information its annual *Review of Humanitarian Action* and keeps a major database of evaluation reports. In 2005, ALNAP led in the production of important guidelines on humanitarian protection.[40] ALNAP also initiated and led a major donor-agency evaluation of the global response to the 2004 Asian tsunami.

Although the recommendation for a humanitarian ombudsman was intended to be taken up by the UN, it quickly became apparent that this was not feasible, and organizations began working on an independent ombudsman project—this eventually became the Humanitarian Accountability Project and in 2003 became HAP-I. Its objectives include the following, among others: developing and maintaining principles of accountability to affected populations; supporting the humanitarian community in adhering to these principles; communicating, advocating, and promoting these principles; and reporting on their implementation. Sphere and HAP-I were incorporated into the Core Humanitarian Standard on Quality and Accountability in 2014 (see Chapter 6).

Alongside JEEAR, other initiatives on humanitarian standards and accountability emerged during the same period. Most notable was the International Federation of Red Cross and Red Crescent Societies/ NGO Code of Conduct, which came out in 1994, but which preceded the genocide in terms of its origins and background. Another was Mary Anderson's work on the principles of "do no harm,"[41] outlining how external assistance can sometimes fuel conflict, but if properly managed can also support peace-building. A major and unresolved debate has raged over whether humanitarian action should be subsumed as part of an over-arching political and security framework or, for reasons of principle and humanitarian access, must stand apart.[42]

The process of humanitarian learning and reform neither began nor ended with the Rwanda and Goma crises. Learning about famines and early warning was rooted in the experiences of the 1970s and 80s—and indeed goes back to the Famine Code in nineteenth-century India. Biafra and the Balkans wars forever taught humanitarians that they had to be astute politically as well as be sensitive to human suffering and loss. But the debacle of Goma triggered a series of transformative reforms that have reverberated throughout the twenty-first century. This is the topic of Chapter 3.

Notes

1 This chapter reuses edited segments from the original book, *Shaping the Humanitarian World*, with permission from the authors of that book (Walker and Maxwell).

2 Two US-based humanitarian agencies, American Friends Service Committee and Mennonite Central Committee, both the humanitarian and service organizations of pacifist churches, had programs in Vietnam that were humanitarian in content but that tended to be political statements about the war. Another American NGO with religious roots, Catholic Relief Services, pulled out of Vietnam when radical members of the church denounced CRS for its attempt to be "neutral." USAID had a large "hearts and minds" program in South Vietnam but, again, its objectives were political, not humanitarian, and it was this program that CRS was seen to be a part of. For details, see Scott Flipse, "The Latest Casualty of War: Catholic Relief Services, Humanitarianism, and the War in Vietnam, 1967–1968," *Peace and Change* 27, no. 2 (2002): 245–270.

3 Ian Smillie, "The Emperor's Old Clothes: The Self-Created Siege of Humanitarian Action," in *The Golden Fleece: Manipulation and Independence in Humanitarian Action*, by Antonio Donini, 1st ed. (Sterling, Va.: Kumarian Press, 2012).

4 Dan Jacobs, *The Brutality of Nations* (New York: Knopf, 1987).
5 Alex de Waal, *Famine Crimes: Politics and The Disaster Relief Industry in Africa*, African Issues (London: African Rights & The International African Institute, 1997).
6 The term "famine" and the powerful images it evokes, is a humanitarian case study in itself. Though thoroughly addressed analytically in Sen's work, it remained curiously undefined for decades—in terms of magnitude and severity on the one hand and manifestation on the other. Sen clearly defined famine as a problem of starvation brought about by a failure of consumption, though he recognized manifestations other than mortality by outright starvation. The seminal work of Alex de Waal in the 1980s on destitution and the impact of famine in terms of health rather than simple starvation helped to better understand the manifestations of famine. The popular usage of the term was perhaps most strongly defined for the current generation by the Ethiopian famine of the mid-1980s. Recent work has helped to define famine better in terms of severity and magnitude. See, for example, Paul Howe and Stephen Devereux, "Famine Intensity and Magnitude Scales: A Proposal for an Instrumental Definition of Famine," *Disasters* 28, no. 4 (December 1, 2004): 353–372; and IPC, *Integrated Food Security Phase Classification: Technical Manual Version 2.0. Evidence and Standards for Better Food Security Decisions* (Rome: FAO, 2012), www.ip cinfo.org/fileadmin/user_upload/ipcinfo/docs/IPC-Manual-2-Interactive.pdf.
7 Kent Glenzer, "We Aren't the World: The Institutional Production of Partial Success," in *Une Catastrophe si Naturelle. Niger 2005*, ed. Xavier Crombé and Jean-Hervé Jézéquel (Paris: Médecins sans Frontières, 2007).
8 Centers for Disease Control, "Nutritional Surveillance in West Africa, Summary Nos. 1 and 2, 20 July 1973," in *Disaster in the Desert: Failures of International Relief in the West African Drought*, ed. Hal Sheets and Roger Morris, Humanitarian Policy Studies (Washington, DC: Carnegie Endowment for International Peace, 1974).
9 John Seaman and Julius Holt, "Markets and Famines in the Third World," *Disasters* 4, no. 3 (1980): 283–297.
10 Richard W. Franke and Bárbara H. Chasin, *Seeds of Famine: Ecological Destruction and the Development Dilemma in the West African Sahel* (Allanheld, Osmun, 1980).
11 Stephen Devereux, "Goats before Ploughs: Dilemmas of Household Response Sequencing during Food Shortages," *IDS Bulletin* 24, no. 4 (1993): 52–59.
12 Devereux, "Goats before Ploughs."
13 Amartya Sen, *Poverty and Famines: An Essay on Entitlement and Deprivation*, Repr. with corrections (Oxford; New York: Clarendon Press; Oxford University Press, 1982).
14 Glenzer, "We Aren't the World."
15 Margaret Buchanan-Smith and Susanna Davies, *Famine Early Warning and Response: The Missing Link* (London: Intermediate Technology Publications, 1995).
16 Gorm Rye Olsen, Nils Carstensen, and Kristian Høyen, "Humanitarian Crises: What Determines the Level of Emergency Assistance? Media Coverage, Donor Interests and the Aid Business," *Disasters* 27 no. 2 (2003): 109–126.

17 Glenzer, "We Aren't the World." 124.
18 Michael Buerk, *BBC News*, October 23, 1984. http://news.bbc.co.uk/2/hi/8315248.stm.
19 de Waal, *Famine Crimes.*
20 Human Rights Watch, *Evil Days: Thirty Years of War and Famine in Ethiopia*, Africa Watch Report (New York: Human Rights Watch, 1991).
21 de Waal, *Famine Crimes.*
22 de Waal, *Famine Crimes.*
23 Jason W. Clay, *Politics and the Ethiopian Famine, 1984–1985*, Rev. ed., Cultural Survival Report; 20 (Cambridge, Mass.: Cultural Survival, 1986).
24 The song was titled "Do They Know It's Christmas?" and came out in time to raise funds during the Christmas season. A later similar attempt, "We Are the World," co-written by Michael Jackson and performed by an all-star cast of musicians that called themselves U.S.A. for Africa, tried an approach to raising funds through music in 1985. Both songs raised awareness about the famine as well as a lot of money for famine relief.
25 Tony Vaux, *The Selfish Altruist: Relief Work in Famine and War* (London: Earthscan, 2001).
26 David Rieff, *A Bed for the Night: Humanitarianism in Crisis* (New York: Simon & Schuster, 2002); Vaux, *The Selfish Altruist.*
27 Rieff, *A Bed for the Night*; Vaux, *The Selfish Altruist.*
28 Rieff, *A Bed for the Night.*
29 The *Convention on the Prevention and Punishment of the Crime of Genocide* was adopted in the aftermath of the Holocaust, in 1948, and has been ratified by 149 countries. It specifies genocide as "intent to destroy, in whole or in part, a national, ethnical, racial or religious group" (Article 2). Countries signatory to the Convention are obliged to intervene to prevent or stop genocide when it is occurring.
30 Peter Uvin, *Aiding Violence: The Development Enterprise in Rwanda* (West Hartford, Conn.: Kumarian Press, 1998).
31 Michael N. Barnett, *Eyewitness to a Genocide: The United Nations and Rwanda* (Ithaca, N.Y.; London: Cornell University Press, 2002).
32 Barnett, *Eyewitness to a Genocide.*
33 For more in-depth accounts, see: Philip Gourevitch, *We Wish to Inform You That Tomorrow We Will Be Killed with Our Families: Stories from Rwanda* (New York: Picador USA; Farrar, Straus, and Giroux, 1999); Johan Pottier, *Re-Imagining Rwanda: Conflict, Survival and Disinformation in the Late Twentieth Century*, African Studies Series; 102 (Cambridge; New York: Cambridge University Press, 2002); Samantha Power, *A Problem from Hell: America and the Age of Genocide* (New York: Basic Books, 2002); Roméo Dallaire, *Shake Hands with the Devil: The Failure of Humanity in Rwanda*, 1st Carroll & Graf ed. (New York: Carroll & Graf: Distributed by Publishers Group West, 2004); Kingsley Chiedu Moghalu, *Rwanda's Genocide: The Politics of Global Justice* (New York: Palgrave Macmillan, 2005); Marie Beatrice Umutesi, *Surviving the Slaughter: The Ordeal of a Rwandan Refugee in Zaire* (University of Wisconsin Press, 2004). There are numerous other accounts as well, most by non-Rwandese authors.
34 John Borton, *The Joint Evaluation of Emergency Assistance to Rwanda: Study III Principal Findings and Recommendations* (London: Overseas

Development Institute, 1996), https://odihpn.org/wp-content/uploads/1996/06/networkpaper016.pdf.
35 Rieff, *A Bed for the Night*.
36 Nicholas Stockton, "In Defence of Humanitarianism," *Disasters* 22, no. 4 (December 1998): 352.
37 Borton, *Joint Evaluation of Emergency Assistance to Rwanda*.
38 Rieff, *A Bed for the Night*.
39 Borton, *Joint Evaluation of Emergency Assistance to Rwanda*.
40 Hugo Slim and Andrew Bonwick, *Protection: An ALNAP Guide for Humanitarian Agencies* (London: Overseas Development Institute, 2005).
41 Mary B. Anderson, *Do No Harm: How Aid Can Support Peace or War* (Boulder, Colo.: Lynne Rienner, 1999).
42 Clare Short, "Principles for a New Humanitarianism" (7 April 1998), https://publications.parliament.uk/pa/cm199798/cmselect/cmintdev/711/8042808.htm.; Joanna Macrae and Nicholas Leader, *The Politics of Coherence: Humanitarianism and Foreign Policy in the Post-Cold War Era* (London: Overseas Development Institute (ODI), 2000), https://www.odi.org/publications/283-politics-coherence-humanitarianism-and-foreign-policy-post-cold-war-era.

3 Humanitarian action in the twenty-first century

- **Humanitarianism post-9/11: between "solidarity and governance"**
- **Darfur: counter-insurgency, genocide, and public outcry**
- **The Indian Ocean tsunami: a multi-country crisis**
- **The Haiti earthquake**
- **The Somalia famine of 2011**
- **South Sudan: independence, disunity, and the world's newest nation in crisis**
- **Syria: "world's worst humanitarian crisis"**
- **The logical culmination: the Mediterranean refugee crisis**
- **Conclusion: humanitarian action in the twenty-first century**

By the dawn of the new millennium in 2000, humanitarian action had changed significantly. It had become much more openly political and, largely due to the reforms that grew out of the post-Rwanda effort, much more institutionalized. It had also expanded dramatically in terms of its funding requirements and profile. By the early 2000s, the budgets of single agencies began to rival the entire global expenditure on humanitarian action a mere decade or two earlier. The most openly political of the humanitarian agencies, MSF, was awarded the Nobel Peace Prize in 1999. MSF staunchly protects its independence of action. But in many ways its activist approach was in the ascendance at the close of the millennium, and the more reserved and neutral approach of the Red Cross movement seemed to be in retreat. A recent book on humanitarian economics notes, "The humanitarian aid market is booming: funding for international humanitarian assistance steadily increased over the last three decades. Hundreds of thousands of professionals work in the humanitarian sector, which has today become a pillar of global governance. Yet humanitarianism is in crisis."[1]

This chapter presents a brief synopsis of the complex history of humanitarian action since the turn of the century by examining some of the game-changing crises and the ways in which humanitarian action has adjusted to new realities. These crises include the "global war on terrorism" (particularly the Afghanistan and Iraq wars), the Darfur crisis, the Indian Ocean tsunami, the Haiti earthquake, the 2011 famine in Somalia, the post-independence civil war in South Sudan, the greater Syria crisis, and the Mediterranean refugee/migration crisis.

Humanitarianism post-9/11: between "solidarity and governance"

The attacks of 11 September 2001 changed much of the face of humanitarian action—with the effects felt most immediately in Afghanistan and Iraq. While humanitarians had enjoyed a relatively free hand in crises during the 1990s—often complaining that they were being used as a substitute for serious political engagement to address problems like the Balkans wars—it quickly became apparent in Afghanistan and Iraq that humanitarian action had become part and parcel of political engagement, and frequently on a highly partisan basis.[2]

Within weeks of the attacks, a coalition of Western nations led by the United States was engaged in a "global war on terrorism" (GWOT)—a war that by their own reckoning would know no borders, would be fought in shadowy hinterlands of countries believed to abet international terrorism, and would be an indefinite and perhaps all-consuming effort. In short order, "humanitarian action lost its prominence and human rights concerns were wiped off the UN agenda," in the words of one long-time observer of Afghanistan.[3]

General Colin Powell—the hero of the short and decisive first war against Iraq, fought in the late winter of 1991—had become the secretary of state in the new George W. Bush administration and quickly declared United States-based humanitarian agencies as a non-lethal asset or, in his own words, a "force multiplier" in the fight against terrorism. This notion—that all resources (humanitarian, developmental, and military) should align towards a single strategic goal—quickly became dominant. And humanitarians, particularly those of the more pragmatic and political persuasions, became at once wary of it, but also more drawn into it by the major donor governments.

An endless war in Afghanistan

Humanitarians had been among the few external agencies present in Afghanistan during the Taliban regime, providing limited assistance to conflict-affected populations at the time, but they were not supportive of the repressive policies of that government. Afghanistan had teetered on the edge of failed statehood for decades following the overthrow of its king in the 1970s and the long Soviet siege of the 1980s. At that point, Western interests favored the Islamists as a counter to the Soviets, and some 7 billion dollars were funneled to their coffers by the United States alone in the 1980s.[4] With the Soviet pullout, however, Afghanistan descended into an internal struggle pitting regional war-lords against one another; and lacking the global organizing rubric of the Cold War, the outside world largely left Afghanistan to its own fate. The Taliban, largely believed to have emerged from the refugee *madrassa* education system in Pakistan, first appeared on the Afghan political scene in a significant way in the mid-1990s. With assistance from Pakistan, they slowly extended their control over much of the country, with perhaps their greatest military success coming just two days before the 11 September attack, when they finally managed to assassinate Ahmed Shah Massoud, the popular commander of the "Northern Alliance," the greatest single threat to continued Taliban rule.

But following 11 September, the Taliban clearly were the first target in the crosshairs of the war against terrorism. Within 48 hours of the attack, foreign humanitarian agencies had all pulled out of Afghanistan in anticipation of an invasion by the United States. The overthrow of the Taliban was relatively swift. By mid-November, most cities in northern Afghanistan had come under the control of the anti-Taliban Northern Coalition, provoking a widespread displacement crisis—ousting the Taliban and installing a government friendly to the West completely trumped concerns for human rights.[5]

For humanitarian actors, the invasion of Afghanistan resulted in the loss of independence, effectively "taking sides" in the conflict—a pro-cess that "was not immediately apparent to aid workers but was to ... the remnants of the Taliban."[6] A debate ensued, unresolved to the present, about the wisdom of situational ethics in determining the independence (and/or neutrality) of humanitarian action in the face of GWOT.[7]

The invasion of Iraq in 2003, ostensibly due to the presence of weapons of mass destruction under the control of the Saddam Hussein regime, only increased these divides. The attack on the UN compound in Baghdad in August of that year killed, among many others, the senior and widely respected UN diplomat, Sérgio Vieira de Mello, who was serving as the special representative of the secretary general. This seemed to underline the widespread perception that the international humanitarian community had sided with Western powers, making it suspect, as well as a legitimate target. The UN withdrew from Iraq following the bombing and, with it, the last pretense of independent humanitarian action by the international community.

The wars in both Afghanistan and Iraq saw an increasing direct involvement of military actors in the provision of aid, to the point that humanitarian assistance has become a central tenet in the "hearts and minds" component of current Western counter-insurgency warfare doctrine. This presented both an opportunity and a risk for humanitarians—it has led to vastly bigger budgets for humanitarian work, but the money came at a high risk to the independence and credibility of the agencies that accepted it.[8]

The "Responsibility to Protect"

Just prior to these re-polarizing events, the International Commission on Intervention and State Sovereignty published *The Responsibility to Protect* (R2P).[9] Growing out of the bitter experience of the Balkans and Rwanda, R2P challenged the diplomatic norms that, since the Treaty of Westphalia in the seventeenth century, have been the basis of most formal diplomacy regarding the intervention of the international community in the internal affairs of nation states. Given the rising numbers of internally displaced persons (IDPs) from the wars of the 1990s, and the continued insistence of belligerent states in those wars that internal displacement was none of the business of the international community, a panel of distinguished diplomats and politicians released this influential report. It challenged the long-standing notion that sovereignty trumped human rights in international affairs and insisted instead that where states could not or would not provide adequate safeguards to the human rights of their citizens, the international community was not only authorized to intervene, it was obliged to do so.

The impact of this report on humanitarian action has been mixed. It has served as an organizing principle for international intervention in civil wars and in failed or failing states with some element of success against a background of extremely difficult circumstances—for example the intervention of the UN peacekeeping mission (United Nations Organization Mission in the Democratic Republic of the Congo, or MONUC) in eastern Democratic Republic of the Congo.[10] At the same time, it was used as one justification for the invasion of Iraq by the Bush administration in 2003. Meanwhile, it never provided adequate grounds for an international force to intervene in the long-running war in Darfur with enough teeth to prevent the killing, rape, and displacement of civilians caught in that conflict. And much later, it was invoked to intervene in Libya to protect civilians in the war that brought down the Gaddafi regime, but without any strategy for what would follow a military intervention. Nevertheless, in contrast to the polarizing influences of the GWOT, the notion of R2P has protected some space for international collective action in defense of the rights of abused individuals and groups.

A major study published in 2006 offered insights into four major issues facing the humanitarian community early in the twenty-first century: the *universality* of humanitarianism, the implications of *terrorism and counter-terrorism* for humanitarian action, the search for *coherence* between humanitarian and political agendas, and the *security* of both humanitarian workers and the populations they seek to serve.[11] The study demonstrates fundamentally that "action aimed at alleviating the suffering of the world's most vulnerable has been for the most part incorporated into a northern political and security agenda."[12] With regard to universality, actually humanitarian action was shown to be perceived largely as the action of Northern and Western agencies, motivated by something other than human need. Terrorism and the GWOT doubtlessly create the need for more humanitarian action, but humanitarians struggled to become adept at navigating the politically charged waters of the GWOT or to advocate policies in the context of GWOT that do not undermine civilian human rights. And in many cases, where notions of R2P were invoked, it was hard to tell whether the motivation was really the protection of human rights or counter-terrorism in disguise.

Darfur: counter-insurgency, genocide, and public outcry

Long ignored by both the central government in Khartoum and the rest of the world, the Sudanese region of Darfur suddenly sprang to public attention in 2003 and 2004 when word began to slip out of a nasty war going on that ostensibly pitted pro-government "Arab" forces against an "African" population from which several insurgent groups had sprung. In fact, the identities and political loyalties of both (all) sides in the conflict were more complex. In the same manner that the famines of the mid-1980s forced humanitarian crises into the public spotlight, the Darfur crisis brought attention to war crimes and demands for public accountability for man-made crises in a way that even the crimes in the Balkans wars or the genocide in Rwanda did not. And it raised public awareness about civilian populations caught in conflict in a manner that perhaps had not been seen since Biafra more than a generation earlier. But while the public perceived the Darfur crisis as a clear-cut, "good guy/bad guy" conflict, the situation on the ground for humanitarian agencies and actors was considerably more complex.

Darfur occupies a huge geographic area in the far west of Sudan. Though part of the historical "north" of Sudan, it was long a political backwater and indeed one of the most neglected parts of Sudan. While almost all of the population is Muslim, Darfur was left out when it came to development budgets, roads, and infrastructure, or access to social services—remaining on the extreme periphery of Sudan through most of the twentieth century. It had briefly come to light as the site of one of the major famines in the mid-1980s,[13] but received far less attention than the more publicized famine in Ethiopia at the same time.

From about 2002 onwards, the Sudanese civil war in the south was grinding to a military stalemate, and negotiations were ending that war. As talks progressed, it became clear that a new political dispensation for Sudan was being hammered out and that only two parties were at the table: the National Congress Party, which controlled the central government in Khartoum and the Sudanese People's Liberation Army (SPLA), which had spearheaded the rebellion in the south. This suddenly focused attention in the other "peripheral" areas of Sudan, mostly in the historic "north." In early 2003, two armed resistance groups in Darfur—the Sudanese Liberation Movement/Army (SLM/A), which had some historical links to the SPLA, and the Justice and Equality Movement (JEM), which had links with Sudanese Islamist parties—successfully launched strategic attacks against the Khartoum government to register their grievances and stake a claim in any talks about the future of Sudan. The most audacious attack struck the Sudanese Air Force in April 2003 at the airport at El Fasher, the regional capital of Darfur.

This caught the government of Sudan off guard and raised the profile of the conflict. Khartoum responded with the tried and tested tactic of mobilizing disgruntled groups to join armed militia, which came to be called *janjaweed*, not so much to fight against the rebel groups themselves but to attack the civilian populations from whom the rebel groups emerged (mostly of Fur, Masalit, and Zaghawa origins). These groups were brutally attacked, their villages were burned or looted, and large parts of the population were forced out of their home areas into displaced camps or into refuge in Chad. For all these reasons, the Darfur conflict has been described as "first and foremost a human rights crisis."[14]

Impacts of the conflict

The worst of the killing and violence took place in 2003 and early 2004. Until about May 2004, Darfur remained off limits to foreigners, including humanitarian groups—despite strong protests from the UN and other bodies. By the time humanitarian organizations were allowed access, the worst of the counter-insurgency—the greatest part of the killing and displacement—was already accomplished. The conflict destroyed the social and economic fabric of Darfur: Farmers were displaced, rural markets were destroyed, and livestock were stolen or killed, all of which disrupted Darfur's agriculturally based economy. Even for groups not displaced by the fighting, livelihood systems were undermined and wealthier households suffered.[15]

The international response

The international humanitarian response picked up rapidly in 2004 and 2005. Given the geographic vastness of Darfur, much of the early response was provided by mobile teams, moving from one IDP area to another. It was mostly food assistance for people displaced from their usual residences and livelihoods and hence from their usual sources of food.

But the extent to which the population was traumatized—and perhaps required a qualitatively different kind of response—was evident to humanitarians on the ground. The Darfur crisis put the programmatic issue of protection—that is, keeping civilians safe in the context of violent conflict—on the humanitarian agenda in a way that no previous crisis had.

The extent of the brutality in Darfur caught the public's attention, particularly in Europe and North America. The Save Darfur Coalition was formed in Washington, DC, in July 2004—almost before humanitarian agencies had access to populations on the ground—and eventually came to represent a group of more than 180 human rights, religious, and political organizations with a full-time staff of 30 people at its peak in 2006.[16] The coalition initially set about to raise public awareness and later sought to press for putting UN peacekeeping troops in Darfur, to bring genocide charges against the regime in Khartoum, and to pressure US and European businesses to divest from Sudan.

This put humanitarian agencies on the ground in an uncomfortable—in many ways untenable—situation. On the one hand, the public pressure to hold the government of Sudan and other parties accountable for their actions created an imperative to stop the violence. On the other hand, agencies on the ground speaking out publicly about abuses were at risk of having their operations curtailed, or even being thrown out of the country, rendering the affected populations even more vulnerable. From their arrival in 2004 to mid-2006, humanitarian agencies had relatively unfettered access to IDP populations, but agencies in the field were also to some degree self-censoring in terms of what they said about the causes of the humanitarian emergency. This made for sometimes-furious in-house debates between field staff (trying to protect their access to affected populations on the ground) and headquarters staff (eager to lead on the advocacy in donor capitals and at the UN).

The Save Darfur Coalition held numerous public events, culminating in a "Rally to Stop Genocide" at the US Capitol in April 2006 attended by high-profile politicians (then-Senator Barack Obama) and celebrities (famously epitomized by George Clooney). The public pressure did have some impact. US Secretary of State General Colin Powell declared the situation in Darfur to be genocide in September 2004. But no other major power did; nor did the UN Security Council. And indeed the United States took no direct action, as a strict interpretation of the Genocide Convention would have required. But all condemned Khartoum's actions in Darfur as crimes against humanity.

In 2006, the African Union mediated the Darfur Peace Agreement (DPA) but, in the end, only Khartoum and one splinter group of the SLA signed it; the main faction of the SLA and the JEM both decided it did not meet enough of their demands. The response in the field was a hardening of positions on all sides and, increasingly, a splintered opposition as Khartoum tried to pick off individual rebel field commanders and make separate deals with them.[17] Khartoum had balked at a UN peacekeeping force in Darfur but had allowed a minimal African Union observer force—ostensibly to monitor a ceasefire. Eventually the African Union and the UN force—under the combined UN/Africa Mission to Darfur, or UNAMID—was allowed to take position in Darfur. But its size and capability was never equal to the task of preventing violence against civilians in an area as vast as Darfur. After the DPA, more localized conflicts emerged which, combined with the splintering of rebel movements, made negotiated access to affected groups ever more difficult.[18]

From "acute" to "frozen" crisis

The number of people affected changed relatively little between 2005 and 2009, as the conflict shifted from all out counter-insurgency operations to more-sporadic and strategic attacks. Estimates of the number of people killed—either from direct violent causes or from malnutrition and disease—varied, but one credible source estimated the excess mortality to be 134,000 in the acute phase of the crisis (2003–05). Some 2.7 million were displaced and more than a quarter of a million were forced to flee to Chad.[19] The extreme level of killing and displacement witnessed in 2003–04 declined, and the large-scale humanitarian operation that began in 2004 brought the extreme levels of malnutrition and associated mortality under control, with the prevalence of malnutrition down substantially by 2006–07—particularly in the displaced camps.

But after the collapse of DPA and the subsequent splintering of the rebel movements, access became more difficult and the conflict essentially became "frozen". In 2009, the UNAMID commander declared that the war was over, and much of the response effort turned to "early recovery". But critics noted that while the level of killing and new displacement had declined, the conflict—and the issues underpinning it—was far from resolved. Millions of people remained displaced, and the emphasis on "early recovery" was either Khartoum's propaganda or posturing by development agencies to cash in on the money still pouring into the response in Darfur.[20]

Investigations of war crimes continued. In July 2008, the International Criminal Court indicted Sudanese President Omar al-Bashir for crimes against humanity and, in March 2009, issued a warrant for his arrest. The response from Khartoum was swift: Ten international agencies were expelled from Darfur—on suspicion of their involvement in the politics behind the indictment and arrest warrant—and an additional three Sudanese agencies were closed down. This was announced as the "Sudanization" of the response—a strategy that only partly succeeded in terms of who was on the ground (many of the international agencies eventually negotiated their return, sometimes in a slightly different configuration), but it was very successful in cowing the agencies into being more circumspect about their advocacy.

Writing in 2011, a long-time Darfur analyst noted that the protracted humanitarian crisis in Darfur had "no end in sight, and despite a massive international humanitarian presence in the region there remained serious unmet humanitarian needs."[21] Seven years later, the situation remained much the same: Bashir was still in power and still under indictment, but had successfully demonstrated that he could travel abroad (at least within Africa) with impunity; most of the people who had been displaced remained displaced; and Darfur was rarely in the news, much less the focus of intense international advocacy as it had once been. The crisis remained, but the world had moved on.

The Indian Ocean tsunami: a multi-country crisis

At 7:58 local time on 26 December 2004, a massive earthquake, registering 9.1 on the Richter scale, struck off the northwestern coast of the Indonesian island of Aceh. The earthquake itself caused significant damage, but within minutes, a tsunami triggered by the tectonic shift crashed into nearby coastlines, completely submerging entire neighborhoods and reaching as far inland as 3 kilometers, depending on local terrain. The city of Banda Aceh, the large-scale human settlement nearest to the epicenter of the earthquake, was destroyed within minutes, with almost no warning and little time to react to the earthquake tremors. Tsunami waves quickly reached the shores of Thailand and the Andaman Islands and eventually affected fourteen countries, with the hardest hit being Indonesia, Thailand, India, Sri Lanka, and the Maldive islands.[22]

Tectonic shocks such as earthquakes and tsunamis are very specific kinds of disasters: They may hit with little warning, and the damage to physical infrastructure is almost instantaneous. Although the affected countries farther from the epicenter of the 26 December earthquake had a bit of warning about the tsunami, few were prepared for a shock of this magnitude. Coastlines were destroyed. Ultimately, an estimated 227,000 people were killed, with an additional 1.4 million displaced, although initial estimates and some subsequent updates suggested a much higher number.[23] The waves generated by the tsunami were estimated to be 65–100 feet high in some places. The total damage caused by the tsunami was conservatively estimated at $10 billion. The knock-on effects were equally damaging if not as instantaneous or dramatic. Much of the artisanal fishing fleet of eastern Sri Lanka was destroyed, along with an estimated 400,000 livelihoods.[24] Infrastructure, trade, and livelihoods were damaged or destroyed along thousands of kilometers of affected coastline. The Maldives suffered damage and economic losses equivalent to 80 percent of its gross domestic product (GDP).[25]

A massive response

For a variety of reasons, the tsunami disaster drew unprecedented public attention, and the response drew unparalleled public donations. The final estimate of funds raised for the response and post-tsunami reconstruction was $13.5 billion—35 percent *more* than the estimated damage. Though this funding could do little to comfort those who had lost whole families in the disaster, it was unprecedented in the annals of humanitarian response. Several factors account for this. First, the disaster struck on the day after Christmas, at a time when millions were at home and watching television—and in a season when at least the Christian world was supposed to be thinking charitably. Second, TV crews didn't take long to reach the scene and indeed even captured the enormity of the waves live in some instances—particularly along the southwest coast of Thailand. Third, Thailand in particular was a popular vacation spot at Christmas time for Europeans, and some 2,400 foreigners (mostly tourists) from northern Europe were killed.[26] This likewise triggered massive voluntary contributions from Western nations. Finally, unlike so many other humanitarian disasters of the era, this one was not triggered by conflict or politics—there were no "bad guys" to blame, just a sense of innocent victims caught in a disaster of unfathomable proportions (though evidence clearly showed that social factors—poverty, gender, environmental conditions—did determine to some extent who was killed).

The tsunami disaster highlighted a number of unique factors in the response. The first was simply the level of individual voluntary contributions. National government and donor countries responded as well, of course, but the number of ordinary people who voluntarily donated to the tsunami response was unique, and in many ways overwhelmed the capacity of agencies. An estimated 41 percent of the funds (roughly $5.5 billion) came from private voluntary donations. At the time, many other populations had urgent humanitarian needs as well—the Darfur crisis in particular, was badly under-funded—but most of the voluntary contributions to the tsunami response were earmarked as such, raising uncomfortable questions for aid agencies about who was and who wasn't considered "worthy" of response.

The second was the large-scale engagement of local and international militaries. Massive logistical capacity was needed almost instantaneously for search and rescue purposes, for providing assistance across enormous areas, and ultimately for reconstruction. Aid agencies arrived quickly, but alone did not have the needed lift capacity, and multiple military actors quickly engaged.

Third, given the circumstances, local actors were of critical importance. With the exception of Thailand, local authorities were not adequately prepared for a disaster of this magnitude. Local actors carried out much of the search-and-rescue activity—some were professional and trained for such a mission; most were not. Local medical staff improvised to meet the demands of such a massive disaster. Unfortunately among the findings of one post-tsunami evaluation was that international actors tended to undermine the efforts of locals. It noted,

"The volume of funds donated to humanitarian agencies enabled them to deploy resources and staff quickly, but it also placed pressure on aid actors—agencies, donors and governments—to be seen to be doing something ... leading to projects not based on assessments, to poor coordination and ... unhealthy competition."[27]

A fourth factor was the effect of the tsunami disaster on local conflict. A long-running, but little-known insurgency for autonomy in Aceh was actually peacefully resolved in the aftermath of the disaster. However, in Sri Lanka, despite a temporary ceasefire between the government and the Tamil Tigers, a dispute over the way in which reconstruction aid was distributed sparked renewed conflict, with a very nasty fight to the bitter end four years later, amid accusations of widespread human rights violations against civilians in the north of the country.

A fifth factor was that with so many actors—international and local; government, non-government, and UN; military and civilian—coordination was a major challenge. Indeed the post-tsunami self-reflection process within the humanitarian community led to a series of major reforms related to both funding and coordination.

And finally, the massive amounts of cash donated to the response—combined with the fact that while the tsunami devastated infrastructure in its path, markets and production facilities nearby were mostly unaffected—meant that for the first time, cash-transfer programs were possible on a large scale. Indeed, while cash transfers had been around for some time as an idea, the tsunami represented an initial "tipping point" in the transformation of humanitarian response away from material assistance and towards market-based programming.

Triggering system-side reforms

The evaluation of the response to the tsunami reached important conclusions, many of which led directly to system-side reforms.[28] First, the "relief" response was effective in providing for the immediate survival needs of the population, but was not based on evidence and was not particularly well coordinated—meaning that some sectors (for example, emergency medical care) were over-resourced while others (water and sanitation) were under-served. Second, the funding response was unprecedented, in terms of both the total and the proportion from private donations. This allowed innovative programming, but highlighted coordination problems and seriously challenged the principle of impartiality—not within the tsunami response, but in comparison to other crises at the time and since. Third, local capacity for response was key to saving lives but was badly underestimated by the international community. International agencies did not engage adequately with local civil society and in some cases directly undermined their efforts. Fourth (and ironically given the undermining of local initiative), the capacity of the international humanitarian system was shown to be limited. Even with massive funding, it was difficult to scale up rapidly. Fifth, international agencies focused too much on "brand promotion" and not enough on getting to grips with the task at hand. This raised serious questions about accountability. And finally, the recovery phase proved a far bigger challenge than the immediate disaster-relief phase. Many agencies were not adequately prepared for the complexity of post-disaster recovery in a crisis of this magnitude.[29]

In response, the Inter-Agency Standing Committee for Humanitarian Response (IASC) initiated a humanitarian reform process after the tsunami that addressed these key findings and instituted some of the architectural models that define the way humanitarian response is coordinated today (see Chapter 5 for more on the IASC). They first established the Central Emergency Response Fund (CERF), a multi-donor pooled fund at the country level, to enable more timely and flexible financing. The reforms also strengthened the position of the "humanitarian coordinator," enabling greater leadership and coordination. Finally, the 2005 reforms set up the contemporary "cluster system" on a sectoral basis to ensure adequate response capacity and coordination (see Chapter 5).

The Haiti earthquake

Just five years after the tsunami, another major earthquake struck just to the south and west of Haiti's capital city, Port-au-Prince, on 12 January 2010. At 7.0 on the Richter scale, it was a hundred times less powerful than the earthquake that caused the tsunami. However, its proximity to a major city, combined with the endemic poverty and poorly enforced building codes of the Western hemisphere's poorest country, caused an enormous humanitarian disaster. Although Haiti was no stranger to natural hazards—suffering hurricane and flood damage on a frequent basis—some time had passed since it had experienced an earthquake, and no preparedness plans were in effect.[30] In proportional terms, the damage to Haiti was worse than the tsunami damage was to any single country it affected.

Nearly a third of Haiti's population of 9.5 million lived in Port-au-Prince and its environs, so a major proportion of Haiti's population was affected. The Haitian government ultimately estimated the death toll at 316,000, with nearly that many more injured by collapsing buildings, and as many as a million displaced. At the epicenter, 80–90 percent of structures were damaged or destroyed, including more than 300,000 homes, creating an enormous crisis of adequate shelter. But the damage was also systemic and widespread: Infrastructure (critically port and airport facilities) was damaged or destroyed; telecommunications links went down; 80 percent of schools and 50 percent of hospitals were damaged. Government ministries and the presidential palace in Port-au-Prince were damaged and unusable. Overall economic damage was estimated at \$7–14 billion—equivalent to 100–200 percent of Haiti's GDP.[31]

Another large-scale international response

Given the extent of the damage and the limited or destroyed capacity of the government to respond, the international response was rapid, but bringing in necessary supplies was severely impeded by damage to the airport and port facilities. The US military took control of the airport and other facilities and tried to introduce military style coordination among the myriad responders to the crisis—although officially the response (including the military response) was coordinated by the US Agency for International Development (USAID). The Haitian government eventually faced criticism from various quarters for its ineffectual response and for effectively ceding national sovereignty to external actors in the aftermath of the crisis.

More traditional humanitarian agencies—some of whom had already been operating in Haiti prior to the earthquake—took on some of the roles needed, particularly the emergency medical care for people injured by collapsing buildings. But the logistical tasks of getting infrastructure up and running, clearing rubble, and addressing the massive shortage of temporary—and eventually permanent—shelter overwhelmed the capacity of the traditional humanitarian agencies, too. Haiti had already been dubbed an "NGO Nation"[32] given the number of small, mostly US-based, organizations (many of them faith-based) operating there. Many more showed up in the aftermath of the earthquake, bringing considerable good will, but not much in the way of experience and sometimes adding to an already high level of confusion.

The overload of agencies combined with the infrastructural hurdles, led to massive coordination problems. The military tried its approach. The UN-led system relied on the Office for the Coordination of

Humanitarian Affairs (OCHA) but OCHA experienced many complaints about the language in which coordination meetings took place and even the restricted access to such meetings. All this meant that local, Haitian organizations, although heavily involved at the local level, were largely left out of efforts to coordinate the response. Many local organizations played crucial roles in addressing the shelter shortfall, but had to improvise and literally scrounge through damaged infrastructure to find the needed materials. Post-disaster evaluation faulted the international system for both ignoring the capacity of Haitian civil society and for largely excluding Haitian agencies from the efforts to coordinate the response.[33]

The urban nature of disaster

The Haiti earthquake was the first of many humanitarian crises of the early twenty-first century that took place in a largely urban environment, making for additional challenges. Not only was the affected population more densely packed into the affected area, but the damage to infrastructure, and especially the environment of mostly collapsed or damaged buildings, contributed to the problems and made the response more difficult. Information gathering was difficult, accurate maps were scarce, and much of the assessment of the crisis was done on a less rigorous "convenience sampling" basis.[34]

On the other hand, the earthquake also saw remarkable innovation in the use of information technology—first in the immediate acute phase of operations when cellphone and social networking technology was used to identify and track down people trapped in collapsed buildings. This information was mapped and relayed to search and rescue teams on the ground, who used real-time crisis mapping technology to locate people, and in many cases extract them from damaged buildings.[35]

Ultimately, the reconstruction phase proved even more difficult than the emergency response to find the dead and rescue the injured or the massive shelter crisis. What the Inter-American Development Bank labeled as the "most destructive event" any country has experienced in modern times—in terms of lives lost or in proportional economic terms—set Haiti's economic development back years, despite the massive inflow of post-disaster funding. Haiti remains vulnerable to natural hazards, suffering both major hurricane damage and an el Niño-related drought in 2016. Cholera was inadvertently introduced to the country by UN peacekeeping troops responding to the earthquake—adding a disaster on top of a disaster. The proliferation of response by international NGOs continues despite the "once in a century" opportunity to identify and bolster local capacity.[36] Haiti is still the least developed nation in the Western hemisphere.

Reform redux?

Substantial reforms to the humanitarian system also resulted—at least partially—from the Haiti response. In 2011, the IASC introduced the "Transformative Agenda," building on the 2005 reforms. This time, the emphasis was on greater predictability, accountability, responsibility, and partnership. In particular the Transformative Agenda aimed for strengthened leadership, improved strategic planning and needs assessments, better information management, improved planning and monitoring and evaluation. It also called for improvements in cluster coordination, more participatory approaches, and strengthened accountability to affected communities.[37]

The theme of learning in response to crises—and from the less-than-expected outcomes from the response—continued to be part and parcel of humanitarian reform.

The Somalia famine of 2011

Somalia in 2011 saw the first instance of actual famine in nearly a decade, and by far the worst famine of the twenty-first century, killing some 258,000 people.[38] The crisis was triggered by a drought and production failures across the Greater Horn of Africa but was also underpinned by a market failure: Somalia is an import-dependent country even in good agricultural years; 2010–11 was a bad year for production that coincided with a dramatic spike in the price of basic food grains on global markets. This drastically reduced people's ability to purchase food at a time when they had to depend on markets for access to food.

But the famine was also the result of the lack of prevention by the fledgling Somali Transitional Federal Government (TFG) or rapid response by the international humanitarian community. An Islamist group known as Al-Shabaab, which had been proscribed as a "terrorist" group, controlled much of South Central Somalia and was at war with the TFG. Counter-terrorism sanctions by donor governments overshadowed humanitarian concerns—meaning that both access and funding were extremely constrained—until an outright famine was declared. A response was quickly mounted, but it was too late to save the lives of hundreds of thousands of Somalis who had already been killed by the famine.

Early warning, late response ... again

The UN declared the famine on 20 July 2011—the first time in history that a famine had been declared in real time using a widely accepted set of technical criteria and based on real-time evidence.[39] The crisis was underpinned by long-term environmental degradation, an underlying crisis of livelihoods in Somalia, and the absence of a functioning central state since the collapse of the Siad Barre regime in 1991. In addition, the World Food Programme (WFP) and other major food aid actors like CARE International had been forced to evacuate from the affected area because of threats from Al-Shabaab. This, combined with the counter-terrorism restrictions, further complicated the situation.

The drought and the food price crisis were predicted by early warning agencies, but little action was taken to prevent or mitigate the crisis. It was only *after* the famine was declared that a proportionately scaled international response began.[40] Early warning, conducted by the Somalia Food Security and Nutrition Analysis Unit (FSNAU) and the Famine Early Warning Systems Network (FEWSNET) issued some 16 special bulletins or other early warning notices up to the time of the declaration of famine.[41] As noted in Chapter 2, the "early warning/late response" phenomenon has been observed over the years.[42] In Somalia in 2011, the main reason was that Al-Shabaab controlled most of the affected areas, and their policies—as well as those of the major donors—restricted the ability of humanitarian agencies to access affected populations. The same drought and food price crisis affected the rest of the Greater Horn of Africa—especially Kenya and Ethiopia—but no famine developed in either of those countries.

Multiple actors

The epicenter of the famine was the riverine and inter-riverine areas of South Central Somalia—primarily Bay, Bakool, and Lower and Middle Shabelle regions. These included the biggest populations of people displaced by the drought and the war. They were also some of the more marginalized clans in Somalia, including the Rahanweyn and Somali Bantu groups. These groups were also the worst affected by the 1991–92 famine.[43] In the Somalia context, social networks play a critical role. For the most part these reflect kin- or clan-based relationships although they can also include friends and neighbors. They are both local and distant, where family members may be in far-away towns and areas within Somalia or much farther away, in neighboring or distant countries. Those who have such connections to town or to the diaspora are possibly much better off than those who do not. Social networks are always important, but having networks *beyond* the immediate (drought- or conflict-vulnerable) context provided an opportunity for support from friends or relatives not facing the same problems.[44] During the crisis, the Somali diaspora was mobilized beyond clan-defined boundaries, particularly after the media images of the famine were broadcast around the world. However, while social networks were critical in protecting people during the famine, the most vulnerable groups were those whose diaspora and domestic social networks were the least well developed, which also explains why the Rahanweyn and Bantu were the worst affected.[45]

The famine saw an increased role of non-Western humanitarian actors. Many of these had been working in Somalia for a long time before the famine, albeit not necessarily in a humanitarian role. These "new" actors included Turkey, Saudi Arabia, and other Gulf states. They also included these countries' various charitable and humanitarian organizations such as the Red Crescent Societies, many of which are major actors in their home countries, as well as Islamic charities and NGOs. Together, these actors pledged one-third of the money for the humanitarian response in 2011. Collectively, many of these agencies sought to operate under the coordinating mechanism of the Organization for Islamic Cooperation (OIC).

Taking innovative programmatic responses to scale

Several programming responses, while not necessarily new, garnered increased attention during the famine—particularly remote management and cash-transfer or market-based programming. Remote management began as a way to maintain a programming presence in highly insecure areas.[46] Humanitarian staff—particularly senior management—had been withdrawing from Somalia since the 1990s, and their absence had reached extreme levels by the time of the famine. Virtually all the implementation was done by local organizations. Not only was physical distance increasing between humanitarian decision-makers and the affected communities. Psychological and emotional remoteness was growing—distinctly reducing the sense of solidarity that had captured the humanitarian spirit in an earlier age.[47] Remote management increased the risk of diversion. And it made adherence to some humanitarian principles more difficult, given the clan linkages to (or even clan control over) the local organizations outsourced to carry out activities. So while remote management did facilitate the provision of aid, it also posed serious threats to the principle of impartiality.

In the absence of a food aid response, the remaining options were for cash transfers or some kind of food voucher program that worked directly with traders. But, while cash transfers were not new in Somalia, nothing had been tried at the scale required. There were several risks. The first was the risk of diversion—no greater for cash than for in-kind food aid—in fact many argued that the risk was substantially lower.[48] The other risk was of even greater food price inflation. Standard analysis showed that it could make populations more vulnerable, not less.[49] But, there were no options on the table in 2011 that presented humanitarian decision-makers with no risks.

Cash transfer programs quickly reached approximately 1.5 million famine-affected people in South Central Somalia and constituted the biggest cash transfer initiative in a single country in history up to that time. The response to the famine was probably the largest market-based response to a crisis of this magnitude in a single country up to that time. Several features of Somalia facilitated this. First, a nation-wide network of money-transfer companies, known as *hawala*, was already functioning and did the actual transfers. Second, the cellphone network functions well; without it the *hawala* system would not have run as well. Third, Somali traders have long been able to negotiate their way across battle lines so the markets were able to respond to increased demand.

Finally, the aftermath of the famine saw the rise of the "resilience agenda." Cycles of crisis and recovery have been the norm in the Greater Horn of Africa for as long as humans have inhabited the region. But governments, donors, and affected communities have all noted that recovery time between crises lengthens after each successive crisis, the time between crises is growing shorter, and in some cases, whole regions of a country seem to be in almost perpetual crisis. Combined with the repeated problems of slow response to early warning and limited investment in prevention and risk reduction, it was clear by the time of the famine that a different approach was needed.[50] In the aftermath of the famine, various stakeholders called for building the resilience of communities regularly affected by crisis. Similar to earlier efforts to reduce vulnerability, resilience purports to hold the key for overcoming the cycle of recurrent crises and humanitarian response.[51] The discourse on resilience has dominated much of the post-famine era not only in Somalia but also in most of the Greater Horn of Africa and the Sahel. All the major donor agencies now have resilience strategies under implementation.[52]

Other key game changers in humanitarian action emerged from the Somalia famine. Given that a number of contemporary humanitarian emergencies occur in contexts where armed non-state actors (whether officially labeled "terrorist" or not) control both geography and human populations, the Somalia famine of 2011 offers valuable lessons about balancing the security concern with the humanitarian imperative. It also offers lessons about the link between early warning and prevention/ response; about how crisis-affected people cope in the absence of external humanitarian assistance; about the emergence of "remote management"; and about the emergence on the global scene of humanitarian organizations that arise from non-Western sources, including Islamic donors and agencies.

South Sudan: independence, disunity, and the world's newest nation in crisis

On 9 July 2011, South Sudan became the world's newest country. Southern Sudan (as it was called before independence) had been in two different wars with the North for five decades before the Comprehensive Peace Agreement (CPA) was signed in 2005—bringing the long civil war to an end. During the first war (1955–72) nearly half a million people lost their lives in the South, but external humanitarian involvement was limited. The second war (1983–2005) was precipitated by the declaration of Sharia law nation-wide, but a variety of grievances underpinned the renewed rebellion. The Sudan People's Liberation Movement/Army (SPLM/A) led the renewed rebellion against the North, and though it had Marxist leanings (and received early support from the Soviet-backed regime in Addis Ababa), the SPLA eventually became a cause célèbre in the West, especially after an Islamist regime seized power in Khartoum in 1989. The war caught the attention of the international community around the time (1988–89) that it led to a massive famine in the South. That, in turn, prompted the founding of Operation Lifeline Sudan (OLS), which subsequently managed most of the humanitarian effort in Sudan throughout the rest of the war.

OLS was a humanitarian cause célèbre itself, but over time it became very controversial, with accusations that it instrumentalized humanitarian aid, relieved the warring parties of their humanitarian obligations, led to aid dependency, amounted to "programmatic expression of the acceptance of continuing violence"[53]—or that it was a thinly veiled means of legitimizing an armed non-state group's claim to sovereignty.[54] Nevertheless, the OLS was credited with saving the lives of millions of Southern Sudanese during nearly two decades of conflict. It became something of a model for UN intervention in conflict zones—for much of the Cold War era, humanitarian efforts had been limited to refugee populations that had successfully fled conflicts.[55]

After the CPA was signed, a six-year transition period ensued culminating in a referendum on independence, which won an overwhelming majority of support in the South. The long-time charismatic leader of the SPLM/A, John Garang, had been killed in a helicopter accident shortly after the CPA was signed, and leadership of the movement, and ultimately the new country, fell to his deputy, Salva Kiir. But deep differences remained within the ruling party that traced back to an internal split—aided and abetted by Khartoum—in the movement in the early 1990s. That split led to "Emma's war" between factions headed by Garang on one hand and Riek Machar on the other. Machar signed a separate peace deal with Khartoum, and was in the Khartoum government for a period in the 1990s, before eventually returning to the SPLM fold.

Independence

Independence saw Kiir become president of the new nation and Machar the vice president. But numerous other factions existed in South Sudan that were heavily armed and not necessarily loyal to the new nation. The SPLM leadership set about to entice these factions into the "big tent" of the movement by buying off the leadership, incorporating rank and file militia members into the SPLA in intact units, giving everyone a salary raise, and paying for it all with the newfound oil wealth.[56] Oil wealth had been—to some extent—a cause of the conflict with the North stretching back to the 1980s. However, the manner of the integration of militias into the SPLA meant not only that the massive expansion of the army after independence had been achieved, but also that the SPLA was not under unified command. On 15 December 2013—during a political showdown among the deeply divided rulers of the country—units of the army were sent to disarm part of the so-called Tiger Battalion, which was part of the Presidential Guard (i.e., outside the SPLA command structure).

The ensuing shoot-out provoked a violent reaction that quickly spread across Juba and took on an ethnic dimension. The vice president and his entourage fled to Jonglei state and formed the SPLM-In Opposition (SPLM-IO, often just referred to as "IO"). This group initially comprised disaffected SLPA leaders—many, but not all, of them originally from the Greater Upper Nile region—including many of the independent militia leaders who had been brought into the SPLA's "big tent" with the rewards of oil wealth.

Renewed warfare

Within months, nearly half of South Sudan's population was directly or indirectly affected. Initially, most of the fighting was restricted to the Greater Upper Nile area (Unity, Upper Nile, and Jonglei states), which comprised the home base of much of the IO. But the political and economic fallout of the conflict rapidly spread to much of the rest of the country. By the end of 2014, an estimated 2 million had been displaced—mostly internally but some 500,000 people fled to Uganda and Ethiopia, with somewhat smaller numbers to Kenya and Sudan itself. But the most vexing problem—particularly for the UN—was the population that had sought refuge in UNMISS bases. These so-called "Protection of Civilians" sites had become semi-permanent IDP camps under UN protection in early 2014, and even four years later, no permanent solution to a very temporary "fix" had been found.

The humanitarian impact of the war

The collapse of the governing consensus, the war, the economic crisis, and the extremely low levels of infrastructure in South Sudan all meant that the humanitarian crisis took on enormous proportions. With little oil wealth left to exploit to pay its still-outsized troop force, the SPLA began a looting spree in the Equatorias in late 2016 and 2017—relatively peaceful up to that point—displacing much of the rural population either into towns like Yei, Kajo Keiji, and Lainza or else across the border to Uganda. By 2018, an estimated four million were displaced—roughly half within the country and half as refugees outside.[57] WFP mounted a massive food aid program. Given the country's poor infrastructure and limited markets, relying on cash transfers was not really possible for much of the affected population. But even with nearly the entire global logistical capacity for air-dropping food aid, the situation could not be contained. Populations in Unity State in particular had been displaced and forced to keep moving for so long that the situation eventually deteriorated into famine conditions—and famine was declared in February of 2017.[58] This resulted in some additional resources, and some improvement—at least locally—in humanitarian access. But even though conditions in Unity improved slightly in 2017, the magnitude of the crisis nation-wide worsened, with more than 6 million people urgently needing food assistance—half the estimated total population—based on pre-war growth rates that did not include the refugees who had fled South Sudan. The actual figure may have been closer to two-thirds of the population remaining in South Sudan by that time.

The emergence of the Protection of Civilians sites, and the difficulties of finding any way out of maintaining these "armed IDP camps" has few contemporary parallels—and is no nearer any solution than it was in January of 2014. After the failure of several peace accords, the international response to the conflict itself dropped off, with the major powers preoccupied elsewhere. South Sudan's earlier benefactors were disgusted by the behavior of the government and the opposition alike; regional powers jockeyed to protect their own interests, but only the regional group Intergovernmental Authority on Development (IGAD) tried to negotiate another peace deal. Writing in 2016, a long-time analyst of South Sudan noted, "The leaders of South Sudan need urgently to reassess their political strategies, because they are heading for collective destruction. Although individually they may appear trapped in the logic of violent competition, they need to explore ways in which they could collectively escape that trap."[59] Two years later, they had made little progress, and the conflict had continued to spread—bringing immiserating humanitarian conditions with it.

Syria: "world's worst humanitarian crisis"

In the spring of 2011, a series of protests against oppressive rule broke out in a number of Middle Eastern countries, following the self-immolation of a despairing Tunisian fruit vendor after municipal authorities destroyed his livelihood. Subsequently dubbed the "Arab spring," the hope was that these protests would bring an end to despotic rule, to be replaced with something more democratic. Rulers were overthrown or removed in Tunisia, Egypt, and Libya. But in Syria, a very heavy-handed response to the protests instead resulted in a civil war that turned into a humanitarian crisis resulting in hundreds of thousands of deaths, millions of people internally displaced (or besieged), and millions more seeking refuge outside of Syria—first in the neighboring countries of Turkey, Jordan, and Lebanon and eventually in Europe as well.

Syria is a country of great ethnic and religious diversity, formed out of the collapsing Ottoman Empire in the aftermath of World War I. Syria was governed in the inter-war period as a French protectorate, becoming independent in 1946. The Soviet-oriented Ba'ath party successfully staged a takeover of the country in 1963, with one of its leaders, Hafaz al-Assad, becoming president in 1971. The country has been ruled by the Assad family ever since. Hafaz al-Assad died in 2000, and the reins were taken over by his son, Bashar.

The anti-government protests in 2011 began as an uprising for democracy, but escalated into full-blown conflict that gave rise to a number of armed groups. These included the Free Syrian Army (a Sunni, anti-Assad but largely pro-Western coalition of many groups), the majority-Kurdish Syrian Democratic Forces (SDF), the Al-Nusra front (a Salafist jihadist organization that eventually aligned with Al Qaeda), and the Islamic State in Iraq and Syria (or ISIS), to name only the major ones. While it appeared in the early part of the war as though the Assad regime might be toppled, Iran, Hezbollah, and eventually Russia all rallied to Assad's cause, stemming any attempt at overthrow and slowly turning the war in the regime's favor. Turkey, the United States, and some Gulf states supported different rebel groups.[60] Rebel groups initially took control of major cities in areas they held, but the regime fought back, destroying wide swaths of the country, leaving city after city as emblems of the total destruction born of urban warfare. Many cities, including Yarmouk, Homs, Aleppo, Raqqa, and eastern Ghouta, bore tragic witness to the carnage. With Russia's formal entry into the conflict in 2015, the war took on even greater international significance. Russia's engagement also undermined any attempts by the international community to contain the crisis or broker an end to the war.

The impact of the conflict

The result in humanitarian terms has been horrific. As of 2016, some 13.5 million people in Syria were in need of some kind of humanitarian support—both protection (by far the biggest single need) and other forms of support (food, health care, water, and shelter). Of these, 5.5 million were in so-called "hard-to-reach areas"—a polite way of saying places where humanitarian access was extremely curtailed—and 600,000 were living in besieged (absolutely inaccessible) areas.[61] More than 100,000 people have "disappeared" after being detained—mostly by agents of the state, although detention by non-state actors has also been reported. Protection has been a constant challenge, including from the regular targeting of civilians by government and armed groups. Grave human rights abuses, crimes against humanity, and violations of IHL have been common. Child soldiers are common in all the parties to the conflict, and the government has used chemical weapons to attack civilians.[62]

Humanitarian access has proved to be a stubborn challenge, making remote management of most humanitarian programming necessary. The humanitarian community remains divided between those based in Syria and those working in neighboring countries or attempting to work cross-border.[63] The UN introduced a "whole of Syria" approach in 2014 to try to address these problems, but fell victim to them instead. Under these circumstances, any sort of principled approach has proven nearly impossible, to put it mildly.[64]

The response to the refugee crisis in neighboring countries was initially a success story with refugees accepted and, in many cases, integrated into host communities in Turkey, Jordan, and Lebanon. But the magnitude of the refugee crisis, and its longevity, began to take a toll by 2016–17. Jordan closed its border in 2016. Lebanon, struggling with a refugee population equal to one-third of its total (pre-war) population, also became an increasingly difficult destination for Syrian refugees. Many of these pressures forced Syrian refugees to look beyond the region for places of asylum—one of the many factors leading to the Mediterranean crisis of 2015–16 (see next section).[65]

Amid all these problems, a massive humanitarian effort was mounted. In areas occupied by the regime, the Syrian Arab Red Crescent (SARC) is frequently the implementing agency. But unlike other members of the Red Cross/Red Crescent movement, serious questions have been raised about the independence of SARC. In opposition-held areas, cross-border programming has been attempted, with remote management as the dominant modus operandi.[66] But local groups have also mounted concerted efforts to begin humanitarian operations in their own areas. Perhaps the most well-known of these is the Syrian Civil Defence—the so-called "White Helmets," for the headgear they wear on search and rescue missions. These local efforts occasionally receive some support from the international community—relief convoys into besieged areas or other high-profile attempts to support—or long-distance financial support.[67]

Remote sensing, drones, and other technology have all been used successfully in Syria. And the greater Syria response—the refugee response in neighboring countries—has without doubt seen the biggest cash transfer and market-based programming in humanitarian history, covering not only food needs (as was the primarily the case in Somalia), but also shelter needs, education and health needs, and a variety of multi-sectoral forms of support.[68]

However, coordination has remained a major challenge, with humanitarians outside of Syria accusing Damascus-based operations of being flagrantly biased towards regime-controlled populations and vice versa. Protection needs have proven almost impossible to address in the Damascus context, and as the war dragged on, protection needs clearly became much deeper than just the immediate requirement for physical safety. Accusations that the regime was using food as a weapon emerged when relief convoys to besieged areas were attacked by Russian and regime aircraft; sexual and gender-based violence has been rampant; and behind the scenes, land confiscation and a variety of other charges lurked.[69] While the search for a conclusion to the war continued, civilian protection continued to be the greatest need in Syria.

A humanitarian nightmare

Like Darfur before it, Syria bore the title "world's worst humanitarian crisis" for years (from about 2013 to 2017) before Yemen assumed that unwanted mantle. But in many ways, Syria remains the quintessentially twenty-first-century humanitarian nightmare: a despotic and predatory state; a deeply divided populace; multiple non-state armed groups, some labeled "terrorist"; a massive civilian population held captive—some in besieged enclaves in destroyed urban areas—and a similarly massive number of refugees outside the country, making for a protection crisis the likes of which have not been seen since World War II; a profoundly divided humanitarian "community" unable to balance the competing demands of protection and access; multiple external actors "stirring the pot"; the closure of borders to neighboring countries; the use of chemical weapons and other atrocities; the inability of IHL to limit the targeting of civilians; and an international community unable to balance the competing demands of sovereignty and the responsibility to protect, and providing little leadership to end the war at the root of the crisis. All of these have been challenges to providing humanitarian response in the greater Syria crisis.

The logical culmination: the Mediterranean refugee crisis

People have been on the move for as long as human history has been recorded (and well before that), but for much of the twentieth century, most of the population movement caused by crisis was limited to nearby countries of refuge. By the beginning of the twenty-first century, the emphasis had shifted, and most people displaced by crisis were concentrated within their countries of origin as IDPs. Globally, the number of IDPs surpassed the number of refugees in the early 1990s, and throughout much of the 1990s and early 2000s, much of the emphasis was on working with IDP populations in war zones or disaster-affected places. However, the almost inevitable outcome of the wars in Syria, Iraq, Afghanistan, and the Horn of Africa—combined with economic collapse and highly repressive states in the Middle East and sub-Saharan Africa—was that population movements would once again be trans-border or even trans-continental. This came to a head dramatically in 2015–16 with the Mediterranean migration crisis.

Population movement—much of it voluntary and motivated more by economic factors than political asylum—had been happening in the Mediterranean for decades. But the war in Syria, and particularly the increasingly crowded facilities in neighboring countries, triggered an increased flow of people to Europe. In 2014, the European Union (EU) received 626,000 applications for asylum—the highest number since the peak of the violence in the Balkans in 1992.[70] Many of these were definitely fleeing conflict and violence in fear for their lives. This flow—combined with the rising trend of nationalism and even xenophobia in Europe—resulted in tighter restrictions on land routes to Europe and forced more people to sea routes. By early 2015, the flow of migrants reached such a volume that the EU convened an extraordinary summit in Brussels to discuss the situation. Media reports of boats filled with immigrants sinking the Mediterranean began appearing as early as 2013, but by 2015 the number of reports—and especially the number of refugees and migrants losing their lives by drowning—had increased dramatically. On 19 April 2015, some 800 people drowned when a boat capsized in the Mediterranean—the largest single incident recorded to that date.[71] These events triggered contradictory responses in Europe. On the one hand, the EU declared that quotas should be issued for the number of immigrants allowed into Europe and that these should be divided among member countries. On the other hand, the massive loss of life on Europe's doorstep triggered demonstrations for the EU to accept more people and voluntary action to save life in the Mediterranean. Hungary—one of the easternmost members of the EU—constructed barbed wire fences along its border with Romania and Serbia, which are not part of the Schengen zone (in which free movement across borders is allowed). And Bulgaria beefed up security on its land border with Turkey. The increased border security within Europe only increased the tendency to attempt sea crossings. But in the summer and autumn of 2015, the crossing from Turkey to Greece—a relatively narrow body of water in the Aegean Sea between the Turkish town of Ayvalik and the Greek island of Lesvos—became one of the key access points to Europe. In August, UNHCR called upon Greece—already in crisis over the collapse of its economy and the possibility of exiting the

EU—to take control of the chaotic situation in its eastern islands, calling the situation there "shameful."[72] Germany, in an attempt to lead in a positive direction, announced that asylum seekers were welcome within its borders—and urged other European countries to do the same, but the situation was spiraling out of control.

On 2 September, the body of a drowned Syrian toddler of Kurdish origin, Alan Kurdi, washed up on the shore in Turkey. A Turkish photographer, Nilüfer Demir, published pictures of the drowned child, and Kurdi became a symbol of all children drowned in the Mediterranean trying to reach safety in Europe. But while the conscience of the world was touched, EU leaders only became more entrenched in opposing positions. While several northern European nations advocated more-open borders, several others opposed, and many put pressure on southern European countries—where the migrants were entering EU territory—to get their borders under control.

By late 2015 and early 2016, the "eastern European land route" was becoming increasingly tightly controlled. This shifted the focus of the crisis to the central Mediterranean—to Italy's outlying islands and Malta. In March 2016 (in the run-up to the World Humanitarian Summit held in Istanbul in May), the EU negotiated a controversial deal with Turkey to return migrants from Greece to Turkey and to put greater pressure on those in Turkey to stay put or return home. This marked the beginning of the "off-shoring" of EU's border security, with other deals to follow with countries neighboring or near to Europe's shores.

The crisis peaked in 2015–16, both in terms of numbers trying to reach Europe and numbers drowned or otherwise killed in the attempt. Some 221,000 people reached Greece, Italy, and Spain by sea in October 2015, but the number dropped to about 10,000 by April 2016—mostly because of increased policing in countries of departure.[73] Numbers stayed at about this level for much of the following two years. Yet the crackdown against "immigrants" in Europe continued, with right-wing political parties campaigning on platforms of protecting European culture from a "siege from migrants" in spite of the sharp decline in numbers. Each year between 2015 and 2018, more than 3,000 people died trying to reach Europe's shores, with more than 5,800 dying in 2016.[74]

A humanitarian response in Europe

The humanitarian response mirrored the crisis itself: Even though many agencies were based in Europe, most were ill prepared to deal with a humanitarian crisis in Europe—or on its doorstep. A heavy focus on "professional" response, and a corresponding lack of professionals, meant that many agencies were paralyzed. In their place a coalition of volunteers and local "pop-up" NGOs mounted a response completely outside both the auspices of the state (especially in Greece) and the formal humanitarian system.[75]

Ultimately, both states and NGOs engaged at a higher and more professional level, but at the height of the crisis in 2015, the response was remarkably non-governmental and not from the "usual suspects." One summary report noted, "The reluctance or inability of mainstream agencies to quickly mobilize resources and presence is symptomatic of how remote the humanitarian system has become from the problems of ordinary people, especially when these problems do not fit in the scripts that agencies are accustomed to."[76] The migration crisis continued—as did the internal reflection on why it had proven so difficult to respond in a timely and adequate way.

Conclusion: humanitarian action in the twenty-first century

To humanitarians active at the time, Darfur and Afghanistan seemed like major turning points: Surely "the system" had learned its lessons in the aftermath of earlier crises and could handle whatever the twenty-first century could throw at it. But nearly every major crisis since then has also seemed like a turning point—to the exasperation and exhaustion of all involved, from affected populations to on-the-ground aid workers, donors, and policy makers. Both the extent to which humanitarian action has expanded and the extent to which it still falls critically short of its lofty ambitions have led to extensive self-criticism and blame-gaming. Much of this came up for reflection in the run-up to the World Humanitarian Summit held, ever so appropriately, in Istanbul—only miles from the on-going migration crisis in the Mediterranean.

Sober judgments at the time suggested that this was simply the "new normal"—that attempting to "resolve" the problems that beset humanitarian action was a fool's errand at best and dangerous self-deception at worst. Humanitarians had made great progress—had developed new approaches with stronger evidence, and had continued to garner committed support from both donors and a weary public—but the challenges they faced seemed to endlessly outpace progress and lessons learned. The twenty-first century was clearly a challenge for the long haul—both for humanitarians themselves, and especially for the crisis-affected populations they sought to serve.

Notes

1 Gilles Carbonnier, *Humanitarian Economics* (London: Hurst, 2015), 4.
2 In an influential summary, Michael Barnett and Thomas Weiss note that at the beginning of the 21st century, contemporary humanitarianism is "precariously situated between the politics of solidarity and the politics of governance" or between its twentieth-century idealistic but relatively marginal position and the twenty-first century's repolarized global political economy. See Michael Barnett and Thomas G. Weiss, *Humanitarianism in Question* (Ithaca, N.Y.; London: Cornell University Press, 2008), 38. This section reuses edited segments from the original book, *Shaping the Humanitarian World*, with permission from the authors of that book (Walker and Maxwell).
3 Antonio Donini, "An Elusive Quest: Integration in the Response to the Afghan Crisis," *Ethics and International Affairs* 18, no. 2 (September 2004): 21–27.
4 Ahmed Rashid, "Afghanistan: Ending the Policy Quagmire," *Journal of International Affairs* 54, no. 2 (Spring 2001): 395.
5 Norah Niland, "Rights, Rhetoric and Reality: A Snapshot from Afghanistan," in *The UN, Human Rights and Post-Conflict Situations*, by Nigel D. White and Dirk Klaasen (New York; Manchester: Juris; Manchester University Press, 2005).
6 Donini, "An Elusive Quest," 24.
7 See for example Nicolas de Torrente, "Humanitarian Action under Attack: Reflections on the Iraq War U.S. Foreign Policy and Human Rights," *Harvard Human Rights Journal* 17 (2004): 1–30; and Paul O'Brien, "Politicized Humanitarianism: A Response to Nicolas de Torrente," *Harvard Human Rights Journal* 17 (2004): 31–40.
8 Sarah Kenyon Lischer, "Military Intervention and the Humanitarian 'Force Multiplier,'" *Global Governance* 13, no. 1 (2007): 99–118; Antonio Donini, Larry Minear, and Peter Walker, "The Future of Humanitarian Action: Mapping the Implications of Iraq and Other Recent Crises," *Disasters* 28, no. 2 (June 1, 2004): 190–204.
9 ICISS, *The Responsibility to Protect: Report of the International Commission on Intervention and State Sovereignty* (Ottowa, Canada: International Commission on Intervention and State Sovereignty, 2001), http://responsibilitytoprotect.org/ICISS%20Report.pdf.
10 Jaya Murthy, "Mandating the Protection Cluster with the Responsibility to Protect: A Policy Recommendation Based on the Protection Cluster's Implementation in South Kivu, DRC," *The Journal of Humanitarian Assistance*, 5 October 2007, https://sites.tufts.edu/jha/archives/55. Note that MONUC operates under a "Chapter 7" mandate in the Congo, meaning that it is not just there to monitor an existing peace agreement, but can engage in enforcement.
11 Antonio Donini, Larry Minear, Sippi Azarbaijani-Moghaddam, Greg Hansen, Tasneem Mowjee, Karina Purushotma, Ian Smillie, Elizabeth Stites, and Xavier Zeebroek, *Humanitarian Agenda 2015: Principles, Power, and Perceptions* (Medford, Mass.: Feinstein International Center, 2006), http://fic.tufts.edu/publication-item/humanitarian-agenda-2015-principles-power-and-perceptions/.

12 Donini et al., *Humanitarian Agenda 2015*, 3.
13 Alex de Waal, *Famine That Kills: Darfur, Sudan*, Rev. ed., Oxford Studies in African Affairs (Oxford; New York: Oxford University Press, 2005).
14 Larry Minear, "Chapter 3, Lessons Learned: The Darfur Experience," in *ALNAP Review of Humanitarian Action in 2004* (London: Overseas Development Institute, 2005), 86, https://www.alnap.org/system/files/content/resource/files/main/alnap-chapter3-rha-2006.pdf.
15 Margie Buchanan-Smith and Abduljabbar Abdulla Fadul, *Adaptation and Devastation: The Impact of the Conflict on Trade and Markets in Darfur* (Medford, Mass.: Feinstein International Center, May 2008), http://fic.tufts.edu/assets/Adaptation-and-Devastation-2008.pdf.
16 Save Darfur Coalition, *Uniting Voices: Save Darfur Coalition 2008 Annual Report* (Washington, DC: Save Darfur Coalition, 2008), https://issuu.com/savedarfurcoalition/docs/2008_sdc_annual_report.
17 Alex de Waal, *The Real Politics of the Horn of Africa: Money, War and the Business of Power* (Cambridge; Malden, Mass.: Polity Press, 2015).
18 Helen Young, Abdalmonium el Khider Osman, Margie Buchanan Smith, Brendan Bromwich, Karen Moore, and Stacey Ballou, *Sharpening the Strategic Focus of Livelihoods Programming in the Darfur Region* (Medford, Mass.: Feinstein International Center, 2007), https://reliefweb.int/sites/reliefweb.int/files/resources/8F2A0D466A219BF2C1257384004CE450-Full_Report.pdf.
19 CRED, *People Affected by Conflict: Humanitarian Needs in Numbers* (Centre for Research on the Epidemiology of Disasters, 2013), https://www.cred.be/publications.
20 Helen Young, "Diminishing Returns: The Challenges Facing Humanitarian Action in Darfur," in *The Golden Fleece: Manipulation and Independence in Humanitarian Action*, by Antonio Donini, 1st ed. (Sterling, VA: Kumarian Press, 2012).
21 Young, "Diminishing Returns," 89.
22 John Telford and John Cosgrove, *Joint Evaluation of the International Response to the Indian Ocean Tsunami: Synthesis Report* (London: Tsunami Evaluation Coalition, 2006), https://www.alnap.org/system/files/content/resource/files/main/889.pdf.
23 Telford and Cosgrove, *Joint Evaluation*.
24 BBC News, "Timeline: Asian Tsunami Disaster," *BBC News*, 7 January 2005, http://news.bbc.co.uk/2/hi/asia-pacific/4154791.stm.
25 Telford and Cosgrove, *Joint Evaluation*.
26 BBC News, "Timeline".
27 Humanitarian Practice Network, "Indian Ocean Tsunami," *Humanitarian Exchange*, January 2006, https://odihpn.org/magazine/editors-introduction-indian-ocean-tsunami/.
28 John Telford and John Cosgrave, "The International Humanitarian System and the 2004 Indian Ocean Earthquake and Tsunamis," *Disasters* 31, no. 1 (14 March 2007): 1–28.
29 Telford and Cosgrove, *Joint Evaluation*.
30 Reginald DesRoches, Mary C. Comerio, Marc Eberhard, Walter Mooney, and Glenn J. Rix, "Overview of the 2010 Haiti Earthquake," *Earthquake Spectra* 27 no. S1 (2011): S1–S21.
31 DesRoches et al., "2010 Haiti Earthquake".

32 Mark Schuller, *Humanitarian Aftershocks in Haiti* (New Brunswick, N.J.: Rutgers University Press, 2015).

33 Abhijit Bhattacharjee and Roberta Lossio, *Evaluation of OCHA Response to the Haiti Earthquake* (UN Office of the Coordination of Humanitarian Affairs, 2011), https://www.unocha.org/sites/dms/Documents/Evaluation%20of%20OCHA%20Response%20to%20the%20Haiti%20Earthquake.pdf.

34 Athena Kolbe and Robert Muggah, "Surveying Haiti's Post-Quake Needs: A Quantitative Approach," *Humanitarian Exchange Magazine*, August 2010, https://odihpn.org/magazine/surveying-haiti%C2%92s-post-quake-needs-a-quantitative-approach/.

35 Patrick Meier, "How Crisis Mapping Saved Lives in Haiti," *Changing Planet, National Geographic* (blog), 2 July 2012, https://blog.nationalgeo graphic.org/2012/07/02/how-crisis-mapping-saved-lives-in-haiti/.

36 Aimee Ansari, *Haiti: A Once-in-a-Century Chance for Change: Beyond Reconstruction: Re-Envisioning Haiti with Equity, Fairness, and Opportunity* (Oxfam International, 26 March 2010), https://www.oxfamamerica.org/static/oa3/files/haiti-reconstruction-paper-03-26-10.pdf.

37 Inter Agency Standing Committee. IASC Transformative Agenda (IASC, n.d.) https://interagencystandingcommittee.org/iasc-transformative-agenda.

38 Francesco Checchi and W. Courtland Robinson, "Mortality among Populations of Southern and Central Somalia Affected by Severe Food Insecurity and Famine during 2010–2012" (Rome; Washington, DC: FAO; FEWS NET, 2 May 2013), www.fsnau.org/in-focus/study-report-mortality-am ong-populations-southern-and-central-somalia-affected-severe-food-.

39 FNSAU, "FSNAU Evidence for Updated Famine Declaration," (Nairobi: FSNAU, 2011), http://www.fsnau.org.

40 James Darcy, Paul Bonard, and Shukria Dini, *IASC Real-Time Evaluation of the Humanitarian Response to the Horn of Africa Drought Crisis: Somalia 2011–2012* (New York: IASC, 2012), https://www.unicef.org/evalda tabase/files/USA-2012-007-1.pdf.

41 Christopher Hillbruner and Grainne Moloney, "When Early Warning Is Not Enough—Lessons Learned from the 2011 Somalia Famine," *Global Food Security* 1, no. 1 (2012).

42 Margaret Buchanan-Smith and Susanna Davies, *Famine Early Warning and Response: The Missing Link* (London: Intermediate Technology Publications, 1995); Rob Bailey, *Famine Early Warning and Early Action: The Cost of Delay* (London: Chatham House, 2012), https://www.chathamhous e.org/sites/files/chathamhouse/public/Research/Energy,%20Environment%20 and%20Development/0712pr_bailey.pdf.

43 Alex de Waal, *Famine Crimes: Politics and the Disaster Relief Industry in Africa*, African Issues (London: James Currey, 1997).

44 Daniel Maxwell and Nisar Majid, *Famine in Somalia: Competing Imperatives, Collective Failures, 2011–12* (New York: Oxford University Press, 2016).

45 Maxwell and Majid, *Famine in Somalia*.

46 Jan Egeland, Adele Harmer, and Abby Stoddard, *To Stay and Deliver: Good Practice for Humanitarians in Complex Security Environments* (New York: UN Office for the Coordination of Humanitarian Affairs, n.d.), xv.

47 Antonio Donini and Daniel Maxwell, "From Face-to-Face to Face-to-Screen: Implications of Remote Management for the Effectiveness and

Accountability of Humanitarian Action in Insecure Environments," *International Review of the Red Cross* 95, no. 980 (2014).

48 Degan Ali and Kirsten Gelsdorf, "Risk-Averse to Risk-Willing: Learning from the 2011 Somalia Cash Response," *Global Food Security* 1, no. 1 (2012).

49 Christopher B. Barrett, Robert Bell, Erin Lentz, Daniel Maxwell, "Market Information and Food Insecurity Response Analysis," *Food Security* 1 no. 2 (2009).

50 DFID, *Humanitarian Emergency Response Review: UK Government Response* (London: DFID, 2011), https://assets.publishing.service.gov.uk/government/uploads/system/uploads/attachment_data/file/67489/hum-emer-resp-rev-uk-gvmt-resp.pdf.

51 Christopher B. Barrett and Mark A. Constas, "Toward a Theory of Resilience for International Development Applications," *Proceedings of the National Academy of Sciences* 111, no. 40 (2014).

52 DFID, *Defining Disaster Resilience: A DFID Approach Paper* (London: DFID, 2011), https://assets.publishing.service.gov.uk/government/uploads/system/uploads/attachment_data/file/186874/defining-disaster-resilience-approach-paper.pdf; Tim Frankenberger, T. Spangler, S. Nelson, and M. Langworthy, *Building Resilience to Food Security Shocks in the Horn of Africa* (Washington, DC: USAID/DFID, 2012), www.fao.org/fileadmin/user_upload/drought/docs/USAID%20%20UKAID%20TANGO_Discussion%20Note.pdf.

53 Mark Bradbury, Nicholas Leader, and Kate Mackintosh, "The 'Agreement on Ground Rules' in South Sudan," in *The Politics of Practice: The Principles of Humanitarian Action in Practice*, HPG Report 4, Study 3 (London: Overseas Development Institute, 2000), 34. https://www.odi.org/sites/odi.org.uk/files/odi-assets/publications-opinion-files/307.pdf.

54 Daniel Maxwell, Martina Santschi, and Rachel Gordon, *Looking Back to Look Ahead? Reviewing Key Lessons from Operation Lifeline Sudan and Past Humanitarian Operations in South Sudan* (London: Secure Livelihoods Research Consortium, 2014), https://securelivelihoods.org/wp-content/uploads/Reviewing-key-lessons-from-Operation-Lifeline-Sudan-and-past-humanitarian-operations-in-South-Sudan.pdf.

55 For more on OLS, see T. A. Aboum, E. Chole, K. Manibe, L. Minear, A. Mohammed, J. Sebstad, and T. G. Weiss, *A Critical Review of Operation Lifeline Sudan* (Washington, DC: Refugee Policy Group, 1990), https://www.alnap.org/help-library/a-critical-review-of-operation-lifeline-sudan; Mark Duffield, Madut Jok, David Keen, Geoff Loane, and Fiona O'Reilly, *Sudan: Unintended Consequences of Humanitarian Assistance. Field Evaluation Study for the European Community Humanitarian Office* (Dublin, Ireland: University of Dublin, Trinity College, 2000), https://www.southsudanpeaceportal.com/wp-content/uploads/2000/04/Sudan-Unintended-Consequences-of-Humanitarian-Assistance-Field-Evaluation-Study.pdf; A. Karim, M. Duffield, S. Jaspars, A. Benini, J. Macrae, M. Bradbury, D. Johnson, G. Larbi, and B. Hendrie, "Operation Lifeline Sudan" (United Nations Department of Humanitarian Affairs, 1 July 1996), https://www.alnap.org/help-library/operation-lifeline-sudan.

56 Alex de Waal, "When Kleptocracy Becomes Insolvent: Brute Causes of the Civil War in South Sudan," *African Affairs* 113, no. 452 (July 1, 2014): 347–369.

57 OCHA, *2018 Humanitarian Response Plan: South Sudan* (United Nations Office for the Coordination of Humanitarian Affairs, 2017), https://relief web.int/sites/reliefweb.int/files/resources/SS_2018_HumanitarianResponsePla n.pdf.

58 IPC in South Sudan, "Localized Famine and Unprecedented Levels of Acute Malnutrition in Greater Unity—Almost 5 Million People in Need of Urgent Assistance," IPC Alert (Integrated Food Security Phase Classification, 20 February 2017), www.ipcinfo.org/fileadmin/user_upload/ipcinfo/ docs/1_IPC_Alert_6_SouthSudan_Crisis_Feb2017.pdf.

59 Alex de Waal, *A Political Marketplace Analysis of South Sudan's "Peace"* (Medford, Mass.: World Peace Foundation, 2016), www.lse.ac.uk/interna tionalDevelopment/research/JSRP/downloads/JSRP-Brief-2.pdf.

60 BBC News, "Syria: The Story of the Conflict," *BBC News*, 11 March 2016, sec. Middle East, www.bbc.com/news/world-middle-east-26116868.

61 OCHA, "Overview: 2016 Syria Humanitarian Response Plan and 2016–2017 Regional Refugee and Resilience Plan" (London: United Nations Office for the Coordination of Humanitarian Affairs, 4 February 2016), https://2c8kkt1ykog81j8k9p47oglb-wpengine.netdna-ssl.com/wp-content/up loads/2016/01/2016_HRP_3RP_Chapeau_Syria_FINAL_hi_res.pdf.

62 Human Rights Watch, "Syria: Events of 2016," *Human Rights Watch* (blog), 12 January 2017, https://www.hrw.org/world-report/2017/country-chapters/ syria.

63 OCHA, *2017 Syrian Arab Republic Humanitarian Needs Overview* (United Nations Office for the Coordination of Humanitarian Affairs, 2016), https://reliefweb.int/sites/reliefweb.int/files/resources/2017_Syria_hno _161205.pdf.

64 Norwegian Refugee Council and Handicap International, *Challenges to Principled Humanitarian Action: Perspectives from Four Countries* (Geneva: Norwegian Refugee Council; Handicap International, 2016), http://reliefweb.int/sites/reliefweb.int/files/resources/nrc-hi-report_web.pdf.

65 Elizabeth Ferris, Kemal Kirisci, and Salman Shaikh, *Syrian Crisis: Massive Displacement, Dire Needs and a Shortage of Solutions* (Washington, DC: Brookings Institution Press, 2013), https://www.brookings.edu/wp-content/ uploads/2016/06/Syrian-CrisisMassive-Displacement-Dire-Needs-and-Short age-of-Solutions-September-18-2013.pdf.

66 Kimberly Howe, Elizabeth Stites, and Danya Chudacoff, *Breaking the Hourglass: Partnerships in Remote Management Settings—The Cases of Syria and Iraqi Kurdistan* (Medford, Mass.: Feinstein International Center, 2015), http://principlesinpractice.org/uploads/Library/Documents/Civil-Mi litaryRelations/fic-breaking-the-hourglass_syria_iraqi-kurdistan.pdf.

67 Kimberly Howe, "No End in Sight: A Case Study of Humanitarian Action and the Syria Conflict," Planning From the Future project (Medford, Mass.: Feinstein International Center, Tufts University, 2016), http://fic. tufts.edu/publication-item/humanitarian-action-in-syria/.

68 Howe, "No End in Sight."

69 Jason Hepps, *Whole of Syria: 2017 Protection Needs Overview* (Protection: Whole of Syria, 2016), http://reliefweb.int/sites/reliefweb.int/files/resources/ wos_protection_needs_overview_2017_oct_2016.pdf.

70 Heather Y. Wheeler, "European Migrant Crisis 2011—Present Day," 2017, www.totallytimelines.com/european-migrant-crisis/.

71 Alexandra Ma, "How Europe's Tragic Refugee and Migrant Crisis Got So Dire," *Huffington Post*, September 15, 2015, sec. The World Post, www.huffingtonpost.com/entry/eu-migrant-crisis-timeline_us_55f345ace4b063ecb fa472f7; Wheeler, "European Migrant Crisis."
72 Ma, "Europe's Tragic Refugee."
73 Patricia Kingsley, "Migration to Europe Is Down Sharply. So Is It Still a 'Crisis'?" *New York Times*, 27 June 2018, https://www.nytimes.com/intera ctive/2018/06/27/world/europe/europe-migrant-crisis-change.html.
74 Kingsley, "Migration to Europe."
75 George Tjensvoll Kitching, H. Haavik, B. Tandstad, M. Zaman, and E. Darj, "Exploring the Role of Ad Hoc Grassroots Organizations Providing Humanitarian Aid on Lesvos, Greece," *PLoS Currents* 8 (17 November 2016).
76 Randolph Kent, Christina Bennett, Antonio Donini, and Daniel Maxwell, *Planning from the Future: Is the Humanitarian System Fit for Purpose?* (London; Medford, Mass.: Humanitarian Policy Group at the Overseas Development Institute; Feinstein International Center at Tufts University; the Policy Institute at King's College London, 2016), 41, http://www.pla nningfromthefuture.org/uploads/4/5/6/0/45605399/pff_report_uk.pdf.

4 Contemporary humanitarian actors

- **Actors: who carries out humanitarian action?**
- **Affected communities and responders of first resort**
- **Traditional established humanitarian system**
- **The wider humanitarian network**
- **Conclusion: understanding the philosophies and objectives of humanitarians**

Defining who comprises the actors in today's humanitarian system is in some ways impossible. With hundreds or even thousands of groups or organizations responding to the same crises, often with competing directives and a wide range of objectives, the humanitarian system is a large, complex, and networked ecosystem of response. As noted by one astute commentator, "It is easy to become entangled in complicated discussions about what exactly constitutes the humanitarian community."[1]

Some of this complexity is linked to how quickly the number of actors has grown. Just 40 organizations responded to the 1980 refugee crisis in Cambodia—a number that would seem shockingly small today. Fifteen years later, during the 1995 crisis in the former Yugoslavia, more than six times that many organizations participated in the response.[2] In 2014, the number of formal humanitarian assistance organizations was estimated to be 5,000, employing over a quarter million people.[3] Yet this number doesn't even begin to cover the actors we now see participating in global humanitarian efforts.

The basics of "who" defines the humanitarian system in terms of major donor budgets has remained remarkably stable during the past 20 years, with the majority of power, resources, and activities still centering around the OECD donors, the UN, the Red Cross movement, and a handful of large NGOs. However, humanitarian response is now often defined as a global responsibility, rather than an effort by a limited number of specialized actors. Humanitarian action has expanded beyond the boundaries of a formal Western system to recognize the vital majority contribution of local and national actors and also to include diverse actors such as the private sector, volunteer organizations, and diaspora groups. In other words, the established institutions, policies, and norms are being stretched and adapted to fit new conceptions of humanitarian action.

This chapter examines the actors that comprise this often unwieldy but vital industry—in short, who participates and who is recognized as a participant. Using references to the historical cases analyzed previously, it provides a guide to the major actors involved in humanitarian action—and the unique roles they play. This chapter aims to also lay the foundation for a thorough understanding of the complex issues and debates surrounding contemporary humanitarian action that will be explored in Chapters 6 and 7.

Actors: who carries out humanitarian action?

Institutionally, individual governments and states are meant to hold the primary responsibility for the protection of their citizens in crises— and are expected to fulfill humanitarian functions. In reality, in today's largest crises, most formal humanitarian action (and the focus of this book) is delivered by a networked ecosystem of international actors who aim to advocate for, provide protection and rapid relief after sudden-onset disasters for, and/or meet the basic humanitarian needs of populations undergoing chronic crisis conditions caused by conflict, repeated disasters, failure of development or governance, or some combination thereof.[4]

Unfortunately, no simple diagram or agreed organizational chart exists that clearly lays out what this networked system of actors looks like and how they relate to one another. Nevertheless, it would appear as something like the framework in Figure 4.1. While it is not meant to be comprehensive or definitive, it gives a simplified structure explaining the variety of actors engaged in humanitarian assistance.

This figure places the affected people and responders of first resort at the center, surrounded by local and national response (the communities impacted, community-based NGOs, local and national governments, etc.) to signify that they are the most critical actors in any crisis response. The next ring is comprised of the traditional established system (UN agencies, Red Cross Movement, major NGOs, donors, etc.), defined as those having humanitarian mandates or established with a core purpose to provide global humanitarian assistance or protection.

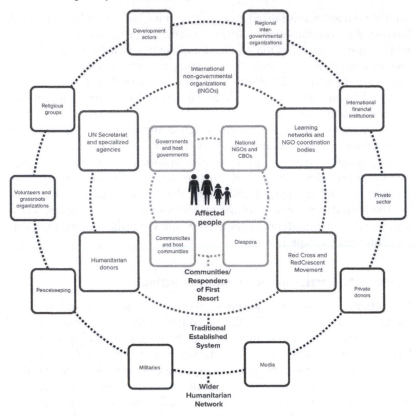

Figure 4.1 Humanitarian actors

The outermost ring is the wider humanitarian network, which includes actors who have mandates that vary in terms of the degree to which humanitarian action is a core function. In some cases, these actors may provide the most effective response in a crisis; in other cases, critical questions are still being asked about whether they are even "humanitarian." The next sections of this chapter describe in detail the roles of these various actors.

Affected communities and responders of first resort

Although global humanitarian response is often presented as Western NGOs and UN agencies flying in and providing aid and expertise, in most cases, local response actually is the most vital for people affected by conflict and disaster. This local response is first and foremost provided by affected communities themselves, their neighbors, local volunteer networks, their own sub-national and national governments, and diaspora.

Affected people and their local host communities

The first response to any crisis is almost always undertaken by the affected communities themselves. In the absence of rapid or adequate external support, communities have long had to rely on their own means to cope with crisis as best they can—and still do in crises that are ignored by or inaccessible to the international humanitarian system. In 2010, Tropical Storm Agatha ravaged central Guatemala, killing hundreds of people and opening up a 200-foot-deep sinkhole in the middle of Guatemala City. Within hours, the mayor, volunteer fire department, and radio station volunteers publicly requested emergency supplies be donated locally to assist those without a home, clothing, or food. Within a day, over 1,000 people had donated and delivered assistance to those who needed it in response to the city's request.[5] Similarly, some of the most important response efforts during the Syrian Civil War (see Chapter 3) have been led by members of the affected community. In response to indiscriminate bombings of population centers, affected people came together and organized the Syria Civil Defence in 2013 to conduct search-and-rescue and medical evacuation operations for civilians. This group became known as the "White Helmets". Their 3,000 volunteers have saved more than 60,000 lives—taking extreme risks in places where international humanitarian actors are either unable or unwilling to go. Although the White Helmets have attracted some international funding and now operate as a local NGO, most of their members are ordinary Syrian citizens.[6]

Likewise, neighbors, host communities, and local volunteers have always provided aid. In 2015, on the island of Lesvos, where some 500,000 asylum seekers arrived on dinghies from Turkey, the Greek host community bore the brunt of the humanitarian response. At the height of the crisis, several thousand refugees arrived each day—with much of their support organized by local people, volunteer networks, the Greek Coast Guard, and an assortment of ad hoc groups.[7] International volunteer networks will be further discussed below.

Some researchers have estimated that the majority of the support for crisis-affected populations worldwide does *not* come from their government or organized humanitarian agencies, but rather from people's own communities, local businesses, volunteers, diaspora groups, and other social networks. Communities themselves are increasingly recognized as the "responders of first resort."[8]

Host-country governments

Almost all major international documents, standards, and resolutions acknowledge that it is the primary role and responsibility of the state to provide assistance. (However, in practice the relationship between state sovereignty and international humanitarian assistance is more complicated, as we will discuss later in the chapter.)

In the last decade an increasing number of countries, following the lead of India and China, are managing their own emergencies, especially in response to disasters caused by "natural" hazards.[9] In situations where international assistance is necessary due to limited resources or other constraints, country governments are becoming more active in coordinating the work of international actors. Another area where governments are taking on more responsibility is in disaster risk reduction.[10]

However, in many crises, governments lack capacity or willingness to effectively address the crisis on their own. The reasons are numerous: violent conflicts in which a government is a belligerent party, lack of pre-existing crisis management systems and infrastructure, or lack of investment and prioritization. In these instances, governments often authorize (or at least tolerate) international humanitarian organizations to work within their borders. Governments that wish to take a leading role in humanitarian response also face structural challenges. In the past, national governments received a sizeable share of international assistance in the form of contributions to their national budget—but such contributions have declined in favor of more-targeted assistance. For example, since 1976, the share of the European Commission's relief budget channeled directly through national governments has fallen from over 90 percent (in 1976) to just 6 percent (in the 1990s).[11]

In other contexts, whether they have capacity or not, host governments impose control over the work and movement of international humanitarian actors (see the case study on Darfur in Chapter 3). Reasons for such restrictions vary. Some governments are particularly motivated to undertake reforms in the aftermath of a major disaster to reduce the impact and cost of recurrent crises. Or, governments may wish to visibly demonstrate control over the situation in order to bolster their political status. But in some cases, particularly in times of conflict, governments actively restrict access of affected people to humanitarian agencies or vice versa, target civilians, or otherwise undermine humanitarian principles and human rights. The role of the government can thus vary dramatically depending on its own interests and the nature of the crisis.

National non-governmental organizations, community-based organizations

National NGOs (NNGOs) and local, community-based organizations (CBOs) are types of civil society organizations that operate within national borders. Such organizations exist both in the developed world and in developing countries. The number of NNGOs and CBOs has grown rapidly in crisis-affected countries, leading to extensive South–South cooperation and widespread recognition that such groups play a critical role in humanitarian action.[12] In remote areas with limited access, their work can be especially important. When violence broke out in Leer, South Sudan, in 2014, residents were forced to flee into the bush. The NNGO Universal Intervention and Development Organisation (UNIDO) came with them—carrying a generator and other supplies. They were able to respond quickly, conduct interviews with local chiefs, and coordinate deliveries from international actors. In such situations, existing community-based networks and knowledge are critical in delivering timely and effective assistance.[13]

These groups are often the first responders in crisis but are often treated as useful subcontractors by international agencies—rather than as humanitarian actors in their own right.[14] One estimate holds that only 0.3 percent of international funds goes directly to local and national NGOs.[15] The rest is channeled through one or more international partners.[16] Calls for greater resources, capacity development, and empowerment of these organizations are now at the forefront of humanitarian reform efforts. This issue will be discussed further in Chapters 5 and 6.

Diasporas

Members of a diaspora are connected to a crisis-affected population but geographically separated. They may have family members and friends who are affected, or plan to return to the community in the future and therefore wish to promote stability. Or, they may simply feel religious or cultural affinity and national pride. Such real or perceived ties often lead to donations and other work on behalf of those affected by emergencies.[17]

The Syrian diaspora, for example, has played a crucial and multi-faceted role in health response. Millions of Syrians were trapped in the country, without access to formal humanitarian assistance. According to a report from MSF, "Syrian diaspora groups, like the Union of Syrian Doctors (UOSSM) … contributed much more to increasing access to medical services than all of the MSF sections combined."[18] Many of the donations and initiatives of diaspora groups are not reflected in official aid flows, making them difficult to quantify. However, we know that remittances are worth billions of dollars and potentially play a huge role in crisis contexts.

Traditional established humanitarian system

The next section (and ring of Figure 4.1) reviews the actors that for the past few decades have received the large majority of funding and been the focus of most discourse on humanitarian action. They are the organizations with the recognized logos (Red Cross and Red Crescent Movement, UN agencies and organizations, international NGOs [INGOs], etc.). If one went to the website of each of these actors, one would find different mandates and missions related to the humanitarian principles, IHL, and other foundational humanitarian frameworks. However, with their different histories and varying roles, these actors have taken on characteristics that distinguish one from another.[19]

These actors, while hopefully recognizing the primacy of national and local institutions, believe that such primacy cannot come at the expense of people themselves. So when social support networks are stretched beyond coping capacity during large-scale or protracted crises, and/or governments are unable or unwilling to respond, these international humanitarian actors aim to respond to needs quickly, with relevant responses, and at the necessary scale. Similarly, where national and local actors undermine or compromise the rights and safety of crisis-affected people, international actors provide assistance and uphold and reinforce the rights of affected people while also stressing relevant international laws and other instruments. Much of this is mandated through UN Resolution 46/182 as described in Box 4.1.

Box 4.1 UN General Assembly Resolution 46/182

GA Resolution 46/182, adopted in December 1991, is generally considered the founding document of the modern UN-established humanitarian system.

One of the most important aspects of Resolution 46/182 was the establishment of national sovereignty as a key component of the humanitarian system. Assistance can only be provided with the consent of the affected country, and state governments are designated as the foremost providers and facilitators of aid in emergencies.[20] It also formally mandated that all humanitarian assistance be delivered in accordance with the four principles of humanity, neutrality, impartiality, and independence that were introduced in the Introduction to the book. Finally since the resolution was created with the goal "strengthening of the coordination of humanitarian emergency assistance of the United Nations"[21] it also formed many of the architectural coordination structures that still exist today: IASC, CERF, and the CAP which will be discussed in Chapter 5.

Red Cross and Red Crescent Movement

The Red Cross and Red Crescent Movement is the world's largest, most established and oldest humanitarian actor. It has a unique institutional role, with characteristics distinct from both intergovernmental organizations like the UN and humanitarian NGOs. With nearly 100 million members, volunteers, and supporters,[22] the movement operates worldwide, operates with the fundamental principles of neutrality and impartiality, and has a mission to provide protection and assistance to people affected by armed conflict and disaster.[23] The movement has a complex structure composed of three parts, including the International Committee of the Red Cross (ICRC), 191 member Red Cross and Red Crescent Societies, and the International Federation of the Red Cross and Red Crescent Societies (IFRC); each are described below.

First, as discussed in Chapter 2, the only organization that has a permanent mandate under IHL is the *International Committee of the Red Cross* (ICRC), and therefore it strictly adheres to the universal humanitarian principles of neutrality, impartiality, and independence and is perhaps the most important actor among those focusing specifically on armed conflict and its consequences.

It defines itself as "an independent, neutral organization ensuring humanitarian protection and assistance for victims of war and armed violence." Its mandate specifically allows it to take impartial action on behalf of the wounded and sick, civilians affected by conflict, and prisoners of war. Its work spans the globe and includes activities such as providing food for displaced people in South Sudan, protecting civilians from violence in Venezuela, and mediating conflict in Ukraine.[24] It also has the unique mandate to visit prisoners of war. This began in WWI and, in 2004, over half a million prisoners of war and detainees received confidential ICRC visits. ICRC also provides a tracing service to put family members in touch with prisoners and displaced people.

ICRC's approach is unique among humanitarian actors. It will often observe, but not take part in, collaborative UN or NGO ventures. It will often work with a local Red Cross or Red Crescent Society, but not at their behest. It will always seek access to victims based on need alone, investing significant resources in quietly building trust and understanding to assure access to affected populations. While ICRC undertakes projects that look similar to those of other agencies, it will often act faster and more impartially.

At a global level, the ICRC seeks to promote knowledge and understanding about international humanitarian law and to develop new areas of humanitarian law. For example, it was central to the ratification of the Land Mines Treaty and discussions held on the banning of laser weapons.

Second, the *National Societies of the Red Cross and Red Crescent* are local autonomous organizations that occupy an important role in emergency response. Each society can only exist if its country has ratified the Geneva Conventions and passed a law to establish the society. Thus, they are mandated by the state but seek to operate independently.

A national society now exists in almost every country in the world. As of 2007, 190 autonomous groups were collectively assisting some 284 million people each year.[25] They work in the fields of public health, disaster preparedness and response, blood supplies, first aid, and the promotion of humanitarian law. In times of war, they may act as auxiliaries to the ICRC, under the ICRC's direction. In times of major non-conflict disaster or crisis, they appeal via their international membership organization, the IFRC, for assistance to be funneled to them from other societies around the world.

Finally, the *International Federation of Red Cross and Red Crescent Societies* (IFRC) is responsible for coordinating and directing assistance specifically for natural disasters and supporting the work of the national societies described above. Together they undertake activities including disaster preparedness, emergency health, disaster law, water and sanitation, and humanitarian diplomacy. The IFRC provides an international voice for the national societies, represents their interests at international conferences and negotiations, and supports their development and capacity building. Although the IFRC headquarters is less than a kilometer from the ICRC headquarters, the two entities have different mandates and work independently in different areas of humanitarian response.

UN Secretariat and specialized agencies

The UN emerged in the aftermath of WWII with three explicit purposes: to prevent and manage future wars, mitigate the worst excesses and failings of capitalism, and promote liberty through the Declaration of Human Rights.[26] Today, the United Nations has expanded to cover a massive range of activities—including sustainable development, peacekeeping, international cooperation in outer space, and the strengthening of civil society. However, one of the UN's most well-known functions is its engagement in international humanitarian action.

The main organization within the United Nations mandated to coordinate global humanitarian assistance is OCHA. Led by an "under-secretary-general"—also called the "emergency relief coordinator" (ERC)—OCHA coordinates the relief activities of all UN agencies as well as NGOs, bilateral organizations, and other humanitarian actors. It oversees the formal humanitarian system and supports advocacy efforts, information management, policy creation and research, and financing.

Other UN agencies have mandates that include the direct provision of assistance to people affected by humanitarian crises. The most relevant are described in Table 4.1.[27] Although each of these agencies plays an important role in humanitarian action, most are also deeply involved in the distinct (but related) field of international development.

International non-governmental organizations

The world of humanitarian INGOs is vast and differentiated, representing a huge range of interests, approaches, capacities, and loyalties. They may be secular or faith-based, multi-mandate or focused on a particular issue. They can have funding structures that rely on donor governments, private foundations, corporations, and/or the general public. Some are small while others operate with budgets as large as major corporations or UN agencies. Their organizational structures also vary—for example, some are directed by national headquarters in a single country, while others have a federated international structure. However, almost all of the largest INGOs are organized based on

Table 4.1 UN agencies, funds, and programs engaging in humanitarian action

Agency	Role in humanitarian action
United Nations High Commissioner for Refugees (UNHCR)	UNHCR coordinates the **protection of refugees** around the world. It provides many types of direct assistance to refugees in host countries, including voluntary resettlement for the most vulnerable individuals. Its primary purpose is to "safeguard the rights and well-being of refugees."[28]
United Nations Children's Fund (UNICEF)	UNICEF supports the **protection and basic rights of children**, including during emergencies. It focuses on the provision of essential services for children, to meet their basic needs and expand their life opportunities.[29]
World Food Programme (WFP)	WFP supports **food security and nutrition** by managing supply chains and delivering assistance to those in need. It has expertise in logistics and emergency telecommunications, and supports the broader humanitarian response during crises.[30]
World Health Organization (WHO)	WHO partners with national and international actors to achieve positive **health outcomes** for all people. WHO plays an important role in preventing disease, strengthening health systems, and monitoring and preparing for public health emergencies.[31]
Food and Agriculture Organization (FAO)	FAO supports **food security, food production, and agriculture** through disaster prevention, early warning systems for food emergencies, and the rebuilding of food systems. It conducts needs assessments, provides agricultural supplies and technical assistance, and supports recovery, especially in rural contexts.[32]
International Organization for Migration (IOM)	IOM focuses on **humane and orderly migration** around the world by promoting international migration law, managing migration logistics, advising governments and migrants, and supporting the human dignity and well-being of migrants. During and after a humanitarian crisis, IOM often works closely with UNHCR to support the voluntary migration of refugees.[33]
United Nations Entity for Gender Equality and Empowerment of Women (UN Women)	UN Women seeks to accelerate progress on **gender equality and the empowerment of women**. The agency "came about as part of the UN reform agenda, bringing together resources and mandates for greater impact." During humanitarian crises, UN Women supports targeted programs and the integration of gender issues throughout the entire response effort.[34]

Agency	Role in humanitarian action
United Nations Development Programme (UNDP)	UNDP supports **sustainable development** in 166 countries around the world—seeking to build local capacity, to improve quality of life and opportunity, and to prepare for and prevent disasters. During a humanitarian crisis, UNDP assists in early recovery, economic recovery, rebuilding of infrastructure, and other immediate and longer-term projects.[35]
UN Population Fund (UNFPA)	UNFPA addresses **reproductive health and population issues** in developing countries and countries with economies in transition. Because reproductive and sexual health needs are often more acute during emergencies, UNFPA plays an important humanitarian role in ensuring health, safety, hygiene, and other basic needs.[36]
UN Office for the Coordination of Humanitarian Affairs (OCHA)	OCHA is the part of the United Nations Secretariat responsible for bringing together humanitarian actors to ensure a coherent response to emergencies. At the global, regional, and country levels, OCHA convenes humanitarian partners for the **coordinated, strategic, and accountable** delivery of humanitarian action.[37]

an international alliance, federation, or network. Together, this group of actors has traditionally been referred to as the "backbone" of humanitarian action.

INGOs are the main implementing partners for the delivery of goods and services on the ground. They are responsible for programming the majority of funds, including those channeled through the UN.[38] However, this funding is not equally distributed. In 2015, just five INGOs were responsible for 31 percent of all non-governmental expenditures on humanitarian aid.[39] These largest INGOs (in descending order) were MSF, SCF, Oxfam, World Vision, and the IRC.

The histories of some of the major NGOs, like SCF, were introduced in Chapter 2. A few additional examples presented in Box 4.2 provide a sense of the scope and scale for humanitarian INGOs.

Box 4.2 Overview of some INGOs

Médecins Sans Frontières (MSF). MSF is an international independent humanitarian organization focused on medical aid, medical infrastructure, and advocacy for people affected by humanitarian crises. MSF operates in more than 70 countries with a team of highly specialized foreign medical and engineering professionals coupled with locally hired staff. The organization is headquartered in Geneva and has a federated structure—in other words, each country section acts as an autonomous legal entity. MSF members are largely known for their willingness to speak out against events or actions they disagree with, and even other actors in the humanitarian space, when other groups do not.[40]

World Vision International (WVI). World Vision is a Christian relief and development organization and the twelfth largest charity in the United States, making it one of the largest humanitarian NGOs. Founded in 1950 to care for children in Asia, World Vision has now expanded its efforts globally to include emergency relief operations, education, healthcare, economic development, and the promotion of justice. The organization places a special emphasis on support for children and approximately half of its programs are funded through child sponsorship programs.[41]

International Rescue Committee (IRC). The IRC was founded in 1933 at the request of Albert Einstein, with a mission to protect victims of the Holocaust. It has grown into a global organization that responds to refugee crises around the world, providing advocacy, direct aid, and resettlement services. One of the unique components of the IRC is that it is one of only nine NGOs that works cooperatively with the US Department of State to resettle refugees inside the United States, providing housing assistance, language training, and other support. Thus, the IRC has extensive operations in cities across the United States as well as in crisis-affected countries around the world.[42]

NGO coordination and advocacy bodies

Although individual NGOs have limited power at the highest levels of the humanitarian system, several important umbrella groups exist to participate in international decision-making processes and influence the system as a whole. NGOs are often collectively represented through different NGO consortia such as the International Council of Voluntary Agencies (ICVA), Voluntary Organizations in Cooperation in Emergencies (VOICE), the Steering Committee for Humanitarian Response (SCHR), and InterAction. While their main function is to bring together NGOs to help influence policy, they also take on various accountability, operational, and learning activities. For example, ICVA (established in 1962) has always been at heart an advocacy grouping and a mechanism for encouraging the flow of resources from richer

Northern agencies to poorer but better placed Southern agencies. The SCHR was one of the first agency groupings to introduce and practice peer review in its programming. InterAction developed the *Private Voluntary Organization Standards* [43] that cover the governance of an organization, its organizational integrity, finances, communications, and human resource systems.

Other consortia have been formed to address global NGO priorities in other contexts; for example, the Emergency Capacity-Building (ECB) Project focuses on developing national-staff skills, facilitating collaboration, and creating practical tools and approaches to disaster preparedness and risk reduction programming. [44] The newest umbrella NGO group that focuses on advocacy is made up of Southern NGOs and called the Network for Empowered Aid Response (NEAR). Launched in 2016, NEAR includes 30 organizations from Africa, 21 from Asia, and 5 from the Middle East. It works to enable local and national organizations and advocates on their behalf at the international level.

Learning networks

Another important category of NGOs is dedicated to conducting research, evaluation, and evidence collection to strengthen humanitarian practice across the sector. Often, these are organized as partnerships or collaborations. ALNAP, for example, emerged after the response to the 1994 Rwandan genocide (see Chapter 2). Its mission is to rigorously evaluate humanitarian responses and make recommendations for improvement—with a particular emphasis on accountability. Another organization, called the Enhancing Learning and Research for Humanitarian Assistance (ELRHA), performs a similar function. ELRHA collaborates with researchers and practitioners to improve humanitarian practice—for example, through its Humanitarian Innovation Fund (HIF) initiative. Other learning networks fulfill roles that are more specialized. The Cash Learning Partnership (CaLP) generates research and evidence to "radically increase the scale and quality of cash transfer programming as a tool for humanitarian assistance." [45] Through its partners, it has collected and published a large body of evidence supporting cash-transfer programs.

Humanitarian government donors

Most humanitarian financing is from governments—either individually or through inter-governmental organizations like the EU and the African Union (AU). The distribution of government donations, however, is quite lopsided. Most financing comes from Western governments, with OECD members making up 94 percent of reported international humanitarian assistance as of 2015.[46] However, some funding from non-Western donors is not included in standard reporting channels and funds spent on humanitarian assistance domestically are not included in these figures. (For example, Turkey was a major international humanitarian donor in 2011–12—and still is—except that most of its contribution is for Syrian refugees inside Turkey, so that funding is not counted as "international humanitarian response.")

According to recent reports, "the system might finally be seeing genuine signs of 'rising donors' from outside the rich Western club."[47] While non-OECD countries have always played a role in humanitarian action, many have increased in visibility and prominence in the last decade. The largest increases in contributions from this donor group during 2012–14 came from Saudi Arabia and other Gulf states such as Kuwait and Qatar, with much of their funding targeted at the crisis in Syria.[48] The sharp rise in donorship from Middle Eastern countries—increasing by a reported 425 percent between 2011 and 2015—prompted hopes that this trend would continue. However, in 2016, levels fell by 24 percent, driven by major decreases from Kuwait, Qatar, and Saudi Arabia.[49] Non-OECD donors tend to give a larger share of their contributions directly to host governments than do other major humanitarian donors, and a far larger portion of their valuated contribution is in the form of in-kind goods and services.

Government donors support humanitarian responses based on commitments to end suffering and save lives, in alignment with national policies and priorities. However, decisions on where and how much to fund are rarely solely based on need.[50] According to humanitarian scholars Michael Barnett and Thomas Weiss, "States will use their interests to determine whose needs matter—and they have the power to get their way."[51] Governments are also influenced by historical, religious, and cultural ties as well as economic, security, and political priorities. These interests can lead to the preferential funding of certain humanitarian sectors and emergencies over others.

To better understand the role of donor governments, Box 4.3 provides a brief overview of some of today's humanitarian government donors.

Box 4.3 Overview of some humanitarian government donors

USAID/OFDA. The United States administers humanitarian support through the US Agency for International Development (USAID) and its subsidiary, the Office of US Foreign Disaster Assistance (OFDA).

OFDA was born 30 years ago in response to the Skopje earthquake in what was then Yugoslavia. The agency is primarily a humanitarian donor, providing financial support for UN agencies and US-based NGOs. However, OFDA also has its own operational components, including its Disaster Assistance and Response Teams (DARTs) and behind-the-scenes negotiations to secure access for humanitarian actors. For example, OFDA negotiated with Angola and Somalia in the 1990s, leading to an agreement in which both states allowed foreign aid workers to access rebel-controlled areas.[52]

Beyond financial and operational contributions, food aid makes up a significant share of US-based response efforts. Such donations are managed by the Office of Food for Peace (FFP) under USAID. In the past, much of FFP's activity has been regulated by laws that restrict much of its aid to in-kind, physical food items. As a result, US food aid was costly and slow to arrive, and some observers noted that such restrictions meant that the aid might not have been suited to the needs and tastes of affected people. Today, while some of FFP's assistance remains in-kind, there has been a significant push for more cash-based programming abroad. As a result, more than half of US emergency food assistance now is in the form of cash whereas traditionally it had all been in-kind food aid.[53] Since the 11 September terrorist attacks in New York, the shape of US humanitarian assistance has undergone radical changes. The old offices and mechanisms mentioned above remain, but they have been radically supplemented by other channels, not least the US military. This is mainly in response to the realization that many of the countries seeking humanitarian assistance—such as Afghanistan, Pakistan, Sudan, and Somalia—are also entangled in the so-called global war on terror.

EU/ECHO. The European Union has been the second largest donor (after the United States) of humanitarian assistance every year since 2000. In a typical year, the European Commission provides nearly 30 percent of global humanitarian aid, primarily through the European Civil Protection and Humanitarian Aid Operations (ECHO) Directorate-General. Unlike USAID, ECHO has no direct operations. Instead, around 60 percent of its funding is channeled through international NGOs (primarily those headquartered in European Union member states). The rest goes to UN agencies, the Red Cross Movement, and directly to disaster-affected states. In recent years, ECHO has had a policy of focusing on so-called forgotten emergencies; it was one of the major funders of the response in Sudan, before Darfur became more well-known.

UK/DFID. The United Kingdom is a leading international donor and supports a variety of development and humanitarian projects through its Department for International Development (DFID). Its foreign assistance programs have historical roots in efforts to establish financial independence among former British colonies during the mid-1900s.[54] In recent years, DFID has established itself as an influential and effective humanitarian donor—for example, leading the donor response to the Syria crisis and promoting important initiatives such as resilience programming and multi-year funding during the lead-up to the World Humanitarian Summit.[55] The UK is one of just a few donor countries to meet the international target for official development assistance (ODA) by contributing 0.7 percent of its gross national income;[56] only five OECD countries contributed a greater share (Denmark, the Netherlands, Norway, Luxembourg, and Sweden). DFID has also set itself apart by consistently contributing the largest share to humanitarian pooled funds, such as the CERF, discussed further in Chapter 5.[57]

China. China has an ancient tradition of philanthropy, largely based on the Confucian concepts of legitimacy and responsibility. The term *rendao* (humanitarian) first appeared in Chinese literature two millennia ago. While Europe was still in its Middle Ages, China already had sophisticated state systems for relief in times of famine or disaster.[58] However, in modern-day China any expansion of the government's role in humanitarian action abroad faces considerable obstacles. The country has historically been suspicious of the West, the Maoist political framework dismisses charity as "bourgeois" and undesirable, and the government has emphasized non-interference in the internal matters of other states. However, most observers expect China to become increasingly active on its own terms in humanitarian action abroad.[59] Recent statements from diplomats and government officials have signaled a new willingness to engage in global cooperation. In 2017, President Xi Jinping declared his intention to "resolutely uphold the authority and status of the United Nations, actively fulfill China's international obligations and duties ... and always be a builder of world peace, contributor of global development and keeper of international order."[60] Although some observers have noted that Chinese assistance, like many other governments, often appears to support its own economic interests,[61] its strengthened role in humanitarian aid and development marks a turning point for the global system. China has recently provided state-sponsored assistance in many crises, including Typhoon Haiyan and the Nepal earthquake in 2013 and 2015, respectively. Numerous more or less independent NGOs and philanthropic groups are also emerging within the country.[62]

Turkey/TIKA. The Turkish International Cooperation and Development Agency (TIKA), along with the Turkish Red Crescent and many Turkish NGOs, was a prominent humanitarian donor during the Somali famine of 2011 and its aftermath. While these organizations have not been in the country since 2014, Turkey's model has been hailed as sustainable for its emphasis on a combination of both humanitarian and development assistance.[63] Turkey has also been a major humanitarian actor in the Syria crisis since it began, with programs implemented both by the state and by NGOs.[64] By 2013, Turkey had become the fourth largest humanitarian donor in the world (although its share has subsequently declined).[65] Istanbul also hosted the World Humanitarian Summit in 2016.

The wider humanitarian network

In addition to the traditional actors described above, numerous organizations have mandates not solely dedicated to providing humanitarian aid but in many cases vital to humanitarian action. These actors have predominantly included militaries, UN peacekeeping forces, media, private donors, and religious organizations. Today, a variety of other players are also contributing to humanitarian action in new ways— for example, private sector businesses, development agencies, and international financial institutions (IFIs) like the World Bank.

While the traditional UN-established system still in many ways represents the public face of humanitarian action, these actors are now involved in every major response—fundamentally reshaping the entire humanitarian system.

Militaries

Foreign and national militaries have a long history of involvement in humanitarian action. The Geneva Conventions specifically require victorious or occupying militaries to address the basic needs of the population, including food, shelter, water, and healthcare. According to Articles 56 and 57 of the Fourth Geneva Convention, "The Occupying Power has the duty of ensuring the food and medical supplies of the population; it should, in particular, bring in the necessary foodstuffs, medical stores and other articles if the resources of the occupied territory are inadequate."[66]

However, the bulk of military-based humanitarian action does not take place within this strict framework. Often the military force is not engaged in combat operations but is providing assistance as part of its country's foreign policy towards the crisis-stricken state. This assistance has traditionally taken the form of logistical support. During the 1980s, for example, many Western states provided air force personnel and equipment for airdrops of food supplies into famine-stricken Sudan and Ethiopia.[67] At the end of the First Gulf War, allied military forces (with the backing of the UN Security Council) created a Kurdish "safe haven" in northern Iraq and then supplied it with humanitarian aid. That same year, allied forces returning from the First Gulf War assisted cyclone victims in Bangladesh. A new set of standards for military operations during disaster recovery was established by the "Oslo Guidelines on the Use of Foreign Military and Civil Defense Assets in Disaster Relief." Released in 1994, the guidelines highlight the principle that foreign military support should be requested only where there is no comparable civilian alternative.[68] The national military in the country experiencing the crisis is also a main player. For example, the Pakistani army and air force have played critical roles in supporting relief activities during the numerous floods and earthquakes experienced in Pakistan over the past decade.

A new military approach to humanitarianism has gradually emerged, beginning with the Kurdish "safe haven" and subsequent operations in the Balkans, Kosovo, Afghanistan, and Iraq, and increasingly blurring the boundaries between traditional humanitarian action and military operations. Militaries have gone beyond provision of logistical support to actively planning and executing what might otherwise be seen as humanitarian operations. Some of the sums involved are massive. The US Commander's Emergency Response Program (CERP) funded local governance, public services, and quality of life projects during the wars in Iraq and Afghanistan—$800 million in 2012–14 for Afghanistan alone.[69]

As discussed in Chapter 3, this blurring of military and humanitarian aims has been controversial over the years. Many individual humanitarian aid workers might well privately support military action in the humanitarian arena. However, the modus operandi of humanitarian action as neutral and impartial complicates their relationship with militaries when they may be actively participating in violent conflicts, still have mandates that allow them to harm civilians, or need to prioritize their own security over the security of the local population.

Peacekeeping

Foreign militaries also provide security during humanitarian operations—as peacekeepers, peace enforcers, military escorts, clearers of land mines, and the like, whether under the umbrella of the UN or as national or regional military forces. In these contexts, the role of external military forces is something that is negotiated and agreed upon by the warring parties. In theory, such a military force is welcomed and trusted by all parties. In practice, however, such forces are often perceived by local populations and combatants as participating in the conflict—or they become targets themselves, as in the case of UNAMIR in Rwanda.

The UN Charter establishes two categories for legitimate peace-keeping operations. Chapter VI of the charter deals with the peaceful settlement of disputes and essentially allows for UN peacekeeping forces to be physically present—to monitor a peaceful settlement and, through their passive presence, discourage violence. In other words, Chapter VI assumes that all parties want and are willing to work for peace. Chapter VII is more robust, addressing threats to peace and unlawful acts of aggression. In such instances, it allows the Security Council to use armed force against warring parties threatening civilians.[70] The UN has mounted 63 peacekeeping and peacemaking operations in its history and had 15 active missions involving over 110,000 personnel during 2017.[71]

Media

The media does not provide humanitarian assistance *per se* but journalists work alongside humanitarians in emergencies—and their work is essential to galvanizing donor resources and political support for international action. Specialized media agencies such as IRIN News exclusively report on humanitarian crises and debates and are regularly republished by other news sources.

The case study of the 1984 Ethiopian famine noted that the media have had a major influence on how global aid is given (see Chapter 2). Such influence continues today; the world was horrified by photos of the drowned three-year-old Syrian boy, Alan Kurdi, who made global headlines in 2015 when photos of his body washed up on a beach in Turkey went viral (see Chapter 3). Consequently, donations to the Syria crisis and other organizations that help migrants spiked in the weeks following the story, though quickly returned to normal. Despite the short-lived nature of the increase in charitable giving, the photos of

Alan published by the media were able to increase awareness and advocacy for the plight of refugees and migrants.[72]

An emerging approach also argues that media and information are themselves critical forms of aid—for example, during the Ebola crisis, media played an important role in sharing information about how to contain outbreaks.[73] Initiatives like First Response Radio seek to rapidly set up radio stations during humanitarian responses, in order to communicate timely and accurate information with affected populations.[74] Of course there are also numerous challenges, such as when media cover certain crises and neglect others, or focus solely on the immediacy of a crisis rather than the vital areas of preparedness, long-term support, or rebuilding efforts.

Volunteer and grassroots organizations

Throughout history, volunteer groups and grassroots organizations have played a significant role in providing aid after crisis. While they often include actors from other categories mentioned in this chapter, especially the "Affected Communities/Providers of First Resort" group, volunteer networks are increasingly being recognized as an independent type of humanitarian actor.

These groups have gained increased attention from humanitarian scholars and organizations, most recently in response to their work supporting the over 1.5 million refugees and irregular migrants arriving in Europe since 2015. A research report in 2016 completed a provisional inventory and counted 216 volunteer groups across Europe as having participated in, or contributed to, the response. These groups took on vital response and advocacy activities, and established both ad hoc and complex coordination arrangements.[75]

Many questions need answering with regard to how these groups will continue to grow and formalize and what their relationship to accountability and protection standards, funding mechanisms, and partnership arrangements will be. Also crucial is how more formalized actors will begin to work with and learn from them.

Religious groups

Religious groups play a wide variety of roles related to humanitarian action. Some INGOs have religious foundations, such as Caritas and Islamic Relief Worldwide. However, other more peripheral actors are also motivated by religious belief—including local religious communities that donate resources and religious leaders who call attention to humanitarian needs. Many religious communities also organize mission trips abroad—inviting ordinary members of the congregation to engage in some type of volunteer work.

Religiously motivated humanitarian action can be effective and valuable. However, groups that combine evangelism with aid work violate the fundamental principles of neutrality and impartiality. Caritas, a global network of locally based Catholic organizations, is careful to provide aid based on need alone, "regardless of race or religion."[76] Other groups that operate outside the formal humanitarian system may not be willing or able to make such a commitment.

Regional inter-governmental and faith-based organizations

Regionally based inter-governmental organizations are beginning to influence development and humanitarian systems around the world. Such entities include the Association of East Asian Nations (ASEAN), the OIC, AU, and many others.[77] For example, the OIC has played a major role during emergencies, including the famine in Somalia in 2011. The emergence of such regional bodies reflects a desire to foster unity among members while also protecting sovereignty. The response from more-established Western actors has included "interest, suspicion, concern, openness and opportunism: interest in their origins and attitudes; suspicion of their motives; concern at a lack of professionalism and coordination."[78]

Nevertheless, regional bodies are playing an increasingly important role in humanitarian coordination and in many other areas (as discussed below). A new effort called the Regional Organisations Humanitarian Action Network (ROHAN) was launched in 2016 to "strengthen capacities and collaboration within and between regional organisations."[79] Its members represent major regional organizations from around the world.

Private donors

The number of non-state funders of humanitarian assistance is growing. One-quarter of funding for humanitarian assistance comes from private donors, the majority of whom are individuals.[80] Some large NGOs rely extensively on individual contributions, including World Vision International and MSF. Individual contributions tend to be a stable and flexible source of humanitarian funding. In comparison, donations from larger institutions can be less predictable and are often earmarked for specific activities.[81] There is also a growing influence of foundations, not only in terms of funding but also policy development.

Additionally, new platforms are making private contributions easier and more popular—in some cases bypassing operational agencies to give directly to the poor. GiveDirectly, for example, is a cash transfer program that allocates funds with minimal overhead to the world's poorest households. This new model has proven successful so far. According to a randomized controlled trial study—considered the gold standard for evidence—the impact per $1,000 in cash transfers was a $270 increase in earnings, $430 increase in assets, and $330 increase in spending on nutrition on average per household.[82]

Private sector

For-profit companies are increasingly involved in humanitarian action, both directly and indirectly.[83] This group of actors is diverse and multi-faceted, and includes large multinational corporations, local businesses in crisis-affected countries, and everything in between. While the private sector has always been involved in humanitarian action to some extent, it has recently begun to play a larger and more integral role.

Rather than simply contributing financial resources, commercial partners are increasingly seen as a resource for technical expertise and sometimes delivery of goods and services.[84] For example, in terms of large global companies, DHL and Ericsson have been working to support humanitarian logistics and telecommunications for years.[85] More recently, companies like Google have played an important role in developing engineering solutions and other innovations to support humanitarian action. One example of private sector partnerships is around the use of humanitarian data. The United Nations Children's Fund (UNICEF) recently launched a new initiative called "Data for Children," collaborating with Facebook and many other organizations to craft a more data-driven humanitarian response.[86] Although such partnerships are now common, most are marginal activities for a large company. Overall, they do not add up to any significant shift in who is carrying out the global humanitarian response.[87] In a different kind of direct engagement, local business communities play an increasingly large role in crisis response, as was seen in the Somalia famine in 2011.[88]

The heightened role of private sector actors raises numerous serious questions. The most common reservation among humanitarian actors is that these actors are motivated primarily by profit—not necessarily by humanitarian principles. Other questions also exist—for example, what does small- and medium-scale local private sector activity look like in emergency response? What are the issues around the role of private security companies being used by states and in some instances humanitarian organizations?[89] And how is the system factoring in the issues around businesses themselves being affected by crises? In a 2014 survey of private sector actors in North and Southeast Asia conducted by OCHA and the World Humanitarian Summit, 96 percent reported being affected by a disaster.[90] Addressing such questions will be necessary to fully integrate the private sector into humanitarian response.

Development actors

Although humanitarian and development actors address different problems and have different approaches, the majority of INGOs have multi-mandates, and bridging the humanitarian–development divide has been a programmatic goal for decades. Today, given the protracted nature of humanitarian crises—and the interrelated drivers of urbanization and climate change—the debate has reemerged along with a policy agenda termed "The New Way of Working", and donor policies looking at the "humanitarian–development nexus". In summary, this initiative involves trying to expand initial programming so that humanitarian organizations can plan to work over multiple years and define shared outcomes between humanitarian and development actors. This reemergence has led to an increase in traditional development actors, such as the United Nations Development Programme (UNDP) and the IFIs (described below) getting more involved in humanitarian action.[91]

Some working in the humanitarian field worry about the implications of including development actors within the wider humanitarian system. One of their main worries is the continuation of the humanitarian principles, which development actors may not always be capable of upholding. For example, many development initiatives involve working closely with country governments to build capacity and institute regulation. In a scenario where a government is viewed as party to a conflict, the principle of neutrality is eroded, and this can cause some to see humanitarian and development organizations as "taking sides." Others worry that the respective organizational structures of humanitarian and development organizations will make it difficult to collaborate effectively. Regardless, due to the current prominence of the humanitarian–development nexus as an aid agenda, future relief efforts will likely see further collaboration between these actors.

International financial institutions

International financial institutions (IFIs) such as the World Bank, the European Investment Bank and many others, play an important role, especially in international development efforts. However, their work is becoming more important in humanitarian action as well.

The World Bank has been among the most prominent IFIs to begin shifting its approach towards humanitarian crises. It has recognized, for example, that developing countries host the vast majority of the 65 million refugees around the world,[92] meaning progress in development is not likely to occur without addressing refugee crises and the emergencies that cause them in the first place. The World Bank has thus implemented a range of programs in recent years targeted specifically at humanitarian crises. For example, in 2017, the organization rolled out a famine response package, which included 17 projects meant to "build social protection systems, strengthen community resilience, and maintain service delivery to the most vulnerable."[93] Additionally, the World Bank hosted the Fragility Forum in the spring of 2018 to address the problems of conflict and violence in fragile states. One of the projects discussed at the forum, for example, addresses forced displacement in the Horn of Africa. Another seeks to improve social cohesion between refugees and a host community in Lebanon.[94]

Conclusion: understanding the philosophies and objectives of humanitarians

This chapter has focused on the major actors, sorting them into categories defined mostly by funding structures, governance models, and mandates. And while these actors can all be placed under this umbrella of "humanitarian action," they have an incredible and sometimes bewildering diversity of aims and objectives, and loyalties. Understanding these differences in loyalties and objectives is also critical to grasping why many of the challenges in providing coordinated humanitarian aid exist. Therefore, this chapter will conclude by reviewing the differing philosophical lenses that researchers have used in the past to interpret why organizations and actors take their various positions.[95]

The first philosophical approach might be labeled as *principle-centered*. Followers consist largely of those in the Dunantist tradition (such as the ICRC and MSF). These actors may closely adhere to the principles that defined classic humanitarianism: humanity, neutrality, impartiality, universality, and independence. In many ways this position could be described as being as concerned with the means of humanitarianism (principles) as the outcomes (impact on humanitarian need). The outcomes they favor are generally a more minimalist, life-saving kind of humanitarianism.

A second approach might be considered more pragmatic or *Wilsonian*. Named after the US president Woodrow Wilson and his interventionist approach to foreign affairs in the aftermath of WWI, this approach is largely defined by a tendency to focus on outcomes, on impact, and relatively less on the means by which these are achieved. These agencies (and often donors) are not afraid to operate in politically charged atmospheres and tend to be aligned with the political agendas of their funders or constituencies.

A third philosophy can be to take a more *solidarist* in approach. This outlook grows out of the principled approach, but has gone far beyond its traditional boundaries. Generally, it includes an expanded definition of humanitarianism that includes looking at underlying causes, human rights, and social transformation in addition to simply saving lives—in general, trying to identify closely with the most affected groups. Some organizations in this group have no problem with humanitarian action that is not only political but sometimes flagrantly partisan. However, many actors that take a "solidarist" approach in programing would also claim to be impartial and non-partisan when it comes to providing assistance, even if most in this group question the notion of neutrality.

An additional, and somewhat more diverse philosophy can come from a *faith-based* approach. Philosophically, the perspectives of faith-based organizations cut across the other three. Although many faith-based organizations have become operationally similar to those in other categories, their fundamental principles are defined by a religious creed, not by secular principles or outcomes.

These categories are by no means mutually exclusive. For example, the "principled" and "solidarist" strains of thought often mix and many actors clearly mix "Wilsonian" pragmatism with "solidarist" philosophies. However, most importantly, over the past decade, these philosophies have become too narrow to define the aims of humanitarian actors.

The first and most obvious deviation is that most of the organizations and actors described in this chapter are not solely, or even primarily, *humanitarian* in their perspective or programming. Many would describe the fight against global poverty or a commitment to social justice as a more over-riding objective. Others have profit motives or political motives. Nevertheless, these organizations have significant humanitarian capacity and programming and are entities that must be understood in assessing global humanitarian response.

Altogether, the multiplicity of actors and their objectives is too great to capture in a few paragraphs. Boundaries, if they exist at all between these categories, are very blurred and will continue to move over time. Therefore, the way this chapter has outlined and categorized the actors will need to continue to change. The most significant changes will ideally happen in terms of giving prominence and power to local structures and actors and learning how to merge differing objectives and philosophies that can truly create a humanitarian system that can assist vulnerable populations.

Notes

1 Paul Currion, *Network Humanitarianism* (London: Humanitarian Policy Group, 2018), https://www.odi.org/sites/odi.org.uk/files/resource-documents /12202.pdf.
2 Linda Polman and Liz Waters, *The Crisis Caravan: What's Wrong with Humanitarian Aid?* (New York: Metropolitan Books, 2010), 9–10.
3 Randolph Kent, Christina Bennett, Antonio Donini, and Daniel Maxwell, *Planning from the Future: Is the Humanitarian System Fit for Purpose?* (London; Medford, Mass.: Humanitarian Policy Group at the Overseas Development Institute; Feinstein International Center at Tufts University; the Policy Institute at King's College London, 2016), www.planningfrom thefuture.org/uploads/4/5/6/0/45605399/pff_report_uk.pdf.
4 Kent et al., *Planning from the Future*.
5 Cultural Survival, "Guatemala Communities Hit Hard by Tropical Storm Agatha," https://www.culturalsurvival.org/news/guatemala-communities-hit -hard-tropical-storm-agatha.
6 Yasmeen Serhan, "Who Are the White Helmets?" *The Atlantic*, 30 September 2016, https://www.theatlantic.com/news/archive/2016/09/syria-white -helmets/502073/.
7 Kent et al., *Planning from the Future*.
8 Kent et al., *Planning from the Future*.
9 Paul Harvey, "International Humanitarian Actors and Governments in Areas of Conflict: Challenges, Obligations, and Opportunities.," *Disasters* 37, no. s2 (22 July 2013): 158.
10 Paul Harvey, *The Role of National Governments in International Humanitarian Response to Disasters* (Kuala Lumpur, Malaysia: ALNAP, 2010), https://www.alnap.org/system/files/content/resource/files/main/26-meeting-ba ckground-paper.pdf.
11 Joanna Macrae, *Aiding Recovery? The Crisis of Aid in Chronic Political Emergencies* (London: Zed Books, 2001).
12 Lesley Bourns and Jessica Alexander, *Leaving No One Behind: Humanitarian Effectiveness in the Age of the Sustainable Development Goals*, OCHA Policy and Studies Series (OCHA; CDA Collaborative Learning Projects, 2016), https://www.unocha.org/sites/unocha/files/LeavingNooneBe hind_20151109_Small.pdf.
13 Stella Madete, "Three Reasons National Organisations Are Vital to Humanitarian Response in South Sudan," *Oxfam Policy and Practice Blog*

(blog), 6 June 2016, https://policy-practice.oxfam.org.uk/blog/2016/06/three-reasons-national-organisations-are-vital-to-humanitarian-response-in-south-sudan.

14 Kent et al., *Planning from the Future.*
15 Development Initiatives, *Global Humanitarian Assistance Report 2017: Executive Summary* (Development Initiatives, 2017), http://devinit.org/wp-content/uploads/2017/06/GHA-Report-2017-Executive-summary.pdf.
16 Kent et al., *Planning from the Future.*
17 Bourns and Alexander, *Leaving No One Behind.*
18 Fabrice Weissman, "Scaling Up Aid in Syria: The Role of Diaspora Networks," *Overseas Development Institute (ODI) Humanitarian Practice Network (HPN)* (blog), July 2013, https://odihpn.org/blog/scaling-up-aid-in-syria-the-role-of-diaspora-networks/.
19 Bourns and Alexander, *Leaving No One Behind.*
20 Kate Burns, "General Assembly Resolution 46/182," Policy Paper, OCHA on Message (OCHA, 2012), https://www.unocha.org/sites/unocha/files/dms/Documents/120402_OOM-46182_eng.pdf.
21 Burns, "General Assembly Resolution 46/182."
22 IFRC, "The International Red Cross and Red Crescent Movement," International Federation of Red Cross and Red Crescent Societies, www.ifrc.org/en/who-we-are/the-movement/.
23 OCHA, "International Humanitarian Architecture," in *Disaster Response in Asia and the Pacific: A Guide to International Tools and Services* (OCHA, 2013), 8–29, https://www.unocha.org/sites/unocha/files/dms/ROAP/Promotional%20Materials/The%20Guide-Web-FINAL.pdf.
24 ICRC, *ICRC Annual Report 2017* (Geneva: International Committee of the Red Cross, 2018), https://www.icrc.org/en/document/annual-report-2017.
25 American Red Cross, "The Global Red Cross Network," American Red Cross, 2018, www.redcross.org/about-us/who-we-are/history/global-red-cross-network.
26 Peter Walker and Daniel G. Maxwell, *Shaping the Humanitarian World*, Global Institutions Series (Abingdon; New York: Routledge, 2009), 33.
27 OCHA, "International Humanitarian Architecture."
28 UNHCR, "UNHCR Mission Statement," UNHCR, 2008, www.unhcr.org/4a2d2e362.pdf.
29 UNICEF, "UNICEF's Mission Statement," UNICEF, 2003, https://www.unicef.org/about/who/index_mission.html.
30 WFP, "Mission," World Food Programme (WFP), https://donate.wfp.org/supporter/casematerial.do?n=gbss&cmdbid=1033610&or=ld; WFP, "Humanitarian Support and Services," World Food Programme (WFP), http://www1.wfp.org/humanitarian-support-and-services.
31 WHO, "Better Health for Everyone, Everywhere," World Health Organization, 2018, www.who.int/healthpromotion/about/goals/en/.
32 FAO, "Mission Statement: FAO's Role in Emergencies," Food and Agriculture Organization of the United Nations (FAO), www.fao.org/focus/e/disaster/mstate-e.htm.
33 IOM, "Mission," International Organization for Migration (IOM), 2018, https://www.iom.int/mission.
34 UN Women, "About UN Women," UN Women, 2018, www.unwomen.org/about-us/about-un-women.

35　University of Minnesota, "Organization: UN Development Programme," University of Minnesota Human Rights Library, http://hrlibrary.umn.edu/UNDP.html.

36　United Nations, "UNFPA Defines Its Mission," United Nations, www.un.org/popin/regional/asiapac/fiji/news/96aug/7.html; UNFPA, "Humanitarian Emergencies," United Nations Population Fund (UNFPA), www.unfpa.org/emergencies.

37　OCHA, "Who We Are," United Nations Office for the Coordination of Humanitarian Affairs, 27 September 2016, https://www.unocha.org/about-us/who-we-are.

38　Bill Morton, "Case Study 7: An Overview of INGOs in Development Cooperation," in *Working with Civil Society in Foreign Aid: Possibilities for South-South Cooperation?*, by Brian Tomlinson (China: UNDP, 2013), 325–352, www.cn.undp.org/content/dam/china/docs/Publications/UNDP-CH11%20An%20Overview%20of%20International%20NGOs%20in%20Development%20Cooperation.pdf.

39　ALNAP, *The State of the Humanitarian System 2015* (London: ALNAP/Overseas Development Institute, 2015), 40, https://www.alnap.org/system/files/content/resource/files/main/alnap-sohs-2015-web.pdf.

40　MSF, "MSF to Pull Out of World Humanitarian Summit," *Médecins sans Frontières* (blog), 5 May 2016, www.msf.org/en/article/msf-pull-out-world-humanitarian-summit.

41　World Vision, "Mission & Values," World Vision, 2018, https://www.worldvision.org/about-us/mission-statement.

42　Center for International Stabilization and Recovery, "International Rescue Committee," James Madison University Center for International Stabilization and Recovery, 2018, https://www.jmu.edu/cisr/_pages/research/gmar/search/international-rescue-committee-irc.shtml.

43　InterAction, "InterAction PVO Standards," June 2017, https://www.interaction.org/document/interaction-pvo-standards.

44　OCHA, "International Humanitarian Architecture."

45　CaLP, "About Us," The Cash Learning Partnership (CaLP), www.cashlearning.org/about-us/overview.

46　Céline Billat, "The Funding of Humanitarian Action by Non-Western Donors: The Sustainability of Gulf States' Contribution" (Geneva: CERAH Geneve, 2015), www.cerahgeneve.ch/files/1714/5268/0956/BILLAT_Celine_-_MAS_Dissertation_CERAH_2015_-_20.11.2015.pdf.

47　ALNAP, *State of the Humanitarian System 2015*.

48　ALNAP, *State of the Humanitarian System 2015*.

49　Sophia Swithern, "Humanitarian Funding: What Were 2016's Key Trends?", *Development Initiatives* (blog), 22 June 2017, http://devinit.org/post/humanitarian-funding-what-were-2016s-key-trends/.

50　Kent et al., *Planning from the Future*.

51　Michael Barnett and Thomas G. Weiss, *Humanitarianism Contested: Where Angels Fear to Tread* (Abingdon: Routledge, 2011).

52　Andrew S. Natsios, *U.S. Foreign Policy and the Four Horsemen of the Apocalypse: Humanitarian Relief in Complex Emergencies*, Washington Papers 170 (Westport, Conn.: Praeger, 1997).

53　USAID, "Fiscal Year 2017 Fact Sheet" (Fiscal Year 2017 Fact Sheet: United States Agency for International Development Office of Food for

Peace, 16 April 2018), https://www.usaid.gov/sites/default/files/documents/1866/FY_2017_factsheet_condensed_4.17.2018.pdf.

54 Barrie Ireton, *Britain's International Development Policies: A History of DFID and Overseas Aid* (Basingstoke; New York: Palgrave Macmillan, 2013), 4–10.

55 OECD, *OECD Development Co-Operation Peer Reviews: United Kingdom 2014* (OECD Publishing, 2014), 89, www.oecd.org/dac/peer-reviews/UK%20peer%20review%202014.pdf; Courtenay Cabot Venton, *Value for Money of Multi-Year Approaches to Humanitarian Funding* (London: Department for International Development, 2013), https://www.gov.uk/government/uploads/system/uploads/attachment_data/file/226161/VfM_of_Multi-year_Humanitarian_Funding_Report.pdf.

56 Ben Quinn, "UK Among Six Countries to Hit 0.7% UN Aid Spending Target," *Guardian*, 4 January 2017, www.theguardian.com/global-development/2017/jan/04/uk-among-six-countries-hit-un-aid-spending-target-oecd.

57 OECD, *OECD Development Co-Operation Peer Reviews*.

58 Hanna Krebs, *The "Chinese Way"? The Evolution of Chinese Humanitarianism*, HPG Policy Brief 62 (London: Overseas Development Institute, 2014), https://www.odi.org/sites/odi.org.uk/files/odi-assets/publications-opinion-files/9140.pdf.

59 Hanna Krebs, "What You Need to Understand About Chinese Humanitarian Aid," *Overseas Development Institute (ODI)* (blog), 6 November 2015, https://www.odi.org/comment/10066-chinese-humanitarian-aid-policy-ideology.

60 Anthony Kuhn, "Emboldened by a Strengthening Economy, China Flexes Its Diplomatic Muscles," *NPR* (blog), 1 January 2018, https://www.npr.org/sections/parallels/2018/01/01/573773442/emboldened-by-a-strengthening-economy-china-flexes-its-diplomatic-muscles.

61 Kuhn, "Emboldened."

62 Kent et al., *Planning from the Future*.

63 Afyare Abdi Elmi, "Ending Famine in Somalia, the Turkish Way," *Al Jazeera*, 19 March 2017, www.aljazeera.com/indepth/opinion/2017/03/famine-somalia-turkish-170319101255256.html.

64 Kent et al., *Planning from the Future*.

65 Kent et al., *Planning from the Future*.

66 Convention (IV) Relative to the Protection of Civilian Persons in Time of War, 12 August 1949, https://ihl-databases.icrc.org/ihl/385ec082b509e76c41256739003e636d/6756482d86146898c125641e004aa3c5.

67 Peter Walker, "Foreign Military Resources for Disaster Relief: An NGO Perspective," *Disasters* 16, no. 2 (1992): 152–159.

68 OCHA, *Oslo Guidelines: Guidelines on The Use of Foreign Military and Civil Defence Assets in Disaster Relief* (United Nations Office for the Coordination of Humanitarian Affairs, 2007), https://www.unocha.org/sites/unocha/files/OSLO%20Guidelines%20Rev%201.1%20-%20Nov%2007_0.pdf.

69 SIGAR, *Department of Defense Spending on Afghanistan Reconstruction: Contracts Comprised $21 Billion of $66 Billion in Total Appropriations, 2002–May 2014* (Special Inspector General for Afghanistan Reconstruction, 2015), 8, https://www.sigar.mil/pdf/special%20projects/SIGAR-15-40-SP.pdf.

70 United Nations, "Charter of the United Nations," United Nations, 10 August 2015, www.un.org/en/charter-united-nations/.

71 United Nations Peacekeeping, "Where We Operate," United Nations Peacekeeping, 2017, https://peacekeeping.un.org/en/where-we-operate.

72 Diane Cole, "Study: What Was the Impact of the Iconic Photo of the Syrian Boy?" *NPR* (blog), 13 January 2017, https://www.npr.org/sections/goatsandsoda/2017/01/13/509650251/study-what-was-the-impact-of-the-iconic-photo-of-the-syrian-boy.

73 Jeffrey Ghannam, *Media as a Form of Aid in Humanitarian Crises* (Washington, DC: Center for International Media Assistance (CIMA), 2016), https://www.cima.ned.org/resource/media-as-a-form-of-aid-in-humanitarian-crises/.

74 First Reponse Radio, "Strategy," First Response Radio, www.firstresponseradio.org/frr-strategy.html.

75 John Borton, *Humanitarian Impulse: Alive and Well among the Citizens of Europe*, HPN Number 67 (London: Overseas Development Institute, September 2016), https://odihpn.org/magazine/humanitarian-impulse-alive-well-among-citizens-europe/.

76 Caritas, "Who We Are," Caritas Internationalis, https://www.caritas.org/who-we-are/.

77 Eleanor Davey, *New Players Through Old Lenses: Why History Matters in Engaging with Southern Actors*, HPG Policy Brief (London: Overseas Development Institute, 2012), https://www.odi.org/sites/odi.org.uk/files/odi-assets/publications-opinion-files/7726.pdf; Pierre Micheletti, *We Need to De-Westernize International Non-Governmental Humanitarian Aid* (Geneva: Security Management Initiative, 2010), https://www.eisf.eu/wp-content/uploads/2014/09/0222-Micheletti-2010-We-need-to-de-westernize-humanitarina-aid.pdf.

78 Davey, *New Players Through Old Lenses*.

79 OCHA, "The ROHAN Network," Agenda for Humanity, (2016), https://www.agendaforhumanity.org/initiatives/3857.

80 Chloe Stirk, *Humanitarian Assistance from Non-State Donors: What Is It Worth?*, Briefing Paper (Bristol: Development Initiatives, 2014), http://devinit.org/wp-content/uploads/2014/05/Humanitarian-assistance-from-non-state-donors-2014.pdf.

81 Stirk, *Humanitarian Assistance*; Kent et al., *Planning from the Future*.

82 Johannes Haushofer and Jeremy Shapiro, "The Short-Term Impact of Unconditional Cash Transfers to the Poor: Experimental Evidence from Kenya," *The Quarterly Journal of Economics* 131, no. 4 (2016): 2057–2060.

83 Steven Zyck and Randolph Kent, *Humanitarian Crises, Emergency Preparedness and Response: The Role of Business and the Private Sector* (London: Overseas Development Institute, 2014), https://www.odi.org/sites/odi.org.uk/files/odi-assets/publications-opinion-files/9078.pdf.

84 Zyck and Kent, *Humanitarian Crises, Emergency Preparedness*.

85 OCHA, "International Humanitarian Architecture."

86 UNICEF, *Data for Children: Strategic Framework* (UNICEF, 2017), 1, https://data.unicef.org/wp-content/uploads/2017/04/Data-for-Children-Strategic-Framework-UNICEF.pdf.

87 ALNAP, *State of the Humanitarian System 2015*.

88 Daniel Maxwell and Nisar Majid, *Famine in Somalia: Competing Imperatives, Collective Failures, 2011–12* (London: Hurst, 2016).

89 Christopher Spearin, "Private Security Companies and Humanitarians: A Corporate Solution to Securing Humanitarian Spaces?," *International Peacekeeping* 8, no. 1 (2001): 20–43.

90 Bourns and Alexander, *Leaving No One Behind.*

91 Lucy Earle, "Addressing Urban Crises: Bridging the Humanitarian–Development Divide," *International Review of the Red Cross* 98, no. 901 (2016): 215–224.

92 UNHCR, *Global Trends in Forced Displacement In 2015* (United Nations High Commissioner for Refugees, 2016), www.unhcr.org/en-us/statistics/unhcrstats/576408cd7/unhcr-global-trends-2015.html.

93 The World Bank, "Fact Sheet: The World Bank Group's Response to the Famine Crisis," *The World Bank* (blog), 28 November 2017, www.worldbank.org/en/topic/fragilityconflictviolence/brief/fact-sheet-the-world-bank-group s-response-to-the-famine-crisis.

94 The World Bank, "Sharing Knowledge to Promote Peaceful and Inclusive Societies," The World Bank, 2018, www.worldbank.org/en/topic/fragility conflictviolence/overview#3.

95 Abby Stoddard, *Humanitarian Alert: NGO Information and Its Impact on US Foreign Policy.* (Bloomfield, Conn.: Kumarian Press, 2006).

5 Contemporary humanitarian architecture and action

- **Architecture: How is the global humanitarian network organized and coordinated?**
- **United Nations-established coordination system**
- **Coordination outside the UN system**
- **Humanitarian action: What happens in humanitarian response?**
- **Conclusion: incomplete and unfinished**

Given all of the actors described in Chapter 4, the next question is: How are they possibly organized? And what do they actually do? Taking a snapshot of some of the most prominent elements of the 2017 response to the crisis in Yemen shows that at least 122 different international humanitarian actors, including NGOs, UN agencies, and other intergovernmental organizations were participating in formal coordinated response efforts.[1]

Their work included activities and programs ranging from the ICRC advocating for civilian protection through efforts to achieve greater adherence to IHL. CARE and similar INGOs that had long-term development programs in place prior to the conflict also began providing short-term life-saving emergency assistance. Islamic Relief sent water tanks to IDPs. MSF carried out emergency medical assistance and condemned attacks on civilians and neutral medical personnel. The UN Humanitarian Coordinator (HC), the Humanitarian Country Team (HCT) and OCHA attempted to coordinate activities by developing strategic response plans and funding appeals. Outside of the coordinated response, over 53 different private sector actors were directly supporting conflict-affected people mostly with financial support, food, and other life-saving assistance as well as early recovery programming through vocational skills training.[2] Finally, local organizations and affected populations were a major source of relief and advocacy for most communities and were acting both independently and in partnership with international actors.

However, this limited example still presents an incomplete picture. Similar to the challenge of comprehensively defining the actors, defining how humanitarian action is coordinated and what happens—or the *objective* of humanitarian action—is not straightforward. Nevertheless, this chapter will first take a step back to describe the formal organizational architecture that attempts to coordinate and govern each of these actors, and also give some examples of what happens outside of this formal architecture. It then will try to zoom in and outline different elements of humanitarian action.

Architecture: How is the global humanitarian network organized and coordinated?

When mapping out how humanitarian action is coordinated, it is important to understand that there are infinite ways in which aid is delivered. While there is a formally established system that revolves around the UN/Red Cross/INGO structure, there is also an incredible array of relationships and frameworks that define how actors work together in crisis.

This section presents some of the main elements of both perspectives on humanitarian coordination and architecture. It will first give an overview of the UN-established and globally mandated coordination system and the governance, fundraising, and policies that define it. While this system is far from able to effectively support all populations in need, it has established terminology and protocols that (as mentioned in the history chapters) have developed in response to crises and continue to slowly evolve and change in response to the growth of the humanitarian system.

However, in many ways this formal system is not the one that dictates how the majority of aid is provided. There is a second perspective which encompasses a much wider network of responders with both established and ad hoc mechanisms for coordinating aid. Understanding what this architecture looks like and how it operates is much more complicated, but in almost every crisis, different elements of this network can be seen.

This section examines both of these realities to help give a more accurate picture of how humanitarian response happens. Understanding this will also lay the foundation for a thorough understanding of the complex issues and debates surrounding contemporary humanitarian policy and action that will be explored in Chapters 6 and 7.

United Nations-established coordination system

The basic blueprint for the formal UN-established humanitarian system—as it exists today—is found in UN General Assembly Resolution 46/182 (see Box 4.1 in Chapter 4). Passed in the wake of the Armenian earthquake and the first Gulf War, this resolution created a system to better coordinate the work of UN agencies, International Non-Governmental Actors, and others in the delivery of humanitarian assistance and protection.

In the decades that have followed, the global humanitarian system has grown and professionalized, and there is an ever-increasing array of standards, coordination, leadership, and resource mobilization tools and frameworks.[3] Even within this formal structure, coordination is not linear, and the reality is that a relatively small number of core actors are at the center of the formal humanitarian system and still hold significant power to determine priorities, allocate funding, and steer the global response.

This group includes some 15 stakeholders comprised of Western donors, UN agencies, the ICRC and Red Cross Movement, and the largest INGOs—who together play an overwhelming role in determining how the system runs. What unites them—beyond a broad commitment to saving and protecting lives—is a common language, culture, and network power.[4]

One way to describe this structure is to look at humanitarian coordination at the global and country levels:

> *Global coordination* is used to determine system-wide priorities, monitor all crises, and make decisions about allocating and sharing resources within and between organizations and crises.
>
> *Country-level coordination* involves policy decision-making and operations in the field in response to a particular crisis.

Figure 5.1 explains what this looks like (though in reality it is not this straightforward and includes many more actors).

United Nations global-level coordination

The *Emergency Relief Coordinator* (ERC)—also referred to as the "Under-Secretary-General" of the UN and the head of OCHA—plays a key role in global coordination activities. He/she is responsible for the oversight of all emergencies happening around the world that require and/or are accepting United Nations humanitarian assistance. ERCs

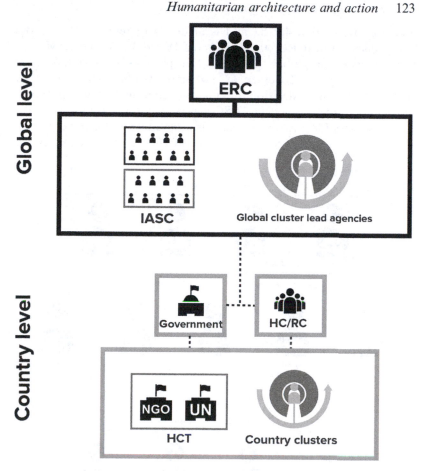

Figure 5.1 Coordination structures

can do everything from speaking out about the need for IHL in the UN Security Council or on news media after bombings in Syria, launching a new policy initiative to promote privacy and security policies on the use of technology in humanitarian aid, and fundraising for forgotten humanitarian needs in Sudan. While the position reports to the secretary-general, the role has the mandate to act as the central focal point for the majority of humanitarian actors discussed above including governmental, inter-governmental and non-governmental organizations, etc.

The ERC is also the chair of the *Inter-Agency Standing Committee* (IASC), one of the main coordinating bodies and forums for global humanitarian action. The IASC was established under General

Assembly Resolution 46/182 and is made up of representatives from UN agencies, the ICRC, the IFRC, the World Bank, the IOM, and representatives of global, US, and European NGO coalitions (see Figure 5.2 below). Together as full and standing members, they attempt to facilitate decision-making and coordination in operations and policies.[5] Every year, the IASC agrees on a set of priorities; in the past these have included topics such as accountability for performance, accountability to affected people, and building national capacity for

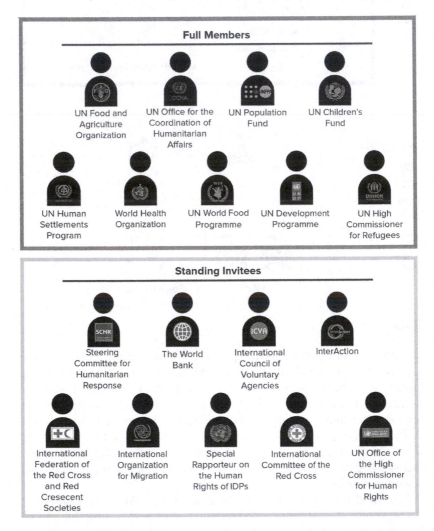

Figure 5.2 The IASC

preparedness. More specifically the IASC also has developed a comprehensive body of handbooks and guidance for use by the entire humanitarian network on topics as diverse as protection and gender. It also coordinates global advocacy on particular emergencies and on topics such as the humanitarian consequences of climate change.

Humanitarian reform and the beginning of the cluster approach

As mentioned in Chapter 3, almost 15 years after GA Resolution 46/ 182, another significant reform helped to establish the humanitarian architecture that exists today.

Following the protection challenges in Darfur and coordination gaps in the 2004 Indian Ocean tsunami response, the ERC commissioned an independent Humanitarian Response Review (HRR) of the current humanitarian system. The review identified major gaps in coordination, especially around who in the system was responsible for what and with what accountabilities. For example, it noticed that no agency was mandated to do camp coordination in an emergency, often leaving this vital response to be coordinated in an *ad hoc* way.

As a result of the review in 2005, the IASC initiated a systematic architectural and coordination reform effort that specifically sought to enhance *predictability, accountability,* and *partnership.* It also launched the formal coordination architecture that still exists today called the Cluster Approach.[6]

The Cluster Approach includes working groups for 11 different critical aspects of humanitarian response. These include those "sectors" listed in Table 5.1.

The idea is that first, having a "cluster lead" will enhance predictability and accountability in response. Cluster leads not only ensure a response in their "sectoral cluster", but also in non-crisis times they do preparedness activities, develop guidance, and build better partnerships. Second, this architectural structure creates an organized "open door" forum for all major humanitarian actors (and actors in this wider humanitarian network) to coordinate with one another and make sure their efforts can fill gaps and not duplicate action.[7] The cluster approach is established at both global and country levels and today is used in almost all countries where an active global humanitarian response is being carried out.[8]

The cluster system has been successful in terms of its significant institutional power: "Though no more than a loose network connecting autonomous organizations, the cluster approach may be understood as an institution in its own right, one that exercises substantial power in

Table 5.1 The cluster system

Cluster	Lead agency
Camp Coordination and Camp Management (CCCM)	IOM/UNHCR
Early recovery	UNDP
Education	UNICEF and Save the Children
Emergency telecommunications	WFP
Food security	WFP and FAO
Health	WHO
Logistics	WFP
Nutrition	UNICEF
Protection	UNHCR
Shelter	IFRC/UNHCR
Water, Sanitation, and Hygiene (WASH)	UNICEF

disaster-affected states."[9] However, it is far from perfect. One critique of the approach is that although it is designed to be a platform for partnership, local and national humanitarian actors are often not involved in decision-making.[10] In other words, the clusters are dominated by the UN agencies and large international NGOs that participate most actively. Evaluations of this system have found that while it has been effective in many contexts, the performance of individual clusters is quite variable.[11] More information about each of the clusters and what they do in a humanitarian response is discussed further below.

United Nations country-level coordination

Effective coordination of humanitarian action at the country level, often referred to as the "field level," hinges upon humanitarian coordination leaders: the *Humanitarian Coordinators* (HCs) or *Resident Coordinators* (RCs). While the principle responsibility for coordinating humanitarian assistance rests with national authorities, if international humanitarian action takes place the HC is responsible for leading the efforts of humanitarian organizations (both UN and non-UN) and ensuring that the humanitarian response in the field is principled, timely, effective, efficient, and contributes to longer-term recovery. This position is in many ways analogous to the ERC at the global level; HCs do everything at the national level, from chairing policy and coordination meetings to working with governments to advocating for funding and protection. For example, the HC for the Central African Republic, Najat Rochdi, released a press statement in June 2018 condemning attacks on hospitals in the central region of the country.[12]

The main decision-making forum for humanitarian matters at the country level is the *Humanitarian Country Team* (HCT)—in some way analogous to the IASC at the global level. It is chaired by the HC and includes both UN agencies and other major humanitarian actors (INGOs, Red Cross and Red Crescent Movement, etc.). The responsibilities of the HCT include setting common objectives and priorities, developing overall strategic plans, finding funding mechanisms to support response, and promoting adherence to humanitarian principles. For example, in 2017 the HCT in Yemen called on all warring parties and those with influence over the parties to ensure the continued functioning of Al Hudaydah Port and to allow the resumption of imports of basic life-saving commodities, the unimpeded passage of humanitarian relief to people in need, and the safe movement of people in search of aid.[13]

At the country level, *clusters* are led by country-level representatives accountable to the HC and, where possible, the national government. The country lead for each cluster is determined based on the specific situation and the capacities of different agencies already operating on the ground. Similarly, the structure of the cluster system is variable and should be adapted to the specific circumstances in each country. For example, the Pacific Humanitarian Team is a regional cluster that focuses on the Pacific due to its high incidence of sudden-onset disasters.[14] During a crisis response, each cluster convenes separate meetings to discuss operational issues related to their specific sector. Coordination meetings are also held between *inter-cluster working groups*, in which each field-level cluster lead reports on activities and discusses crosscutting issues in the response.

Coordination outside the UN system

The architecture of the UN-established system is not synonymous with the entirety of humanitarian action, which we will discuss more later in this chapter. Increasingly, other bodies—for example, regional organizations and national institutions—are taking different approaches. Many local and other informal networks are forming new coordination mechanisms. Humanitarian architecture and the actors that participate are de-Westernizing—becoming more global, more inclusive, and more varied. Where this trend will lead is not yet clear, and largely depends on the choices made by humanitarian professionals in the years ahead.

What we may see in the future can be derived from a few models of coordination that are already in operation.

For example, the ASEAN Coordinating Centre for Humanitarian Assistance on Disaster Management (AHA Centre) has become a promising model for regional coordination and relief. It has helped facilitate not only crisis response, but also disaster monitoring, preparedness, and capacity building, such as training national actors so that they can manage responses in their own countries, as was seen in the relief efforts for the landslides in Indonesia and flash floods in Laos. The AHA Centre is also coordinating public–private partnerships.[15] Similarly, the OIC has a goal "to safeguard and protect the interests of the Muslim world in the spirit of promoting international peace and harmony among various people of the world."[16] It includes 57 member states that coordinate on a variety of issues, including humanitarian aid. Its Department of Humanitarian Affairs mobilizes disaster assistance, distributes funds for response, and strengthens institutional capacity. Its coordinated efforts include aid assistance in Gaza, Iraq, and Chad.[17]

In terms of local and civil society coordination, a good example is from 2015 when thousands of refugees fled to Austria following a wave of tightening border control regulations in Europe. While the Austrian Red Cross was involved in the response, the majority of the humanitarian action was coordinated by several Austrian volunteer organizations created in response to the influx of refugees. These groups organized hundreds of everyday Austrian citizen volunteers to distribute donations such as food, water, and blankets to incoming migrants. The Austrian government and police force also contributed to the effort by registering and assisting refugees in transit. Without a formal response mechanism, these groups were able to coordinate and provide aid for nearly 13,000 refugees over the course of only a few weeks.[18]

In 2018, the gap between numbers of people in need and the UN-led system's ability to respond emphasizes the necessity of increasing support for actors outside of the UN System. In 2018, formal global assessments estimated that 135.7 million people were in need, but the UN acknowledged that only 90.9 million people were being targeted for assistance by the formal UN-led system participating in the appeal to respond. For the almost 45 million *other* people, affected communities would be supporting themselves the best they could with their own resources and assisted by their own governments and other actors. Because of access or capacity constraints, some Western aid organizations would not be able to reach those they knew were in need. These trends, as well as the significant funding gaps talked about in the Introduction, foreshadow that the next decade will see continued change in humanitarian action.

Humanitarian action: What happens in humanitarian response?

After asking how actors are organized, the next question is: What they do? As mentioned in the introduction to this chapter, defining what comprises humanitarian action is not straightforward. Ultimately (and ideally) for most actors, the objective of humanitarian action is as presented in the Introduction to this book: to "save lives, protect livelihoods, alleviate suffering, and maintain human dignity during and in the aftermath of crisis, as well as prevent and strengthen preparedness for the occurrence of such situations."

However, there is often variation to this definition and disagreement over how the scope and purpose of this objective is interpreted and what modality of aid is used. Box 5.1 presents four definitions of humanitarian action. There are major disparities between them: To some groups, humanitarian action is intended for short-term relief; to others, it encompasses longer-term rehabilitation, reconstruction, and development programming. Some clearly indicate a provision of concrete services like food, water, and shelter, while others talk about maintaining human dignity. Different groups also tend to disagree on the target of humanitarian action and who is involved.

Box 5.1 What is the definition of "humanitarian action"?

- "Humanitarian action includes the protection of civilians and those no longer taking part in hostilities, and the provision of food, water and sanitation, shelter, health services and other items of assistance, undertaken for the benefit of affected people and to facilitate the return to normal lives and livelihoods."[19]
- "[Humanitarian action is] a needs-based emergency response aimed at preserving life, preventing and alleviating human suffering and maintaining human dignity wherever the need arises if governments and local actors are overwhelmed, unable or unwilling to act."[20]
- "Humanitarian action" encompasses all activities falling within the scope of linking relief, rehabilitation and reconstruction/ development. This concept of humanitarian action fulfills all the criteria of relief and rehabilitation but also gives input into the

> process of reconstructing disaster struck societies aiming for sustainable development in the longer term."[21]
>
> • "Humanitarian action refers to assistance and protection provided in a short-term programme focusing on the crisis event and the needs of people directly affected."[22]

This section attempts to further illustrate "what humanitarian action is" by reviewing two frameworks. First, it provides a snapshot of humanitarian action by looking at the objectives and some activities of different global sectors or clusters and some of the funding trends. Second, it gives an overview of humanitarian action by describing the broad areas of humanitarian planning and programming.

Global sectoral response

On a global level, one way to understand the scope and scale of what comprises humanitarian action is to take a closer look at the work of the various "clusters" discussed above and review the funding trends on how resources are distributed globally between various sectors and humanitarian activities.

While no humanitarian activity necessarily falls squarely into one category, Table 5.2 attempts to give a broad overview of the objectives and examples of activities carried out in recent crises by different actors within the individual clusters.

To further understand the scale of actions taken, reviewing some of the funding trends within these different sectors is helpful. Between 2014 and 2016, the food-related sectors (agriculture, food security, and nutrition) accounted for the largest share of humanitarian funding (24 percent) on average.[43] The next largest sector was health (13 percent).[44] Although requirements for other critical sectors such as protection, shelter, non-food items, education, and water and sanitation and have all grown over 200 percent in the last 11 years, they continue to be underfunded. Funding for safety and security of staff and operations has also received less than half of its requested amount every year for the past 11 years.[45]

Some of this underfunding in specific sectors may be explained by the increase in "multi-sector" funding. Between 2005 and 2015, the amount requested for multi-sector programs has increased more than 13-fold, reaching US$6.2 billion in 2015—almost one-third of the requirements for all sectors. "Multi-sector programming" refers to activities that combine different sectors, such as the assistance provided

Table 5.2 Examples of cluster objectives and activities

Cluster	Overview of objective	Examples of humanitarian activities
Camp Coordination and Camp Management (CCCM)	"Ensure equitable access to services and protection for displaced persons living in communal settings, to improve their quality of life and dignity during displacement, and advocate for solutions while preparing them for life after displacement."[23]	The CCCM Cluster conducted a training session in Somalia to help organizations strengthen their programs to mitigate gender-based violence.[24]
Food security	Coordinate the response to food security in a crisis, including "addressing issues of food availability, access and utilization."[25] Sometimes includes addressing underlying livelihood constraints.	USAID provided cash transfers to households affected by drought in Afghanistan to help them purchase food.[26]
Early recovery	Address recovery needs that arise during response, build community resilience, and ensure sustainability.	UNDP helped remove debris in the Philippines following Hurricane Yolanda.[27]
Education	"[Ensure] predictable, well-coordinated and equitable provision of education for populations affected by humanitarian crises."[28]	UNICEF constructed classrooms for crisis-affected children in Afghanistan.[29]
Emergency telecommunications	"Provide timely, predictable, and effective information and communications technology (ICT) services in humanitarian emergencies."[30]	WFP supported Puerto Rican agencies to restore internet access after Hurricane Maria.[31]
Health	"Relieve suffering and save lives in humanitarian emergencies," specifically as it relates to health.[32]	MSF launched mobile health clinics in South Sudan to reach people injured by conflict.[33]

Cluster	Overview of objective	Examples of humanitarian activities
Logistics	Be responsible for "coordination, information management, and for facilitating access to common logistics services to ensure an effective and efficient logistics response takes place in humanitarian emergency missions."[34]	The UN Humanitarian Air Service scheduled flights for aid delivery to the mountains of Nepal after the earthquake.[35]
Nutrition	"Safeguard and improve the nutritional status of crisis affected populations."[36]	UNICEF opened clinics in Somalia to provide nutritional support to children in a period of drought.[37]
Protection	Ensure that "all people affected or threatened by a humanitarian crisis have their rights fully respected in accordance with international law and their protection assured by relevant and timely actions through all phases of the crisis and beyond."[38]	The ICRC called for the protection of civilians following an attack on a port in Yemen.[39]
Shelter	"Support people affected by natural disasters and internally displaced people affected by conflict with the means to live in safe, dignified and appropriate shelter."[40]	Catholic Relief Services distributed tarps and iron sheeting to help families construct shelters after the Nepal earthquake.[41]
Water, Sanitation, and Hygiene (WASH)	Support humanitarian response with water and sanitation services.	The IRC helped restore sources of clean water in the Central African Republic following violence.[42]

by UNHCR for refugee populations. As the number and scale of regional refugee-related appeals have grown—including the Syria Regional Response Plan—so has the scale of these requirements.[46] The increased use of cash transfers to meet multiple sectoral needs at once has also contributed to increases in multi-sector funding.

As implied by the growth in multi-sector budgets, looking at humanitarian action as a series of separate, distinct activities—each aimed at meeting some component of overall need—gives an overly simplified view of what humanitarian actors actually do. While some agencies do have sectoral specializations, the entire point of humanitarian action is to address the combination of needs at a population level. This is easier to understand if the predominant need is for food, or shelter—or any specific "thing." If the need is for protection against violence or human rights abuse, it is more difficult both to understand and to actually *do*. So reviewing humanitarian programs—as opposed to sectors or clusters—offers a more comprehensive view of humanitarian response.

Humanitarian planning and programming

A second way to understand humanitarian action is to review the analytical planning and programming tasks. However, every organization and actor does this differently, contextual differences are huge, and it is *not* a linear or straightforward iterative process.

The broad areas of programming include

- information gathering and needs assessment,
- response planning and analysis,
- fundraising and fund management,
- program implementation and project management, and
- (ideally) monitoring and evaluation of the responses.[47]

The short paragraphs below do not do justice to the complexity of what happens on the ground in a response, but shouldy give some insights to what many of the humanitarian actors described in Chapter 4 do on a daily basis.

Information gathering and needs assessment to understand the needs of the affected community is the critical first step in humanitarian action. Ideally, a community or local or national government would have undertaken emergency preparedness activities that provide an initial sense of potential needs. However, in many cases, reliable baseline information is lacking. In addition to assessing needs at the outset of an operation, assessments should continue because needs are constantly changing.[48] Improvements in assessment and information management are one of the success stories of humanitarian professionalization in the past decade or so.

Information gathering and needs assessments can appear as simple as aid workers with a clipboard going house-to-house to find out how people have been affected by a crisis. But it can also include remote sensing, aerial footage taken by an unmanned aerial vehicle (UAV), call centers that affected communities can ring up, or data collected from social media accounts. Many needs assessments are done at an organizational level or on a cluster-by-cluster basis, but increasingly efforts are made to do multi-sectoral assessments that are widely shared between actors. The changing role of needs assessments in driving evidence-based programming is discussed further in Chapter 6.

But information and analysis needs go well beyond assessment. Humanitarians have long relied on "early warning"—or the forecasting of likely conditions three to six months out. In the past, food aid took that long to get to places affected by famine, and the prediction or early warning of famine was imperative for intervening with any kind of effectiveness.[49] More recently, humanitarians have had to include the analysis and early warning of conflict, mass migration, and longer-term climate change in addition to the expected seasonal rainfall and agricultural production that have been part of early warning since the 1980s.

After needs are assessed, *response planning and analysis* is critical. This is when actors usually begin to agree on their objectives and develop response plans and specific projects to assist those in need. This can be done at a strategic or ad hoc level and alone or as part of a coordinated response. For example, in Yemen in 2017, the overall UN-led coordinated strategic objectives by the HCT were to the following: save lives, prioritize the most vulnerable; integrate protection and gender-related concerns across the response; support maintenance of basic services and institutions; and strengthen coordination, accountability, and advocacy.[50]

In the past, there were often few strategic choices for response: When a population was assessed as food-insecure, for example, the only real choice was to provide them with food aid (usually donated in kind and shipped long distances to reach affected populations).[51] However, with a greater range of options today (indirect support for livelihoods, cash transfers, or voucher programs), "response analysis" tools such as market surveys, recipient preference surveys, and other relatively recent inventions help donors and agencies choose the best option for response.[52]

Overall, the established traditional humanitarian community, through the HC, aims to have a harmonized approach in responding to an emergency and tries to have all actors ensure their programing is in line with the priorities and implementation plans of the broader HCT and specific cluster under which the project falls. Most of the traditional donors in emergencies look for these synergies in project proposals. However, achieving this is extremely difficult, and it is debatable who can best decide what the priorities should be (Box 5.3 further illustrates this).

Once organizations know what they want to do, they usually need to *raise and manage funds* to carry out these activities. This can be done in any number of ways: An individual organization might run a public campaign asking for donations via text message or bid to gain a large government donor contract. A smaller NGO might become an implementing partner and receive funding from a larger agency. Most large organizations have donor-relations departments that undertake activities related to fundraising, such as writing proposals, maintaining budgets, and creating reports for donors, but even smaller groups have to undertake these critical functions.

Currently, financing humanitarian action is itself a complex field, with many types of instruments and increasingly varied approaches. Some funding coordination mechanisms, such as the CERF and Pooled Funds (described in Box 5.2) are well established. But today more innovative funding mechanisms are also being tried, such as impact investing and social impact bonds. Funding will be further discussed in Chapters 6 and 7.

Box 5.2 Selection of formal funding mechanisms and tools

While most of humanitarian funding flows straight from a bilateral donor to an implementing agency or government, the formal established humanitarian system has established a variety of funding mechanisms and tools. Below are a few.

Central Emergency Response Fund (CERF). This global fund is managed by the UN Emergency Relief Coordinator. Although donors often prefer to target their contributions at particular crises—sometimes in order to pursue self-interested foreign policy goals—the CERF provides funding on the more neutral basis of needs. It focuses on providing funding for both rapid response and under-funded emergencies.

Pooled Funds. One tool used in numerous emergencies is the country-based pooled funds (CBPFs) that are established at the country level and managed by the Humanitarian Coordinator. Like the CERF, these funds are allocated based on documented needs and in support of priorities established in Humanitarian Response Plans. Outside the UN system are other pooled-funding mechanisms, like the Disasters Emergency Committee (DEC). This consortium of 13 major humanitarian NGOs appeals and collects donations in a central fund and then disburses funds to its members. The Start Fund, the first multi-donor pooled fund managed by NGOs, provides "rapid financing to underfunded small to medium scale crises" and acts "in anticipation of impending crises."

Financial Tracking Service (FTS). This open-source data platform enables all agencies working in a crisis to aggregate and curate their data. The goal is to provide a single public database of all humanitarian funding requested, pledged, and delivered. It monitors funding progress on all formal UN-led humanitarian response plans and appeals and provides information to inform coordination, decision-making, and advocacy.

Implementing programming and project management is what most people think of when they think of humanitarian aid. It includes aid workers running food distributions, setting up and managing refugee camps, delivering vaccines, providing basic health services, constructing and managing water-distribution networks, and a host of other activities related in one way or another to the sectors or clusters outlined in the previous section. All of these interventions are comprised of projects and activities that aim to address specific sets of needs and deliver specific results. Usually, they are time-bound activities that involve the distribution of goods and services and include specific budgets. The 2018 United Nations Global Humanitarian Overview gives some examples of such activities carried out: In 2017, 1.2 million young children and young women received medical attention in Sudan, 130,000 people received emergency shelter in Fiji, and 27 million square meters of land was freed from the threat of mines and explosive remnants of the war in South Sudan.[53] Box 5.3 provides further examples.

Providing services in humanitarian contexts also includes procurement and logistics. Shelter cannot be provided and food cannot be distributed without access to supplies and the means of transporting, storing, and distributing them. This is the domain of logistics, which comprises all of supply-chain management: acquisitions, storage, inventory management, transportation, and distribution. In some operations, this can be the most expensive and complex part. For example, after the Haiti earthquake, the main airport had only 14 spaces for airplanes bringing in relief supplies, roads were covered in rubble, and there was a lack of fuel and storage facilities, making the distribution of vital relief extremely challenging for logistics teams. On the other hand, the rise of cash transfers and market-based programming by definition outsources a good deal of the logistics to private traders.

An area of increasing importance in humanitarian action is protection activities: protecting people from violence and human rights violations in the context of both conflict and disasters triggered by natural hazards. Humanitarian actors (with the exception of militaries and peacekeeping forces) are not armed, so providing "hard protection" is usually not an option. Sometimes simply by being present, humanitarian actors can influence militaries or armed groups towards behavior that respects the rights of civilians. Sometimes protection activities involve direct negotiations with armed actors; in other cases, they educate about or highlight the laws of warfare or IHL—and attempt to create an environment in which human rights violations are less likely. Sometimes inevitably, protection is also about remedial services—providing counseling or psycho-social support to victims of rape or gender-based violence; providing "safe spaces" for children or specialized services, such as legal aid, family tracing, and reunification services; supporting demobilization of child soldiers; and facilitating refugee registration.[54] Protection has become an increasingly important consideration in the provision of material forms of assistance as well. How IDP camps are laid out, or serviced, has implications for protection: Are gender-segregated sanitation facilities provided? Is lighting adequate at night? And increasingly, the provision of cooking fuel (be it firewood, charcoal, or other fuel) has been recognized as a significant factor in protection, as women are routinely attacked and raped when looking for firewood for cooking outside of a settled area. Protection is a relatively recent element of programming, and probably the most difficult.

Box 5.3 Humanitarian Needs Overview (HNO) and Humanitarian Response Plans (HRPs) and appeals

In most humanitarian crises around the world, the UN has established mechanisms and a process for assessing and coordinating response through the production of HNOs and HRPs. In 2018, over 30 HRPs and appeals were created, including for highly publicized crises such as the Syria conflict and the Rohingya crisis in Myanmar and Bangladesh, but also for lesser-known emergencies such as those in Niger, Burundi, Libya, and Mauritania.

The objectives of this process and these plans are to facilitate effective, rapid, and coordinated responses to humanitarian crises and to bring organizations and donors together. But they also serve as a donor funding appeal by laying out what objectives and projects the coordinated UN-led system wants to carry out and how much money they need to achieve them.[55]

Humanitarian Needs Overview (HNO). This is a document that represents the "shared understanding of the impact and evolution of a crisis and [is used] to inform response planning ... [It] presents a comprehensive analysis of the overall situation and associated needs."[56] At the national level, the HCT manages the HNO and uses the cluster approach to categorize needs in different areas. The HNO may also include a severity ranking that communicates the urgency of each type of need. For any given crisis it should be produced twice per year.

Humanitarian Response Plan (HRP)/UN Coordinated Appeal. The step after the initial needs assessment is strategic planning, yielding an HRP. The HRP indicates the amount of international assistance likely to be required and serves as a "UN Consolidated Appeal" for fundraising. Its target audience is policymakers and international donors.

Most crisis HRPs have three components. First, they outline an agreed strategic approach "consisting of a narrative, strategic objectives and indicators."[57] The cluster partners, together with national actors, come together to devise the prioritized objectives for the crisis response. For example, in 2018–2021 the Afghanistan HRP aimed to assist 2.8 million people with three strategic objectives: "(SO1) Save lives in the areas of highest need; (SO2) Reduce protection violations and increase respect for International Humanitarian Law; and (SO3) People struck by sudden onset crises get the help they need, on time."[58]

Second, HRPs provide detailed plans of the activities and projects, by cluster, that participating organizations want to undertake to fulfill the overall objectives.[59] Finally, HRPs also detail how much money is being requested by each organization to carry out each activity. For Afghanistan, the total being asked for was US$430 million.

Although this process happens on a global level (and ad hoc in a sudden-onset emergency), not all HRPs are equally funded. For example, in 2016 Burundi received 99 percent of its requested amount, while Gambia received just 4 percent. The largest appeals have continued to dominate the global funding stream—the five largest accounted for 57 percent of the total, with two Syria-related appeals accounting for 38 percent.[60] Globally, as presented in the Introduction to this book, a major funding shortfall is being seen in HRPs—in 2016, just 40 percent of the amount requested by HCTs was given.[61]

In addition, not all crises have HRPs, and not all humanitarian partners participate in the development of HRPs. The Red Cross auxiliary organizations—the ICRC and IFRC—coordinate additional funding mechanisms and appeals. The ICRC divides its annual budget into "headquarters" and "operations", with each having its own international appeal for funding. This gives transparency to the process of how much funding is used for logistical and administrative overheads and what goes to fund its operations in the field. The IFRC appeal system is centered on pooling funding to distribute to national societies and acting as a liaison to assist national societies in their fundraising efforts. And, as discussed above, there are many other coordination structures and funding mechanisms that contribute to humanitarian response.

Finally, and some feel most importantly, is *monitoring and evaluation* (M&E). Information management doesn't end with good assessments. It is a critical component of project management and implementation. It consists of collecting data, but is associated more with analyzing, visualizing, and disseminating information such that it is readily available to aid workers for making decisions in a crisis—decisions about targeting and about tracking a project, both in terms of its finances and its progress towards its specified objectives. This type of information management mostly falls under the category of M&E.

M&E used to be almost non-existent in humanitarian action—the assumption was that money spent on information collection and analysis took money away from response. Some of the harmful unintended consequences of humanitarian action outlined in Chapters 2 and 3, along with demands for greater accountability, have led to major changes in the past decade or so—not only in short-term monitoring but also in measuring effectiveness and making a more deliberate effort to learn and establish best practices. By closely observing project activities and understanding their impact in the community, adjustments can be made to ensure that project design and activities are relevant, effective, and efficient and yield meaningful results for the community. Donors are putting more and more emphasis on M&E and are requiring clear, measurable and results-based updates.[62] Improving the quality of humanitarian response is a growing area of policy and practice; it will be discussed more in Chapter 6.

Conclusion: incomplete and unfinished

Though most of the types of humanitarian action and coordination structures described here fit into formally established humanitarian systems and frameworks, it is clear that humanitarian action takes various forms, and there is not one global humanitarian response that has been able to coordinate the diversity of humanitarian action taking place. Affected people and communities are often the first and longest-term responders in any crisis. For them, humanitarian action might consist of providing a place for a neighbor to sleep or cooking and distributing food for others. On the opposite end, for populations far away from a crisis but still interested in humanitarian aid, action may consist of promoting a video of Beyoncé singing as part of a World Humanitarian Day advocacy campaign, or texting donations to an NGO after an earthquake. As mentioned by the president and CEO of the International Rescue Committee, David Miliband, "The classic definition of humanitarian action is simple: We exist to save lives. But in fact we have other priorities too. Protecting women and girls from violence, investing in disaster risk reduction, promoting economic livelihoods are part of the humanitarian enterprise."[63]

Therefore, coordinating aid, given all of these differing priorities, whether within an organization or between this constellation of varied actors, is no easy feat. A 2014 journal article noted response challenges: "Three years after the devastating earthquake in Haiti, coordination failures take the blame for the interminable pace of the recovery effort."[64]

The good news is that understanding how to most effectively provide humanitarian action and what coordination architecture can best support that is a policy area that is continuously assessed and discussed. The hope is that, as one observer has noted, "Regardless of an organization's size, experience, or resources, everyone who is here shares the responsibility for cooperating with one another and coordinating relief efforts."[65]

The previous chapters and historical case studies have already demonstrated that action and architecture have continually changed over the past few decades. So while the frameworks presented in this chapter for understanding humanitarian coordination and action do not provide a comprehensive picture or the final word, we hope that, together with the illustrations of action throughout the preceding historical chapters, the basics about what happens in an emergency are becoming clearer. The next step is to further understand what changes may continue to take place. The next two chapters discuss this.

Notes

1 OCHA Yemen, *2017 Periodic Monitoring Review: January-April 2017. Yemen* (United Nations Office for the Coordination of Humanitarian Affairs, 2017), https://reliefweb.int/sites/reliefweb.int/files/resources/2017_PMR_YEMEN_final_EN.pdf.
2 UNDP Yemen, "Private Sector Organizations/Companies Engagement in Emergency Preparedness, Response and Recovery" (United Nations Development Programme, 2017), https://www.humanitarianresponse.info/sites/www.humanitarianresponse.info/files/documents/files/survey_i_presentation_v2.pdf.
3 Lesley Bourns and Jessica Alexander, *Leaving No One Behind: Humanitarian Effectiveness in the Age of the Sustainable Development Goals*, OCHA Policy and Studies Series (OCHA; CDA Collaborative Learning Projects, 2016), https://www.unocha.org/sites/unocha/files/LeavingNooneBehind_20151109_Small.pdf.
4 Randolph Kent, Christina Bennett, Antonio Donini, and Daniel Maxwell, *Planning from the Future: Is the Humanitarian System Fit for Purpose?* (London; Medford, Mass.: Humanitarian Policy Group at the Overseas Development Institute; Feinstein International Center at Tufts University; the Policy Institute at King's College London, 2016), 48, www.planningfromthefuture.org/uploads/4/5/6/0/45605399/pff_report_uk.pdf.
5 IASC, *Introduction to Humanitarian Action: A Brief Guide for Resident Coordinators* (Inter-Agency Standing Committee (IASC), 2015), https://reliefweb.int/sites/reliefweb.int/files/resources/rc_guide_31_october_2015_webversion_final.pdf.
6 Logan Boon, *The Cluster Approach: Working Towards Best Practices in Humanitarian Response*, Issue-Specific Briefing Paper: Humanitarian Aid in Complex Emergencies (Denver, Colo.: University of Denver, 2012), https://www.du.edu/korbel/crric/media/documents/logan_boon.pdf.
7 IASC, *Guidance Note on Using the Cluster Approach to Strengthen Humanitarian Response* (Inter-Agency Standing Committee (IASC), 2006), https://interagencystandingcommittee.org/system/files/legacy_files/Cluster%20implementation%2C%20Guidance%20Note%2C%20WG66%2C%2020060611115-.pdf.
8 Boon, *The Cluster Approach.*
9 J. Benton Heath, "Managing the Republic of NGOs: Accountability and Legitimation Problems Facing the UN Cluster System," *47 Vanderbilt Journal of Transnational Law* 239, 2014, 241, https://ssrn.com/abstract=2250835.
10 Heath, "Managing the Republic of NGOs."
11 Peter Walker and Daniel G. Maxwell, *Shaping the Humanitarian World*, Global Institutions Series (Abingdon; New York: Routledge, 2009).

12 OCHA, "The Humanitarian Coordinator Condemns the Intrusion of Armed Groups into Bambari Hospital" (Bangui: Office of the Humanitarian Coordinator for the Central African Republic, 9 June 2018), https://reliefweb.int/sites/reliefweb.int/files/resources/Press%20release%20-%20Intrusion%20of%20armed%20men%20in%20Bambari%20hospital%20-%200906 2018.pdf.

13 Yemen HCT, *Statement on Behalf of the Humanitarian Country Team in Yemen on the Critical Importance to Maintain Al Hudaydah Port Open* (Yemen: UN Office of the Humanitarian Coordinator in Yemen, 2017), https://reliefweb.int/sites/reliefweb.int/files/resources/hct_statement_on_the_critical_importance_to_maintain_al_hudaydah_port_open.pdf.

14 OCHA, "International Humanitarian Architecture," in *Disaster Response in Asia and the Pacific: A Guide to International Tools and Services* (OCHA, 2013), 8–29, https://www.unocha.org/sites/unocha/files/dms/ROAP /Promotional%20Materials/The%20Guide-Web-FINAL.pdf.

15 Michael Barnett and Peter Walker, "Regime Change for Humanitarian Aid," *Foreign Affairs*, July 2015, https://www.foreignaffairs.com/articles/ 2015-06-16/regime-change-humanitarian-aid.

16 OIC, "History," Organization of Islamic Cooperation, 2018, https://www. oic-oci.org/page/?p_id=52&p_ref=26&lan=en.

17 OIC, "Humanitarian Affairs," Organization of Islamic Cooperation, 2018, https://www.oic-oci.org/dept/?d_id=18&d_ref=12&lan=en.

18 Agence France-Presse, "Refugee Crisis Intensifies as Thousands Pour into Austria," *Guardian*, 20 September 2015, https://www.theguardian.com/worl d/2015/sep/20/thousands-of-refugees-pour-into-austria-as-european-crisis-in tensifies.

19 GHD, "23 Principles and Good Practice of Humanitarian Donorship," Good Humanitarian Donorship (GHD), 2016, https://www.ghdinitiative. org/ghd/gns/principles-good-practice-of-ghd/principles-good-practice-ghd.h tml.

20 Council of the European Union, Representatives of the Governments of the Member States, "The European Consensus on Humanitarian Aid: Joint Statement by the Council and the Representatives of the Governments of the Member States Meeting within the Council, the European Parliament and the European Commission," *The Official Journal of the European Union* 1, no. 25 (2008).

21 EUPRHA, *The State of Art of Humanitarian Action: A Quick Guide on the Current Situation of Humanitarian Relief, Its Origins, Stakeholders and Future* (European Universities on Professionalization of Humanitarian Action, 2013), http://euhap.eu/upload/2014/09/the-state-of-art-of-humanita rian-action-2013.pdf.

22 Doris Schopper, "Humanitarian Communication: Addressing Key Challenges," Coursera, 2017, https://www.coursera.org/learn/humanitarian-com munication#syllabus.

23 Global CCCM Cluster, "Global Camp Management and Camp Coordination Cluster," Global CCCM Cluster, 2018, www.globalcccmcluster.org.

24 Somalia CCCM Cluster, "CCCM Somalia Cluster Dashboard," Dashboard (Global Camp Coordination and Camp Management Cluster, May 2018), https://reliefweb.int/sites/reliefweb.int/files/resources/CCCM%20Dashboard %20-%20May%202018.pdf.

25 Global Food Security Cluster, "About Food Security Cluster," Food Security Cluster, 2018, http://foodsecuritycluster.net/page/about-food-securi ty-cluster.

26 USAID, *Food Assistance Fact Sheet: Afghanistan* (Washington, DC: United States Agency for International Development Office of Food for Peace, 2018), https://reliefweb.int/sites/reliefweb.int/files/resources/FFP% 20Fact%20Sheet_Afghanistan_6.4.18.pdf.

27 UNDP, "Philippines Recovery Work," United Nations Development Programme, 12 December 2013, https://stories.undp.org/philippines-recovery-w ork.

28 Global Education Cluster, "Who We Are," Global Education Cluster, 2018, http://educationcluster.net.

29 Afghanistan HCT, *2018–21 Humanitarian Response Plan: January 2018– December 2021* (Afghanistan: UNOCHA, 2018), https://www.humanitaria nresponse.info/sites/www.humanitarianresponse.info/files/documents/files/af g_2018_humanitarian_response_plan_7.pdf.

30 Global Emergency Telecommunications Cluster, "About ETC," ETC, n.d., https://www.etcluster.org/about-etc.

31 Emergency Telecommunications Cluster, *Caribbean: Hurricane Irma. ETC Situation Report #1* (Emergency Telecommunications Cluster, 2017), http s://www.etcluster.org/document/hurricane-irma-sitrep-1.

32 Global Health Cluster, "About Us," Health Cluster, 2018, www.who.int/ health-cluster/about/en/.

33 MSF, "South Sudan: Violence against Civilians Forces Thousands to Flee in Leer and Mayendit Counties," *Médecins sans Frontières* (blog), 31 May 2018, https://www.doctorswithoutborders.org/what-we-do/news-stories/news /south-sudan-violence-against-civilians-forces-thousands-flee-leer-and.

34 Global Logistics Cluster, "About," Logistics Cluster, 2018, https://logclus ter.org/about-us.

35 WFP and Logistics Cluster, "How Does Humanitarian Logistics Work in Nepal?" (World Food Programme, 2015), https://reliefweb.int/report/nepal/ how-does-humanitarian-logistics-work-nepal.

36 Global Nutrition Cluster, "What We Do," Nutrition Cluster, 2018, http:// nutritioncluster.net/what-we-do/.

37 Mike Pflanz, "Travelling Clinics to Help Children in Somalia's Remotest Areas Stay Healthy," *UNICEF Somalia* (blog), 20 September 2011, https:// www.unicef.org/somalia/nutrition_9587.html.

38 Global Protection Cluster, "Who We Are," Global Protection Cluster, 2018, www.globalprotectioncluster.org/en/about-us/who-we-are.html.

39 Reuters Staff, "U.N., Red Cross Call for Protecting Civilians after Coalition Attack on Yemen Port," *Reuters*, 13 June 2018, https://www.reuters.com/a rticle/us-yemen-security-aid/un-red-cross-call-for-protecting-civilians-after-c oalition-attack-on-yemen-port-idUSKBN1J90O7.

40 Global Shelter Cluster, "About Us," Global Shelter Cluster, 2018, https:// www.sheltercluster.org/about-us.

41 CRS, "Nepal Earthquake Response," Catholic Relief Services, 2015, https: //www.crs.org/media-center/nepal-earthquake-response.

42 IRC, "Central African Republic," International Rescue Committee, 2018, https://www.rescue.org/country/central-african-republic#how-does-the-irc-h elp.

43 Average funding by sector, 2013–2016 was calculated from Financial Tracking System (FTS) "Global Overview," specifically from FTS, "Total Reported Funding 2013," Financial Tracking Service (FTS), 2013, https:// fts.unocha.org/global-funding/overview/2013; FTS, "Total Reported Funding 2014," Financial Tracking Service (FTS), 2014, https://fts.unocha.org/ global-funding/overview/2014; FTS, "Total Reported Funding 2015," Financial Tracking Service (FTS), 2015, https://fts.unocha.org/global-fund ing/overview/2015; FTS, "Total Reported Funding 2016," Financial Tracking Service (FTS), 2016, https://fts.unocha.org/global-funding/over view/2016.

44 Average funding by sector, 2013–2016 was calculated from Financial Tracking System (FTS) "Global Overview," specifically from FTS, "Total Reported Funding 2013"; FTS, "Total Reported Funding 2014"; FTS, "Total Reported Funding 2015"; FTS, "Total Reported Funding 2016."

45 Development Initiatives, "International Humanitarian Assistance: Volumes and Trends," in *Global Humanitarian Assistance Report 2016*, (Global Humanitarian Assistance Report (GHA), 2016), http://devinit.org/wp-con tent/uploads/2016/06/Global-Humanitarian-Assistance-Report-2016_Chapt er-3.pdf.

46 Development Initiatives, "International Humanitarian Assistance: Volumes and Trends."

47 OCHA, "Humanitarian Program Cycle," Humanitarian Response (OCHA), https://www.humanitarianresponse.info/en/programme-cycle/space.

48 OCHA, "Needs Assessment: Overview," Humanitarian Response (OCHA), https://www.humanitarianresponse.info/en/programme-cycle/space/page/ass essments-overview.

49 Daniel Maxwell and Benjamin Watkins, "Humanitarian Information Systems and Emergencies in the Greater Horn of Africa: Logical Components and Logical Linkages," *Disasters* 27, no. 1 (2003): 72–90.

50 Humanitarian Response Plan for Yemen 2017, https://reliefweb.int/sites/ reliefweb.int/files/resources/2017_HRP_YEMEN.pdf.

51 Christopher B. Barrett and Daniel G. Maxwell, *Food Aid after Fifty Years: Recasting Its Role*, (London: Routledge, 2005).

52 Daniel Maxwell, John Parker, and Heather Stobaugh, "What Drives Program Choice in Food Security Crises? Examining the 'Response Analysis' Question," *World Development* 49, no. September 2013 (2013): 68–79.

53 OCHA, *Global Humanitarian Overview 2018* (United Nations Office for the Coordination of Humanitarian Affairs (OCHA), 2017), https://reliefweb. int/sites/reliefweb.int/files/resources/GHO2018.PDF.

54 OCHA, "OCHA on Message: Protection," OCHA on Message (United Nations Office for the Coordination of Humanitarian Affairs (OCHA), 2012), https://www.unocha.org/sites/dms/Documents/120405%20OOM%20 Protection%20final%20draft.pdf.

55 More can be found at OCHA, *Global Humanitarian Overview 2018* (2018), http://interactive.unocha.org/publication/globalhumanitarianoverview.

56 OCHA, *Needs Assessment: Overview*.

57 OCHA, "Strategic Response Planning: Overview," Humanitarian Response (OCHA), https://www.humanitarianresponse.info/programme-cycle/space/p age/strategic-response-planning.

58 OCHA, *Humanitarian Response Plan for Afghanistan 2018–2021*, (United Nations Office for the Coordination of Humanitarian Affairs (OCHA), 2018), https://reliefweb.int/report/afghanistan/afghanistan-humanitarian-res ponse-plan-2018-2021-revised-financial-requirements.

59 OCHA, *Humanitarian Response Plan for Afghanistan*.

60 Development Initiatives, *Global Humanitarian Assistance Report 2017: Executive Summary* (Development Initiatives, 2017), http://devinit.org/wp -content/uploads/2017/06/GHA-Report-2017-Executive-summary.pdf.

61 Development Initiatives, *Global Humanitarian Assistance Report 2017*.

62 IOM, "Monitoring and Evaluation in Emergencies," *IOM Emergency Manual*, n.d., https://emergencymanual.iom.int/entry/36852/monitoring-a nd-evaluation-me-in-emergencies.

63 David Miliband, "It's Time to Reassess the Goals of Humanitarian Aid," *The Guardian: Poverty Matters Blog* (blog), 28 February 2014, www.thegua rdian.com/global-development/poverty-matters/2014/feb/28/humanitarian-a id-goals-david-miliband.

64 Heath, "Managing the Republic of NGOs," 241.

65 Building a Better Response E-Learning; https://buildingabetterresponse.org; 5.

6 Changes in policy and practice

- **From rural and camp contexts to urban response**
- **From annual to multi-year programming**
- **From the presumption of international assistance to the recognition of locally led humanitarian action**
- **From in-kind assistance to market-driven programming and the rise of cash transfers**
- **The call for greater multi-stakeholder accountability**
- **Recognizing the imperative of protection**
- **The growth of evidence-based and data-driven programming**
- **The emergence of the innovation agenda and use of technology**
- **Conclusion: continual change**

In many contemporary humanitarian policy briefs and papers, it is common to see phrases like "the humanitarian system is at a crossroads" or "we are facing a turning point in the definition of humanitarian action" (in fact both authors have written documents that say these things). But as the previous chapters have shown, the boundaries and definitions of "humanitarian action" and the policies defining it have changed and are always changing. As noted by the former Under-Secretary General for Humanitarian Affairs, "The pace of change is accelerating; what used to take a generation now happens in five years. Humanitarian organizations need to be in a constant state of review, adapting and reinventing ourselves, if we are to remain relevant ..."[1]

Some of this change is driven by shifting crisis contexts, politics, or institutional frameworks, but ideally also by new evidence and learning. Major failures in places like Rwanda and Haiti led to calls for reform and helped develop new standards and operating procedures. Funding shortfalls have made it necessary to operate more efficiently and strategically. And new technologies have opened up possibilities that simply did not exist previously. Therefore, today the humanitarian world and its activities are much broader than ever.

This chapter highlights the major operational and policy trends that show how humanitarian action has changed over the past decade. These trends pick up some of the lessons that humanitarians have learned from the historical case studies in Chapters 1 through 3 and help illustrate how the contemporary response system discussed in Chapters 4 and 5 is working. The trends covered in this chapter are (1) from working in rural and camp contexts to urban response, (2) from annual to multi-year funding, (3) from in-kind assistance to market driven programming, (4) from the presumption of international assistance to recognition of locally-led humanitarian action, (5) the call for greater multi-stakeholder accountability, (6) recognizing the imperative of protection, (7) the growth of evidence-based and data-driven programming, and (8) the emergence of the innovation agenda and use of technology. While by no means an exhaustive list of the policy issues now being developed, these topics demonstrate key examples of how humanitarian action is changing.

From rural and camp contexts to urban response

The historic, traditional image of a humanitarian crisis depicts people in rural, underdeveloped areas or in camps. A trend in humanitarian aid is the emergence of policies and programs to respond to needs in urban areas. This could happen when a shock occurs in an urban area, when mass displacement causes people to seek refuge in cities, or when camps slowly transition into more permanent cities of their own. In 2017, more than 60 percent of refugees and 80 percent of IDPs were living in urban centers.[2] Some examples of urban humanitarian contexts include Syria, Turkey, Lebanon, Jordan, the Horn of Africa, and Malaysia.

Providing aid for affected people in urban areas is very different from traditional encampments. To begin, how do you locate people in need within a larger city? How do you provide aid for refugees and displaced people while members of the host community may also struggle with poverty? And how do you navigate the issues of sovereignty that come with working within the jurisdiction of local and national governments, which may even be hostile to affected people? The changing nature of crisis contexts from rural to urban is likely to change aid operations significantly in years to come.

In terms of humanitarian response, while crises have always occurred in urban contexts, the humanitarian community only began reviewing its policies on urban response in the 1990s. In 1997, UNHCR produced its first "Comprehensive Policy on Urban Refugees." As highlighted in Chapter 3, during the 2010 earthquake response in Haiti, the humanitarian community began to design policy and programs on a larger scale that could adapt aid to urban contexts.[3] When humanitarian organizations arrived in Port-au-Prince, they found it difficult to distinguish between those affected by the earthquake and those suffering from long-term structural poverty. Aid distribution points soon turned into large-scale slums; people would move from their homes to these areas to more easily receive aid, regardless of whether they were affected by the earthquake. Humanitarian organizations also faced difficulties navigating jurisdictions and collaborating with the many layers of government in the urban centers of Haiti.[4] Due to its urban context and the many actors involved, Haiti has been called "the humanitarian disaster of the future,"[5] from which humanitarian organizations have much to learn.

Another example is the large number of Syrians now living in cities in Turkey, Lebanon, Jordan, Iraq, and across the European Union.[6] The refugee crisis presents significant challenges due to its global scale but has been the setting for new tools, such as cash transfers and online information provision and communication channels, that help organizations adapt to providing aid in urban contexts.

Protection also takes on a different meaning in urban contexts. Urban refugees and other displaced people face threats different from those of affected people living in a camp or rural area. A 2017 report revealed that refugees living in Lebanon are typically only able to rent single rooms for their entire family, paying much higher than the market price and often in terrible conditions that can lead to disease.[7] Providing accurate and timely information to allay fears and ensure that legal processes are followed is increasingly difficult in urban areas, as some affected people may be isolated and unsure of where to go for information.[8] An increasingly large role for humanitarian organizations is advocating for affected people's rights to live and work in the country where they reside.[9] Aid organizations walk a fine line between respecting the sovereignty of host country governments that wish to protect employment and opportunities for their own citizens, and speaking out for the rights of affected people.

Above all, urban contexts present a significantly increased need for humanitarian organizations to collaborate with local and national host governments. In UNHCR's 2014 report on alternatives to camps, 11 of the 14 action initiatives it described involved working more closely with local government and host communities to strengthen response.[10]

Humanitarian organizations must also work with host governments to promote resilience and sustainability as cities grow rapidly. This concept of collaboration harkens back to the "ambiguous boundaries" graphic in the Introduction: in modern times, humanitarian action increasingly overlaps with other agendas in politics, resilience, and government capacity building.

To address the specific difficulties of providing aid in urban contexts, organizations and initiatives have been created, such as the Global Alliance for Urban Crises,[11] Urban Refugees,[12] and UNHCR's internal Urban Refugee Steering Group. These groups and organizations work to improve the aid provided in urban contexts and strengthen the resiliency of cities, governments, and affected people themselves to cope with the challenges of displacement and crisis.[13] Organizations like these will have a greater role to play in coming years as an increasing number of people flock to urban centers and urban crises and displacement become progressively more common.

From annual to multi-year programming

Historically, humanitarian action has prioritized immediate assistance to those affected by disasters and conflict. Most donors have 12-month funding cycles, and so humanitarian country teams typically adopt strategic plans and funding appeals on an annual basis. However, the reality today, as discussed in many of the crises covered in Chapter 3, is that most emergencies are neither temporary nor straightforward to address; they are increasingly complex, protracted, and difficult to remedy. Humanitarian needs almost always persist for longer than a single year and sometimes stretch into decades. Even in situations where the cause of the emergency is clear, recovery usually takes a long time.

For example, seven years after the earthquake in Haiti, tens of thousands of people were still living in makeshift camps.[14] On a macro level, in 2017, UN funding appeals were published for 29 crises around the world—all of which had issued funding appeals for the same crisis in the preceding year.[15] According to OCHA, more than 90 percent of humanitarian appeals last longer than three years and have an average length of seven years.[16] The Democratic Republic of the Congo, one of the poorest countries in the world, has had annual funding appeals for the past decade, and Somalia, Ethiopia, and Sudan (among others) have received global humanitarian aid for decades.[17] For refugees displaced by conflict, the average length of displacement is over 20 years.[18]

Therefore, some donors and agencies are attempting to pivot towards multi-year planning (MYP). In the simplest terms, this change can be described as expanding program cycles to span multiple years in contexts where the continuation of crisis is relatively predictable.

While humanitarian managers on the ground in many contexts like South Sudan came up with ways to operate long term in contexts that had short-term budgets, only in 2011 was one of the first major multi-year response plans adopted, in Kenya. The crisis there was multifaceted, involving a large refugee population, violence, disease outbreaks (including HIV/AIDS), seasonal natural hazards, climate change, and food insecurity. Thus, a strategic multi-year plan was designed to prepare for predictable future needs (such as food shortages), invest in resilience (such as stronger local governance), and meet the immediate needs of affected populations (such as water and sanitation).[19] Though this first MYP attempt faced many challenges, humanitarian actors in neighboring Somalia who were facing similar problems adopted a multi-year funding appeal for 2013–15 with the goal of ensuring more-cohesive and stable funding streams for humanitarian action.[20] By 2014, 14 countries had adopted multi-year strategic response plans.[21]

Perhaps the best example of a cohesive, multi-year approach comes from Sudan. The humanitarian coordinator adopted a multi-year strategy for 2017–19 that encompasses annual response plans for each year. In other words, this approach combines a medium-term forward-looking strategy with annual planning for specific activities. The document specifically prioritizes links to development actors, especially the UNDP, and capacity building at all levels.[22] The plan recognizes the persistent nature of the challenges facing Sudan, including violent conflict, long-term displacement, natural hazards, and poverty.

Multi-year planning is an administrative reform with the potential, many argue, to reshape the way that aid is provided and to boost both its effectiveness and its efficiency. The OECD lays out a few specific reasons.[23] First, during protracted crises, future needs are to some extent predictable. Multi-year strategic planning (and the funding required) can allow humanitarian actors to make decisions that anticipate needs, build better partnerships, and incorporate local perspectives. MYP also makes it possible to address the root causes of the crisis by supporting long-term development, resilience, and risk-reduction projects. Second, during predictable sudden-onset events, such as hurricanes or cholera outbreaks, an MYP approach allows aid agencies to pre-position stocks of aid supplies while investing in strategies to mitigate future harm. For example, vulnerable groups can be identified and provided with materials to weatherproof their homes and thereby reduce storm damage. Finally, during unpredictable sudden-onset events like earthquakes, media and donor interest tends to intensify in the days after the event—but drops off precipitously even as the acute needs persist for years. Longer planning cycles can counteract that problem by explicitly planning for the future.

Multi-year planning can also increase the effectiveness of humanitarian action by increasing both flexibility and cooperation. Aid can be delivered more quickly if the funding is already in place before a new crisis occurs or worsens. Likewise, projects have more time to adapt to the real needs expressed by the affected population. Staff can be hired for longer periods, allowing better understanding of the local context. Lastly, greater investment in training, equipment, and other resources is possible. These factors have major implications for the structure of humanitarian action—potentially leading to a more coherent response that supports related longer-term goals, builds local capacity, and is more accountable to affected groups.

Implementation of the MYP approach faces practical challenges. No single model exists for what a multi-year plan should look like; existing plans vary widely in scope and purpose. Some practitioners have described a "prioritization dilemma" in which short- and long-term goals compete for priority,[24] making it difficult to include both in a single plan. In addition, more funding tied up in multi-year contracts means that fewer resources will be available for unforeseen crises.[25] It is therefore critical to ensure that the humanitarian system retains its capacity to fulfill its core function of rapidly delivering aid during emergencies. Finally, the MYP approach may not be successful without critical thinking and engagement that spans all years—one major risk is that second- and third-year plans are just copy-and-paste duplicates of the first year.

Despite such challenges, MYP is becoming increasingly commonplace. Though these efforts will likely differ in each unique context, MYP will likely become the norm for humanitarian responses.

From the presumption of international assistance to the recognition of locally led humanitarian action

While much of the focus throughout the history of humanitarian action has been on the formally organized—and mostly Western or Northern—humanitarian agencies such as the UN, the Red Cross, or the INGOs, formal and non-formal humanitarian actors especially at the local and national level have always been present. In the past decade, greater attention is finally being given to local and national actors both at the level of *implementation* and *policy attention*. Despite the massive involvement of local and national actors in carrying out programs and projects, they are mostly stuck in the role of sub-contractors to the UN or INGOs. There are calls for national and local humanitarian actors to increasingly be empowered to take a greater role in the leadership, coordination and delivery of humanitarian preparedness and response in their countries; and for funding and policy to help make this possible.

There were many arguments that led to this policy shift. In the last decade it was increasingly recognized that in situations of extreme constraints on access (for example, the Somalia famine or the Syria conflict described in Chapter 3), local organizations are often the only ones able to reach the most vulnerable populations. It was also acknowledged that local organizations are on the ground more quickly, and they are widely recognized to be more culturally sensitive in their approach, less expensive than their international counterparts, and more likely to be around for the long term. There is also the potential that a local leadership and decision-making can build and strengthen traditional practices and communities and maximize local, national, and regional capacity.

However, some concerns persist about local capacity to scale up rapidly, and about local communities' long-term funding stability (obtaining funding for an acute emergency response is often easier than for long-term recovery or post-disaster reconstruction). While it does not oppose localization per se, MSF published an influential rebuke of blanket statements in favor of localization: "The current thinking driving the localisation agenda fails to make an essential distinction between the different humanitarian contexts, and ignores the challenges faced by local actors in conflict settings."[26] MSF argues that local actors could be less likely to be perceived as impartial and more likely to be involved in local disputes—especially in the context of violent conflict.

Several new initiatives and organizations have emerged recently to advocate for localization, generate evidence, and shift funding and power structures. As part of the Grand Bargain launched at the World Humanitarian Summit in 2016 (discussed in the conclusion below) 30 of the largest humanitarian donors committed themselves to changes in working practices and funding allocations to local and national actors. The NEAR network was also launched in 2016 and represents local and national NGOs from Africa, Asia, the Pacific, the Middle East, and Latin America to help give these individual organizations a stronger collective voice in the international system, as well as conduct research; and has begun piloting its own independent pooled financing mechanisms.[27] Another initiative, the Charter for Change, calls for commitments to shift funding and power from international to local and national actors. There are also numerous other initiatives and research being carried out by academics, INGO partners, and learning organizations.

Therefore, the issue of the "localization" of humanitarian action has gained increased attention, but not necessarily greater levels of direct funding support. The 2018 Global Humanitarian Assistance report shows a slight increase in direct funding to national and local organizations between 2016 and 2017, but even so, local organizations only receive 0.4 percent of all humanitarian funding directly—albeit substantially more through sub-contracts. But in future local organizations will, with little doubt, continue to play an increasingly critical role in humanitarian action, and the policies and practices to support this will continue to need to be strengthened. As mentioned in a 2015 report on Syria, "With a keen local understanding of the conflict, the people and the area, diaspora and local aid organisations are uniquely qualified to know what is most needed, in which areas, and how to gain access to those in need. But still they struggle for recognition."[28]

From in-kind assistance to market-driven programming and the rise of cash transfers

Humanitarian actors do their best to identify and fulfill the needs of those affected by emergencies, but they have not always been successful. Recipients of aid have often expressed frustration with aid agencies. For example, in a recent survey conducted in the Middle East, aid recipients gave agencies a score of three points out of ten for "meeting priority needs."[29] One way to make sure affected people receive the goods and services they actually need is to provide them with purchasing power, rather than traditional in-kind items, so that the market can respond to needs. The idea of giving people cash has existed for a long time, but only in the past decade has the humanitarian system begun to consider making it a dominant form of aid. As mentioned in the influential High Level Panel on Cash Transfers,

> Many of us are familiar with images of a convoy with crucial supplies … Today a family may instead receive an envelope of cash, a plastic card or an electronic money transfer to a mobile phone, with which they can buy food, pay rent and purchase what they need locally.[30]

This new trend reflects a growing body of evidence that giving cash directly to affected populations can lead to more efficient, dignified, and sustainable outcomes. In practice, the terms "cash transfer programming" (CTP) and "market-based programming" encompass a variety of delivery mechanisms that provide some form of purchasing power for use in private markets. In some cases this means handing people cash in envelopes, but it also includes electronic money transfers, debit cards, and vouchers for specific types of product or for specific values. These may be unconditional transfers or "cash-for-work" programs that provide temporary employment. Each method has particular advantages and drawbacks, but all reinforce the core idea that affected populations should have the ability to make decisions on their own behalf.

Giving cash directly to those affected by emergencies has a long history. The Red Cross delivered cash during the 1870–71 Franco-Prussian War, during nineteenth-century famines in India, and in Botswana in the 1980s.[31] However, from its inception in 1954, US foreign assistance in the form of food aid was primarily a means of domestic price supports and surplus disposal, and the policies of other exporting countries were similar. In-kind food aid has long been a major form of humanitarian assistance (though it also served many other functions).[32] Agricultural surpluses are no longer the domestic political issue that they once were, and as humanitarian budgets have grown in the past decade, reliance on donations of in-kind food aid have declined, with cash resources now eclipsing in-kind food assistance even in US budgets.[33] Food may still be provided to recipients, but is more likely to have been purchased with cash in the affected country or region itself.[34]

As discussed in Chapter 3, during the 2004 Indian Ocean tsunami many aid agencies began to provide cash on a large scale for the first time.[35] Cash was used explicitly to support local economic recovery and resilience, and was found to be effective in a wide range of contexts. Evaluations showed that affected populations with access to markets preferred cash over other forms of in-kind assistance. However, a strategic and coherent approach to cash programming had yet to be developed.[36]

A true turning point in the global recognition of "cash-transfer programming" and "market-based programming" happened in 2011, during the response to the famine in Somalia. During this crisis, the largest amount of unconditional cash transfers to date, US$86 million was provided directly to households in the form of cash or vouchers, or in cash-for-work programs.[37] Market-based programing in this context was driven by insecurity in the region, which made it difficult for many of the major humanitarian INGOs and UN agencies to deliver in-kind food assistance. Many donors and aid agencies were at first reluctant to deliver cash instead, fearing food price inflation, fraud and theft, disruption of local markets, and challenges surrounding targeting and monitoring.[38] While disagreement caused delays at first, the devastating famine forced aid agencies to act. The subsequent program evaluation found that "cash and vouchers made a quantifiable difference in reducing hunger and improving food security."[39] Many of the fears about market-based programming turned out to be unfounded: There was no greater incidence of fraud and theft than with in-kind aid programs; food prices were not inflated by the injection of cash resources; and the vast majority of cash was used either to buy food or to pay off debts (much of which had been incurred to buy food prior to the program)—it was not used for frivolous expenditure.[40] The success of the program in the Somalia famine led the way for more actors and donors to promote cash-transfer and market-based programming.

Cash-transfer programming has generally reduced the transaction costs of transportation and distribution, increasing the proportion of total budgets that reach recipients. Whereas in-kind aid procured elsewhere had the potential to undermine local economic recovery, cash transfers can in many instances stimulate production, employment, and higher wages in the affected region. CTPs can allow money to be transferred remotely to cellphone-linked accounts. Mobile-money transfer platforms make it possible to send, receive, and save money—even for people who lack access to traditional banking services.[41]

While most humanitarian actors agree that CTPs should be used more often and on a larger scale, some broad disagreement still exists as to when cash is the most appropriate response. Some concerns remain about inflation and other market distortions; cash cannot be effective when local markets are not functional or accessible. Pure cash-based responses may risk ignoring needs that cannot be met with cash, including specific nutritional programs, education, and protection. All of these issues can be addressed with good analysis of local markets and response options. And indeed, one positive spinoff from cash programming has been the rise of response analysis—leading to evidence-based choices for the most appropriate way to respond to need.[42] A final detriment to the use of cash—and especially mobile-money platforms—is that it may reduce interactions between humanitarian staff and affected populations, which could have consequences in terms of protection, solidarity, and mutual understanding.

Recent estimates suggest that approximately 7 percent of all humanitarian assistance was cash- or voucher-based in 2015 and that number has likely already risen.[43] Despite challenges, prominent humanitarian agencies have pledged to scale up their cash programming well beyond 7 percent.[44] The rise of CTP will also bring coordination challenges and new operational protocols and partnerships. Although proponents are careful to note that cash transfers are not appropriate in all contexts, they have the potential to create far-reaching changes in humanitarian action.

The call for greater multi-stakeholder accountability

Humanitarian organizations do not operate in a vacuum. Rather, they are one component of a complex system of other entities (mainly donors, affected people, and other organizations). The idea of finding ways to ensure accountability among and between all of these entities is central to recent reform efforts in the humanitarian system. Aid agencies are increasingly expected to be responsive to both the affected populations they serve and the donors that fund their work, and in addition to other partners and implementing organizations.

To date, an accepted definition of accountability in the humanitarian context does not exist.[45] Over the years the definition has grown, and for most it now includes this strong focus on carrying out humanitarian action based on how affected people perceive their needs. It has become much more holistic and has a focus on community empowerment that prioritizes the transfer of decision-making power to local populations. Between 2000 and 2012, the number of humanitarian "quality and accountability" initiatives and instruments more than tripled, from 42 to 147.[46]

The accountability reform agenda emerged over several decades of increasingly complex humanitarian responses. After a series of high-profile response failures, many stakeholders—including agency staff, donors, affected populations, and the public—began to ask how humanitarian action could avoid such mistakes in the future. As discussed in Chapter 2, the JEEAR made a wide range of policy recommendations in 1996, but its most important legacy was a system-wide shift towards accountability and performance standards.[47] Several of the initiatives that followed—the Sphere project, the Humanitarian Accountability Partnership, and People In Aid—eventually merged to form the Core Humanitarian Standard (CHS) Alliance and create the Core Humanitarian Standard approved in 2014. The CHS combines and adapts earlier accountability initiatives into nine consolidated commitments, depicted in Box 6.1 below.

Box 6.1 The nine commitments of the Core Humanitarian Standard

1   Humanitarian response is appropriate and relevant.
2   Humanitarian response is effective and timely.
3   Humanitarian response strengthens local capacities and avoids negative effects.
4   Humanitarian response is based on communication, participation, and feedback.
5   Complaints are welcomed and addressed.
6   Humanitarian response is coordinated and complementary.
7   Humanitarian actors continuously learn and improve.
8   Staff are supported to do their job effectively and are treated fairly and equitably.
9   Resources are managed and used responsibly for their intended purpose.

The CHS is voluntary, but organizations that officially adhere to the commitments are expected to be accountable to affected people, donors, and the public. The effects of the CHS can be seen in a variety of contexts. For example, in Pakistan in 2018, organizations strengthening their commitment to the third principle—increasing local capacities—invested in training sessions on accountability and the Sphere Standards for local staff members.[48]

One of the most prominent trends in accountability is that many initiatives are now prioritizing information sharing and communication as important areas of reform. Traditionally, humanitarian actors often prioritized other aspects of the response, such as food and shelter, at the expense of communication. Affected populations need accurate and timely information to ensure their safety and to plan for their future. Aid agencies are stressing that communication and information access are basic human needs or rights. Likewise, humanitarian actors need the perspectives of the affected population—as a form of accountability and to ensure that actual needs are being met. The Communicating with Disaster Affected Communities (CDAC) initiative has argued: "As relief arrives, communication, listening and engagement with those most affected is essential to help create a better and more accountable response."[49]

However, implementation of these initiatives is not always clear. One expert noted that accountability commitments published in annual reports "don't always trickle down to the field operation sites."[50] In other words, even as the standards themselves improve, more work is needed on the implementation side. Another challenge is ensuring accountability happens in a "360 degree" manner. Accountability to donors is more straightforward, as donors can restrict funding based on results. However, accountability to affected populations and between peer organizations has been harder to implement. The short-term, urgent and often political nature of humanitarian action makes it difficult to establish balanced power relationships. In some cases, humanitarian agencies do not comply with the wishes of affected people—whether due to negligence, or legitimate logistical, financial, or even ethical constraints.

As recently as 2016, the accountability agenda has taken shape in the form of concrete proposals for reform. For example, the CHS Alliance report on preparation lists value for money, community-based monitoring and evaluation, and better communication strategies as major areas for improvement.[51] The Accountability to Affected Populations (AAP) agenda promotes the idea that affected people should be included in decisions as they are made. Sphere has launched a handbook that focuses on the need to support local actors, current issues of urban response, use of cash transfers, and protection as a cross-cutting issue.[52]

Despite these achievements, truly achieving accountability in the humanitarian sector still has a long way to go. This is especially evident with regard to sexual abuse and exploitation, as Box 6.2 indicates. Even in 2018, the humanitarian community is still plagued with the lack of accountability in fundamental ways and continual progress and a more robust, accountable aid policy is necessary.

Box 6.2 Sexual abuse and exploitation

Early in 2018, Oxfam, one of the largest humanitarian organizations worldwide, faced allegations that senior officials had been covering up evidence that staff members in Chad and Haiti had hired prostitutes in areas where the organization was delivering aid. Though Oxfam received a large amount of attention for this scandal, with some calling for the British government to end donations to the organization,[53] it is neither the first nor the only humanitarian organization to engage in this type of behavior. Even more unacceptable is that this is not the only type of sexual abuse and exploitation that takes place.

Sexual exploitation and abuse by aid workers is happening in the aid sector and it has been happening for a long time. High-profile reports of sexual abuse by aid workers date back to the 1990s in Cambodia and West Africa.[54] In 2002, an assessment by UNHCR and Save the Children uncovered 67 documented allegations of sexual abuse and exploitation of refugee children. Staff from 40 aid agencies were implicated.[55] Many more equally atrocious cases have been reported over the years, but even more terrifying is the number of cases that have not been reported.

The cause of sexual abuse in humanitarian contexts lies in the exploitation of the power dynamics between aid providers and affected people. In settings where people are desperately in need of essentials, aid workers are easily able to take advantage of the power imbalance that exists between themselves as providers of aid and affected people as recipients. Abuse is further perpetuated due to the lack of reporting mechanisms and the vulnerability of affected people in such situations.[56]

In light of the Oxfam scandal, many are calling for greater inspection of the way organizations handle accountability and allegations of sexual abuse in crises. Reform is urgently needed, and time will tell if organizations are committed to the accountability and change required to protect affected people from abuse in future.

Recognizing the imperative of protection

In broad terms, protection actions generally seek to "save people from violence, coercion, or deliberate deprivation."[57] This means that humanitarian agencies should work to not only meet material needs, but also reduce exploitation and abuse and protect basic rights. In the past several decades, the continued reality of violence against civilians has caused humanitarian actors to rethink their approach to protection. One famous example comes from the coalition war against Iraq in 1991: In a photo, a child IDP wears a sign around her neck that reads, "We don't need food. We need safety."[58]

As mentioned in the 2016 Report of the Secretary-General for the World Humanitarian Summit, "There is outrage that national sovereignty and security are being placed above people's rights to protection and assistance and that the most basic tenets of international humanitarian and human rights law are being violated every day without accountability."[59]

Chapter 3 highlighted the Darfur crisis, one of the first to be designated as a "protection crisis" when armed conflict broke out between government forces and local armed groups. All sides committed atrocities, but pro-government militias perpetrated the worst examples. There were clear violations of international law, yet no clear enforcement mechanism existed; nor were there mechanisms for helping affected people seek safety and deal with the trauma.[60] This complex situation reaffirmed the need for effective protection strategies.[61]

Following the Darfur crisis, more humanitarian actors began to formally document abuses and advocate for adherence to international law. Today, protection activities are taking place on multiple levels and carried out by many different actors. For example, in the context of Syria, both state and non-state actors engage in continual attacks on schools, hospitals, and other civilian sites.[62] Humanitarian actors and agencies struggle to provide even the most basic supplies even as access is restricted and aid convoys are attacked. Nevertheless, local actors, such as the Syrian White Helmets discussed in Chapter 3, as well as international humanitarian actors have demonstrated a strong commitment to integrate protection programming throughout the response.

Beyond the context of armed conflict, natural disasters and famines are now widely recognized as requiring protection strategies, because extreme deprivation and vulnerability are often accompanied by risks to personal safety and wellbeing. As humanitarian actors have expanded both the language and the practice of protection over the past several decades, disagreements have emerged over the scope and proper application of protection principles.

Controversy around protection raises fundamental questions about the purpose of humanitarian action. As discussed in the Biafra crisis case study in Chapter 2 and in the various mandates of actors outlined in Chapter 4, while some actors perceive their work more narrowly as providing immediate life-saving assistance, others take a broader view that may include political advocacy to stop human rights violations. The latter perspective is surprisingly uncommon, with research reporting a "widespread perspective among humanitarians that they do not have a role to play in countering abusive or violent behaviour."[63] Instead, many humanitarians try to avoid provoking any criticism from governments that could impede their access to populations in need.[64]

Even where most actors agree, protection is an inherently challenging task. Providing material aid, such as tarps and food, is more straightforward and often easier than ensuring protection and dignity. Influential researchers and practitioners have long recognized the failures around protection and advocated for more effective and comprehensive strategies.[65] Protection activities are now often linked to programs on education, livelihoods, dignity, and other basic rights enumerated in international law. In the end, given the scale and scope of violence in today's crises, humanitarian protection is vital and will continue to require resources and action.

The growth of evidence-based and data-driven programming

Humanitarian action requires constant decision-making about who, where, when, and what to target. Such decisions are shaped by a wide variety of factors that include data and evidence, but often in the past humanitarian decision-making relied on assumptions and "educated guesses."[66]

In the past decade, substantial investments have been made in data collection and evidence-based programming to help reduce biases and other sources of error. Some of the major changes have included a much greater reliance on actual assessments rather than presumptions about need, better overall context monitoring and improved early warning, stronger standards for monitoring and evaluation (M&E), use of standardized indicators, more willingness to invest in research— actually testing which interventions are most appropriate—and deliberate attempts at post-crisis reflection and "lessons learned" exercises.

As one example, where once aid workers would travel in person with paper surveys to conduct interviews, mobile communications have made it possible to receive responses via text message. There has been a massive growth in data platforms and digital data flow, such as mobile phone records, social media posts, satellite imagery, and financial transactions, all of which can be used to make aid delivery more effective and timely. Flowminder has pioneered the use of mobile phone operator data to track large population movements. In 2014, it collaborated with a Nepali cell phone company called Ncell and the two were able to provide up-to-date population mapping data using mobile phone records. The first maps were released less than two weeks after the earthquake occurred and included gender and age distributions of the population in each area.[67] The Internal Displacement Monitoring Centre (IDMC) also publishes a public database with data from around the globe, as well as an annual report that analyzes current displacement and identifies areas where data are lacking.[68] The Humanitarian Data Exchange (HDX), formed in 2014, seeks to address problems of data availability and consolidation by providing a single, shared platform with consistent data standards that can be used to generate better evidence.

However, major challenges in collecting data and ensuring evidence-based programming persist. A central problem in the adoption of evidence-based approaches is ambiguity over what may constitute "evidence." Some use the term broadly to refer to any assessment yielding empirical information; others apply it more narrowly to theories of change that establish cause-and-effect relationships. A report published by ALNAP identified four major difficulties related to the use of evidence in decision-making:[69] Priorities are often unclear, making it difficult to know which information should be considered; gaps in data and analysis exist; addressing such problems is costly; and needs and operational contexts are constantly shifting, causing information to quickly become outdated. Finally, political and bureaucratic barriers are also major hurdles for evidence-based programming. An extensive survey of humanitarian practitioners concluded that the main limiting factor so far has been the lack of political and organizational will to act on evidence and to deploy the necessary resources to tackle problems using the best available solutions.[70] Even more striking, a study on the constraints and challenges of information and analysis states that humanitarian information and evidence is frequently meddled with, undermined and manipulated for political purposes—particularly in extreme crises such as famines.[71]

Like all humanitarian interventions, data collection carries the possibility of causing harm. Recent research has demonstrated serious risks involved in humanitarian data collection. Studies have argued that information technology "exposes critical, unaddressed gaps in the legal and ethical frameworks that have traditionally defined and governed humanitarians' professional conduct."[72] An urgent need is to define human rights—such as expectations of privacy and data security—in the context of new technologies. Crowd-sourced data can also lead to problems in terms of accuracy and reliability. In many cases, social media posts share rumors (for example, about which borders were open during the European migrant crisis) that have not been validated. Ensuring data privacy is extremely important—for example, data sharing faced major challenges during the Ebola crisis in West Africa in 2015, due to the lack of appropriate anonymization.[73] Many of these challenges remain unresolved. However, humanitarian groups have already begun to catalogue potential risks and make suggestions for their mitigation.

Due to the relative newness of the large-scale use of technological data and evidence-based programming in humanitarian response, much of its potential remains unexplored. With more time and investment, these processes have the potential to substantially reshape the way that aid is delivered.

The emergence of the innovation agenda and use of technology

Innovation has always occurred in the humanitarian context, often driven by resource constraints and other challenges in the field. However, a policy agenda and intentional organizational approach to innovation did not gain institutional momentum until 2009, when donors began to provide funding for innovation-specific programs, and agencies began establishing dedicated innovation-development teams. Three major motivations drove this change. First, the system lacked an effective framework for encouraging change and progress. Second, budgets were stretched thin and crises were lasting longer than ever before, requiring new partnerships and ways of working. Finally, many of the tools and services utilized for humanitarian action were outdated.

In this context, several institutional efforts emerged to directly foster innovation. Academic centers were established and operational agencies and INGOs dedicated innovation units. In a 2016 interview, David Miliband, president and CEO of the IRC, revealed that he had set up an independent research and development lab to develop technologies "ranging from malnutrition-measuring devices for nurses in Africa to computer based education software for schools in refugee camps."[74] The innovation agenda was growing rapidly in the lead-up to the World Humanitarian Summit in 2016—and it became one of the core policy agendas and focuses of the event. As a result, a new initiative, the Global Alliance for Humanitarian Innovation (GAHI), was launched as a public–private partnership to use innovation to "build bridges between actors with different comparative advantages in order to ensure that the right assistance reaches the people who need it."[75]

Examples of innovation "labs" trying to change operations are many and interesting. Response Innovation Labs, established after the Nepal earthquake in 2015, and Start Network Innovation Labs, are based in different crisis contexts but both aim to shift towards "bottom-up" innovation, driven by local entrepreneurs or crisis-affected communities, rather than "top-down" innovation driven by headquarters staff in international organizations.

Some of the boldest innovations are in the realm of financing. In the past few years, the ICRC launched the first social impact bond for humanitarian action, generating an investment of €22 million in humanitarian response over a five-year period. Insurance-based financing for humanitarian assistance is being explored by several actors, including the World Bank, whose increased engagement in humanitarian settings is expected to drive further financial innovation. Another example is the use of biometric data. The UNHCR has established a "Common Cash Facility" in Lebanon to distribute cash to Syrian refugees through a network of ATMs—each equipped with iris-scanning technology to verify the account holder.[76] While the use of biometric technology is itself notable, the Common Cash Facility has also pioneered an innovative public–private partnership approach to CTP. Aid agencies collaborate with the Cairo Amman Bank and the biotechnology company IrisGuard to deliver the services. Because each agency utilizes the same distribution platform, refugees can access cash from different sources in a single transaction. In 2016, 10 humanitarian organizations used the Common Cash Facility to deliver $118 million to 40,000 refugee families.[77]

One of the biggest problems with innovation in the humanitarian sector is institutional bureaucracy and inertia. Innovation requires taking risks and, in many cases, failing. Humanitarian agencies are notably risk-averse, leading to a situation in which "field workers often wish to keep their initiatives to themselves rather than sharing what they have learned, for fear of intervention from headquarters."[78] Another problem is the fact that few, if any, innovations that have emerged in the past decade have been widely adopted or have brought about significant improvement in how humanitarian assistance is delivered. There is what is called a "scaling" challenge, with innovation focusing mostly on prototyping and piloting. This is a core challenge that must be addressed in order for the sector to reap the full benefits of innovation.

Other concerns are ethical in nature. While businesses can easily roll out experimental new products to consumers, humanitarians risk putting lives in danger if they veer too far from established norms. While innovators are aware of these risks, there is no clear guidance on how to reconcile experimental approaches with core humanitarian principles. A small number of high-profile mistakes could derail the innovation agenda.[79]

A broader critique of the expansion of technological approaches suggests that it risks undermining one of the central purposes of humanitarian action. Remote data technologies make it possible for humanitarian agencies to have a smaller field presence—which could reduce the accuracy of needs assessments and make it harder to monitor aid as it is delivered. Physically present aid workers can make nuanced judgments about a situation and ensure that supplies are not being diverted by parties to conflict. This is much harder when operations are managed remotely. Furthermore, the absence of direct oversight by senior managers and technical experts may result in inappropriate forms of aid delivery, harming overall program quality.[80] And of course, human solidarity has always been a core element of the humanitarian imperative—technological remoteness undermines this element more than anything else.

Despite these challenges, innovation remains a trend in the contemporary humanitarian world. However, the innovation agenda is not likely to solve the most fundamental issues in humanitarian action, such as the need for greater accountability. In other words, it is not a panacea. However, innovation is already yielding major improvements in certain areas that could exponentially improve both the quality of aid and the efficiency with which the humanitarian system operates.

Conclusion: continual change

In 2015, some organizations in the humanitarian sector were asking if the humanitarian system was "broken" or "just broke." In other words, is humanitarian action fundamentally failing to achieve its goals, or does it simply lack the necessary resources? Recent trends seem to suggest that the answer is "both," and as this chapter aims to point out, the humanitarian system is working to find ways to address these challenges.

An overarching initiative that attempted to address the "broke" and "broken" system and make progress on many of the policy issues discussed in this chapter was the World Humanitarian Summit, held in Istanbul in 2016. It brought together over 9,000 participants representing 180 member states, including 55 heads of state and government and over 700 local and international NGOs, representatives from the private sector and academia, and other stakeholders. Together, they generated more than 3,500 commitments to action and launched more than a dozen new partnerships and initiatives. These included the "New Way of Working", which promoted policies to bridge the humanitarian–development divide and have a diverse set of actors working together for collective outcomes. The "Grand Bargain" was launched as an agreement between more than 30 of the biggest donors and aid providers to promote critical changes in the aid system, including gearing up cash programming, improving needs assessments and reporting, increasing funding for national and local responders, integrating gender as a cross-cutting issue, improving transparency and accountability of funding, reducing bureaucracy with harmonized reporting requirements,[81] and promoting multi-year funding. As discussed throughout this chapter, progress has been made on many of these initiatives. However, leadership, political will, and the ability for policies to be more nimble and able to adapt to the wider humanitarian environment and find results at the country level are still needed to bring real change.[82]

So although humanitarian action faces real obstacles, the trends discussed in this chapter illustrate that possibilities exist and effort will be forthcoming for the global system to engage in the collaboration, creativity, and hard work needed to improve outcomes for those affected by crises. For example, new approaches to accountability and protection suggest an acknowledgement of past failures. And the potential for cash transfers and other innovations is often framed in terms of efficiency and "value for money"—allowing humanitarian agencies to achieve more with increasingly tight budgets.

How much and to what degree change happens is and will continue to be a source of debate. As mentioned by a long-time observer of the humanitarian system, "Whether change is a constant of humanitarian life … is open to debate: many observers have complained that the humanitarian system fails to change, or does not change enough. Nevertheless, most humanitarians would accept that change initiatives are a constant of their working lives."[83]

For many humanitarian practitioners, the current environment is challenging but also exciting—as necessity and urgency drive the creation of new approaches with enormous potential to save lives and reduce human suffering.

Notes

1 Stephen O'Brien, cited in Lesley Bourns and Jessica Alexander, *Leaving No One Behind: Humanitarian Effectiveness in the Age of the Sustainable Development Goals*, OCHA Policy and Studies Series (UNOCHA; CDA Collaborative Learning Projects, 2016), 3, https://www.unocha.org/sites/unocha/files/LeavingNooneBehind_20151109_Small.pdf.
2 Michel Maietta, Eilidh Kennedy, and Francois Bourse, *The Future of Aid: INGOs in 2030* (Inter-Agency Regional Analysts Network (IARAN), 2017), http://futureofaid.iaran.org/The_Future_Of_Aid_INGOs_In_2030.pdf.
3 Richard Pallardy, "Haiti Earthquake of 2010," *Encyclopaedia Britannica* (Encyclopaedia Britannica, Inc., 15 December 2017), https://www.britannica.com/event/Haiti-earthquake-of-2010.
4 Elizabeth Ferris, "Haiti and Future Humanitarian Disasters," *Brookings Institution* (blog), 12 January 2011, https://www.brookings.edu/blog/up-front/2011/01/12/haiti-and-future-humanitarian-disasters/.
5 Ferris, "Haiti and Future Humanitarian Disasters."
6 Phillip Connor, "Most Displaced Syrians Are in the Middle East, and About a Million Are in Europe," *Pew Research Center* (blog), 29 January 2018, www.pewresearch.org/fact-tank/2018/01/29/where-displaced-syrians-have-resettled/.

7 Ground Truth Solutions, *Refugee Perceptions in Lebanon: Summary of Focus Group Discussions, Round Two*, Mixed Migration Platform (Ground Truth Solutions, 2017), https://reliefweb.int/sites/reliefweb.int/files/resources/Refugee%20perceptions%20in%20Lebanon_Round%202.pdf.

8 Nora Danielson, *Urban Refugee Protection in Cairo: The Role of Communication, Information and Technology*, New Issues in Refugee Research 236 (Oxford: United Nations High Commissioner for Refugees, 2012), www.unhcr.org/en-us/research/working/4fbf4c469/urban-refugee-protection-cairo-role-communication-information-technology.html.

9 UNHCR, *Policy on Alternatives to Camps* (United Nations High Commissioner for Refugees, 2014), www.unhcr.org/protection/statelessness/5422b8f09/unhcr-policy-alternatives-camps.html.

10 UNHCR, *Policy on Alternatives to Camps*.

11 Global Alliance for Urban Crises, "Global Alliance for Urban Crises," 2016, http://urbancrises.org/.

12 Urban Refugees, "Urban Refugees," www.urban-refugees.org/.

13 Global Alliance for Urban Crises, *Adapting Humanitarian Action to an Urban World* (Global Alliance for Urban Crises, 2016), http://urbancrises.org/sites/default/files/2016-10/Global%20Alliance%20for%20Urban%20Crises%20Brief%20-%20Final.pdf.

14 Julie Harlet, "Humanitarian Aid: 7 Years After the 2010 Earthquake, Who Remains Displaced?" *International Organization for Migration—Haiti* (blog), 2017, http://haiti.iom.int/humanitarian-aid-7-years-after-2010-earthquake-who-remains-displaced.

15 Cyprien Fabre and Courtenay Cabot Venton, *Multi-Year Humanitarian Funding*, Commitments into Action Series (Organisation for Economic Co-operation and Development (OECD), 2017), www.oecd.org/development/humanitarian-donors/docs/multiyearfunding.pdf.

16 Rodolpho Valente and Romano Lasker, *An End in Sight: Multi-Year Planning to Meet and Reduce Humanitarian Needs in Protracted Crises*, Policy and Studies Series (OCHA Policy Development and Studies Branch, 2015), https://www.unocha.org/sites/unocha/files/An%20end%20in%20sight%20Multi%20Year%20Planning.pdf.

17 Valente and Lasker, *An End in Sight*.

18 UNHCR, "Protrated Refugee Situations, EC/54/SC/CRP.14" (United Nations High Commissioner for Refugees, 10 June 2004), 2, www.unhcr.org/40c982172.pdf.

19 OCHA Kenya, *Kenya 2011+ Emergency Humanitarian Response Plan* (United Nations High Commissioner for Refugees, 2010), https://www.humanitarianresponse.info/sites/www.humanitarianresponse.info/files/documents/files/2011_kenya_ehrp.pdf.

20 OCHA Somalia, *Somalia Consolidated Appeal 2013–2015* (United Nations Office for the Coordination of Humanitarian Affairs, 2013), www.jccp.gr.jp/_src/sc2325/3_CAP_2013_Somalia.pdf.

21 Development Initiatives, *Global Humanitarian Assistance Report 2014* (Development Initiatives, 2014), http://devinit.org/wp-content/uploads/2014/09/Global-Humanitarian-Assistance-Report-2014.pdf.

22 OCHA Sudan, *Multi-Year Humanitarian Strategy 2017–2019: Sudan* (United Nations Office for the Coordination of Humanitarian Affairs,

2017), https://reliefweb.int/sites/reliefweb.int/files/resources/Sudan_Multi-Year_Humanitarian_Strategy_2017-2019.pdf.

23　Fabre and Cabot Venton, *Multi-Year Humanitarian Funding.*

24　Valente and Lasker, *An End in Sight.*

25　Anna Patton, "Yemen: DfID's Test Case for Multiyear Humanitarian Programming," *Devex* (blog), 12 June 2014, https://www.devex.com/news/sponsored/yemen-dfid-s-test-case-for-multiyear-humanitarian-programming-83665.

26　Ed Schenkenberg, *The Challenges of Localised Humanitarian Aid in Armed Conflict* (MSF, 2016), 3, https://www.alnap.org/system/files/content/resource/files/main/msf-egs03-the-challenges-of-localised-humanitarian-aid-in-armed-conflict-.pdf.

27　"What We Do," NEAR Network, 2016, www.near.ngo/what-we-do.

28　Eva Svoboda and Sara Pantuliano, *International and Local/Diaspora Actors in the Syria Response*, (London: Overseas Development Institute, March 2015), https://www.odi.org/publications/8714-international-and-local-diaspora-actors-syria-response.

29　UN report cited in Louise Redvers, "What Refugees Really Think of Aid Agencies," IRIN, March 2015, www.irinnews.org/analysis/2015/03/05/what-refugees-really-think-aid-agencies.

30　High Level Panel on Humanitarian Cash Transfers, *Doing Cash Differently: How Cash Transfers Can Transform Humanitarian Aid* (London: Overseas Development Institute (ODI) & Center for Global Development (CGD), 2015), 15, https://www.cgdev.org/sites/default/files/HLP-Humanitarian-Cash-Transfers-Report.pdf.

31　High Level Panel on Humanitarian Cash Transfers, *Doing Cash Differently.*

32　Christopher B. Barrett and Daniel G. Maxwell, *Food Aid after Fifty Years: Recasting Its Role*, (London: Routledge, 2005).

33　USAID, "Fiscal Year 2017 Fact Sheet" (Fiscal Year 2017 Fact Sheet: United States Agency for International Development Office of Food for Peace, April 16, 2018), https://www.usaid.gov/sites/default/files/documents/1866/FY_2017_factsheet_condensed_4.17.2018.pdf.

34　WFP, *WFP Strategic Plan 2008–2013* (Rome, Italy: World Food Programme, 2007), https://documents.wfp.org/stellent/groups/public/documents/communications/wfp228800.pdf?_ga=2.121773583.501948251.1533737580-2781514 84.1532996909.

35　High Level Panel on Humanitarian Cash Transfers, *Doing Cash Differently.*

36　Lesley Adams, *Learning from Cash Responses to the Tsunami: Final Report* (London: Humanitarian Policy Group, 2007), https://www.odi.org/sites/odi.org.uk/files/odi-assets/publications-opinion-files/4860.pdf.

37　Degan Ali and Kirsten Gelsdorf, "Risk-Averse to Risk-Willing: Learning from the 2011 Somalia Cash Response," *Global Food Security* 1, no. 1 (2012): 57–63.

38　Ali and Gelsdorf, "Risk-Averse to Risk-Willing."

39　Kerren Hedlund, Nisar Majid, Dan Maxwell, and Nigel Nicholson, *Final Evaluation of the Unconditional Cash and Voucher Response to the 2011–12 Crisis in Southern and Central Somalia* (Humanitarian Outcomes, UNICEF, Unite for Children, 2013), 3, https://reliefweb.int/sites/reliefweb.int/files/resources/SOM_resources_cashevalsum.pdf.

40　Hedlund et al., *Final Evaluation.*

41 Louisa Seferis, "Cash Transfer Programming: Benefits and Risks," *Professionals in Humanitarian Assistance and Protection (PHAP)* (blog), 14 March 2014, https://phap.org/thematic-notes/2014/march/cash-transfer-p rogramming-benefits-and-risks; Gabrielle Smith, "New Technologies in Cash Transfer Programming and Humanitarian Assistance," *Humanitarian Exchange*, May 2012.

42 Daniel Maxwell, John Parker, and Heather Stobaugh, "What Drives Program Choice in Food Security Crises? Examining the 'Response Analysis' Question," *World Development* 49, no. September 2013 (2013): 68–79.

43 Alexandra Spencer, Chloe Parrish, and Charlotte Lattimer, *Counting Cash: Tracking Humanitarian Expenditure on Cash-Based Programming*, Working Paper 505 (London: Overseas Development Institute (ODI) and Development Initiatives, 2016), https://www.odi.org/sites/odi.org.uk/files/resource-documents/11296.pdf.

44 For example, International Rescue Committee, *Commit to Cash* (International Rescue Committee, 2016), https://www.icvanetwork.org/system/files/versions/WHS_Cash.pdf.

45 Y. S. Andrew Tan and J. von Schreeb, "Humanitarian Assistance and Accountability: What Are We Really Talking About?", *Prehospital and Disaster Medicine* 30, no. 3 (2015): 264–70.

46 Tan and von Schreeb, "Humanitarian Assistance and Accountability."

47 John Borton, *The Joint Evaluation of Emergency Assistance to Rwanda: Study III Principal Findings and Recommendations*, (London: Overseas Development Institute, 1996), https://odihpn.org/wp-content/uploads/1996/06/networkpaper016.pdf.

48 Community World Service Asia, "Promoting Accountability, and Quality Humanitarian Assistance to Disaster and Crisis Affected Communities in Pakistan," *Community World Service Asia* (blog), 16 May 2018, https://corehumanitarianstandard.org/news/promoting-accountability-and-quality-humanitarian-assistance-to-disaster-and-crisis-affected-communities-in-paki stan.

49 CDAC Network, "CDAC Network," Communicating with Disaster Affected Communities (CDAC), www.cdacnetwork.org.

50 IRIN, "Put Accountability into Practice," *IRIN News*, July 2012, https://reliefweb.int/report/world/how-put-accountability-practice.

51 CHS Alliance, *On the Road to Istanbul: How Can the World Humanitarian Summit Make Humanitarian Response More Effective?* (CHS Alliance, 2015), https://www.chsalliance.org/files/files/CHS-Alliance-HAR-2015.pdf.

52 The Sphere Project, *The Sphere Handbook 2018: Draft 2* (The Sphere Project, 2017), www.sphereproject.org/handbook/revision-sphere-handbook/draft-re ady-for-feedback/#download.

53 Nicola Slawson, "Oxfam Government Funding Cut off After Haiti Scandal," *Guardian*, 16 February 2016, https://www.theguardian.com/world/2018/feb/16/oxfam-government-funding-cut-off-after-haiti-scandal.

54 Amy Costello, "The Oxfam Scandal Shows That Reform Is Needed in the Humanitarian Aid Sector," *PRI*, 15 February 2018, https://www.pri.org/stories/2018-02-15/oxfam-scandal-shows-reform-needed-humanitarian-aid-s ector.

55 House of Commons International Development Committee, *Sexual Exploitation and Abuse in the Aid Sector: Eighth Report of Session 2017–19*

170   *Changes in policy and practice*

(London: House of Commons, 2018), 9, https://publications.parliament.
uk/pa/cm201719/cmselect/cmintdev/840/840.pdf.
56 Costello, "The Oxfam Scandal."
57 Global Protection Cluster, *Humanitarian Country Team Protection Strategy* (Global Protection Cluster, 2016), www.globalprotectioncluster.org/_a
ssets/files/tools_and_guidance/essential-protection-guidance/gpc-_-hct-guida
nce.en.pdf.
58 Hugo Slim and Andrew Bonwick, *Protection: An ALNAP Guide for Humanitarian Agencies* (London: Overseas Development Institute, 2005).
59 Ban Ki-moon, *One Humanity: Shared Responsibility (Report of the Secretary-General for the World Humanitarian Summit)* (New York: United Nations, 2016), 3, https://reliefweb.int/sites/reliefweb.int/files/resources/Secre
tary-General%27s%20Report%20for%20WHS%202016%20%28Advance%
20Unedited%20Draft%29.pdf.
60 Sara Pantuliano and Sorcha O'Callaghan, *The "Protection Crisis": A Review of Field-Based Strategies for Humanitarian Protection in Darfur*, HPG Discussion Paper (London: Overseas Development Institute (ODI), 2006), https://www.odi.org/sites/odi.org.uk/files/odi-assets/publications-opin
ion-files/267.pdf.
61 Pantuliano and O'Callaghan, *The "Protection Crisis."*
62 Global Protection Cluster, *Whole of Syria Humanitarian Strategy for Protection* (Global Protection Cluster, 2015), www.globalprotectioncluster.
org/_assets/files/field_protection_clusters/syria/files/ssg-wos-humanitarian-st
rategy-for-protection-with-protection-advocacy-strategy_26-09-2015.pdf.
63 Norah Niland, Riccardo Polastro, Antonio Donini, and Amra Lee, *Independent Whole of System Review of Protection in the Context of Humanitarian Action* (Norwegian Refugee Council, 2015), https://reliefweb.int/sites/
reliefweb.int/files/resources/final_whole_of_system_report.pdf.
64 Niland et al., *Independent Whole of System Review.*
65 Slim and Bonwick, *Protection*; Haidi Willmot, Ralph Mamiya, Scott Sheeran, and Marc Weller, eds., *Protection of Civilians*, 1st ed. (Oxford: Oxford University Press, 2016); IASC, *Growing the Sheltering Tree: Protecting Rights through Humanitarian Action* (Geneva: Inter-Agency Standing Committee (IASC), 2002), www.globalprotectioncluster.org/_assets/
files/tools_and_guidance/IASC_Growing_Sheltering_Tree_2002_EN.pdf.
66 James Darcy, Heather Stobaugh, Peter Walker, and Dan Maxwell, *The Use of Evidence in Humanitarian Decision Making*, ACAPS Operational Learning Paper (Medford, Mass.: Feinstein International Center, 2013), 8, http://fic.tufts.edu/assets/TUFTS_1306_ACAPS_3_online.pdf.
67 "Case Study: Nepal Earthquake 2015," Flowminder, 2015, www.flowm
inder.org/case-studies/nepal-earthquake-2015.
68 IDMC, "About IDMC," Internal Displacement Monitoring Centre (IDMC), 2017, www.internal-displacement.org/about-us/.
69 Alice Obrecht, *Using Evidence to Allocate Humanitarian Resources: Challenges and Opportunities*, ALNAP Working Paper (London: ALNAP/
Overseas Development Institute, 2017), https://www.alnap.org/system/files/
content/resource/files/main/alnap-eaar-resource-allocation-2017.pdf.
70 James Darcy and Charles-Antoine Hofmann, *According to Need? Needs Assessment and Decision-Making in the Humanitarian Sector*, HPG Report

(London: Overseas Development Institute, 2003), https://www.odi.org/sites/odi.org.uk/files/odi-assets/publications-opinion-files/285.pdf.

71 Daniel Maxwell, Peter Hailey, Jeeyon Janet Kim, Erin McCloskey, and Maria Wrabel, *Constraints and Complexities of Information and Analysis in Humanitarian Emergencies: Evidence from Nigeria* (Medford, Mass.: Feinstein International Center, 2018), http://fic.tufts.edu/assets/AAH-Nigeria-Case-Study-Report-FINAL1.pdf; Daniel Maxwell, Peter Hailey, Jeeyon Janet Kim, Erin McCloskey, and Maria Wrabel, *Constraints and Complexities of Information and Analysis in Humanitarian Emergencies: Evidence from South Sudan* (Medford, Mass.: Feinstein International Center, 2018), http://fic.tufts.edu/assets/SouthSudan-Case-Study-Report.pdf.

72 Daniel P. Scarnecchia, N. A. Raymond, F. Greenwood, C. Howarth, and D. N. Poole, "A Rights-Based Approach to Information in Humanitarian Assistance," *PLoS Current Disasters*, no. 1 (December 2017).

73 UNOCHA, *Building Data Responsibility into Humanitarian Action*, Policy and Studies Series 018 (United Nations, 2016), https://www.unocha.org/sites/unocha/files/Building%20data%20responsibility%20into%20humanitarian%20action.pdf.

74 Matthew Shaer, "Inside The IRC: How A Visionary Aid Organization Is Using Technology to Help Refugees," *Fast Company* (blog), 21 November 2016, https://www.fastcompany.com/3065447/how-a-visionary-aid-organization-is-using-technology-to-help-refugees.

75 Global Alliance for Urban Crises, *Adapting Humanitarian Action to an Urban World*.

76 Heidi Gilert and Lois Austin, *Review of the Common Cash Facility Approach in Jordan* (Cash Learning Partnership (CaLP) and UNHCR, 2017), https://reliefweb.int/sites/reliefweb.int/files/resources/59fc362e7.pdf.

77 Gilert and Austin, *Review of the Common Cash Facility Approach*.

78 Alexander Betts and Louise Bloom, *Humanitarian Innovation: The State of the Art*, Policy and Studies Series 009 (UNOCHA, 2014), 22, https://www.unocha.org/sites/unocha/files/Humanitarian%20Innovation%20The%20State%20of%20the%20Art_0.pdf.

79 Betts and Bloom, *Humanitarian Innovation: The State of the Art*.

80 Joe Belliveau, "Humanitarian Access and Technology: Opportunities and Applications," *Procedia Engineering* 159 (2016): 300–306.

81 Agenda for Humanity, "World Humanitarian Summit," Agenda for Humanity, 2016, https://www.agendaforhumanity.org/summit.

82 Victoria Metcalfe-Hough and Lydia Poole, with Sarah Bailey and Julie Belanger, *Grand Bargain Annual Independent Report 2018*, HPG Commissioned Report (London: Overseas Development Institute, 2018), https://www.alnap.org/system/files/content/files/main/12256.pdf.

83 Paul Knox-Clarke, *Changing Humanitarian Action?* ALNAP Working Paper (London: ALNAP/Overseas Development Institute, 14 February 2017), 6, https://www.alnap.org/system/files/content/resource/files/main/alnap-31-am-background-paper.pdf.

7 Unresolved (and unresolvable?)

Understanding the humanitarian world in the twenty-first century

- Multiple agendas and competing imperatives
- Access, sovereignty, principles and the challenge of protection
- Growing funding gaps
- A humanitarian malaise?
- Conclusion: towards the future of humanitarianism

As the second decade of the twenty-first century comes to a close, the profile of humanitarian action has never been higher. Certainly budgets, expectations, and the demand for humanitarian services have never been higher. But at the same time, the "system" shows signs of being stretched to the breaking point, and even though budgets are at an all-time high, so are the gaps in the system—resulting in people it cannot protect and needs it cannot meet.

Humanitarian action continues apace—in part because there is no alternative, no "panic button" that can be pushed to stop out-of-control, major crises in a dozen or more countries until some of the thorny issues that have arisen can be decided and addressed. One senior humanitarian observer described the process of humanitarian reform as "lifting the bonnet on an automobile to work on the engine while the car is speeding down the road at 60 miles per hour."[1] And so it is likely to remain.

Humanitarian action is thus at least partly the art of managing some of these constant issues, since "resolving" them seems to be out of the question. For students of humanitarian action and humanitarian leaders alike, understanding what these are, and how they will shape the future is important. In closing this short book, a few of the on-going and unresolved challenges are worth highlighting.

Multiple agendas and competing imperatives

Many different objectives define humanitarian action, from the *core objectives of saving and protecting lives* in violent conflict to the wider objectives of laying the foundation for reducing poverty and inequality, reducing human rights abuses, or contributing to peace building, resilience, and market strengthening.

Each of these agendas has its advocates, and each tugs the enterprise in a different direction. Donors continue to want humanitarians to act to some degree in the political interests of the government(s) offering funding, and that will always be the case, despite the principle of independence. But competing imperatives run deeper. In Somalia in 2011, the counter-terrorism imperative completely outweighed the humanitarian imperative until an actual famine was declared (by which time it was too late to save the lives of a quarter million people).[2] Similar security concerns of governments or regional powers outweigh the protection of civilians in Syria, Yemen, and a dozen other violent contemporary conflicts around the world. As a community of practice, humanitarians are relatively powerless to counter political and security imperatives, but speaking out on behalf of the even more powerless people caught up in violent conflict will continue to be part of what humanitarian action means.

Humanitarians by definition do a lot of different things, and the boundaries between what is "humanitarian" and what is rightfully something else are as blurred as ever (see Figure 2 in Chapter 1). Some have tried to clarify boundaries by declaring humanitarian action to be about all these things. Others have tried to ring-fence the purely life-protecting or life-saving elements of humanitarian action in an acute crisis and define everything else as something other than "humanitarian." Some have tried to define "pure" humanitarian action along a kind of Dunantist line, where actors prioritize the key principles and work only under IHL, and define everything else—even if done in a principled way in conflict situations—as "relief" but not necessarily "humanitarian". None of these have proved satisfactory. Some humanitarians will always engage in activities that other humanitarians think is someone else's business—because it is too political, or too transformative, or because it helps to pick winners and losers. At the same time, nearly all will agree that, while at times all humanitarians can do is to try to protect life and dignity, at other times it makes little sense to continue providing emergency assistance year after bloody year while doing little to address the drivers of the crisis that are causing the bloodiness in the first place.

In recent years, several initiatives have emerged that try to close some of these divides. Growing out of a concern with linking humanitarian action to the Sustainable Development Goals introduced in 2015, a major agenda of the World Humanitarian Summit in 2016 was to adopt a "New Way of Working" that, at a minimum, involved not only addressing the acute symptoms of crisis but also addressing their underlying causes (see Chapter 6). In some cases, this implies a much broader range of services, provided in a manner that can be mobilized rapidly if a crisis demands them; in other cases it means explicitly linking poverty reduction objectives and humanitarian objectives—frequently in the form of social safety net programs that can also rapidly scale up to address large-scale shocks. But in both cases, these imply host-government management—and as the case studies have demonstrated, sometimes governments cannot provide this level of engagement—indeed sometimes they are a party to the conflict causing the problem in the first place. Too much "coherence" between independent and impartial humanitarians on the one hand and governments or militaries that have political agendas on the other will always be problematic for humanitarians.

The other initiative, which is less specifically defined but probably broader in application, is the whole notion of "resilience." Although more complicated in practice, resilience implies the ability to "bounce back" after a shock or crisis. The way in which humanitarian assistance is managed can either enable or undermine this ability to bounce back, but building more resilient communities (which most observers would label as a "development" activity) can prevent people from being as badly affected by shocks in the first place. Governments have a major role to play in this, but humanitarian agencies can and do work on resilience-building agendas even in areas outside government control or where governments don't have the capacity to lead. And part of building resilient communities necessarily embraces concerns about governance, about human rights, and about conflict management. So some of these activities will continue to overlap with humanitarian action—and humanitarian actors will continue to be called upon to engage in some of these activities. But humanitarian action will never be "all things to all people." For every Clare Short urging humanitarian actors to embrace a broader vision and provide a wider set of responses, there will be a David Rieff calling them back to their origins of simply providing a "bed for the night."[3]

Access, sovereignty, principles and the challenge of protection

The access that humanitarian actors have to crisis-affected populations—and perhaps more importantly, the access that affected populations have to protection and assistance—lies at the heart of the humanitarian endeavor. The most commonly cited reason for several of the core humanitarian principles of neutrality, impartiality, and independence is to ensure access to affected populations. Humanitarian access is mandated by Resolution 46/182 of the UN General Assembly 1991 that laid the foundation for much of contemporary humanitarian action.

During the Cold War, the bulk of humanitarian action was on the fringes of conflict zones—refugees across a border from a warring country being perhaps the most common example (there were some important exceptions to this, Biafra being a seminal example; see Chapter 3). During the 1990s, working *in* conflict zones became much more common—and indeed to try to contain the crisis within the country affected to prevent large-scale flows of refugees—the wars in the former Yugoslavia being the seminal example (see Chapter 3). In nearly every serious humanitarian crisis today, humanitarian access is constrained and sometimes nearly impossible. With the rise of counter-insurgency or counter-terrorism warfare, both national militaries and armed non-state actors have restricted or denied access to even the most principled of humanitarian actors—creating what is frequently referred to in the literature as "the collapse of humanitarian space."[4]

The most common restrictions to access include bureaucratic restrictions on personnel and humanitarian supplies (including counter-terrorism restrictions that limited access in Somalia or Gaza for example), the level of violence in conflict, direct attacks against aid workers, and the potential diversion of aid. Note, however, that for the most part these restrictions constrain humanitarian actors. Sometimes, other factors constrain the ability of affected populations to access assistance.

Growing constraints to access, and the refusal of states to protect their own citizens, were behind the rise of the R2P doctrine, which held that sovereignty comes with responsibility: Where national governments would not or could not protect the rights of their own citizens, the international community had an obligation to intervene (a "responsibility to protect")—overturning centuries of international relations doctrine that states were sovereign over all matters within their own boundaries. R2P has been invoked several times, but has not addressed the constraints to humanitarian access.

However, resurgence in the assertion of national sovereignty followed quickly in response to the global consensus around R2P, with new laws curtailing both national civil society and international humanitarian actors. Such laws were used to control or expel humanitarian agencies from Darfur in 2009 (in response to the issuing of an arrest warrant for the president of Sudan by the International Criminal Court) and to significantly curtail the ability of humanitarian agencies to operate independently in other countries such as Ethiopia or South Sudan.

While R2P was predominantly about the responsibility of state actors, protection at a more localized level remains a concern for humanitarian actors themselves. In many cases, advocacy is their only tool, although a new kind of agency has emerged in the twenty-first century that puts itself at the interface of humanitarian action, peace-building, and human rights protection, that is not, first and foremost, concerned with the provision of assistance, but rather with addressing the conditions that put people at risk of violence of abuse.[5] Nearly every crisis reviewed in Chapter 3 highlighted the need for protection of civilians, and many of them have been labeled as primarily protection crises, with other needs taking a secondary place.

Constraints on access have led to the rise in the "remote management" of humanitarian assistance, where international agencies or international staff manage programs from a third (and less restricted) country, while local organizations or local staff manage programs on the ground.[6] But remote management, while enabling some degree of continuity in programming under complex environments, presents its own issues—especially vis-à-vis the issue of protection.

And quite delinked from the issue of access, the issue of humanitarian protection took a serious hit in 2018 when one of the most respected agencies in the humanitarian world, Oxfam, was accused of over-looking allegations that staff brought prostitutes into agency quarters during the response to the Haiti earthquake and other disasters (see Chapter 6).[7] Earlier reports—that ironically didn't generate the public reaction that the Oxfam scandal did—suggested even more worrisome abuses, including demanding sex (including sex with children) in exchange for assistance, or to be considered for refugee resettlement programs.[8] How, reporters and donors asked, could humanitarians claim to be concerned about protection when they do not even protect vulnerable people from their own predatory staff?

Growing funding gaps

As Table I.1 in the Introduction makes clear, humanitarian budgets have never been larger, but the demands made on those budgets are higher still and, on average, less than two-thirds (sometimes only half) of assessed humanitarian need is funded. And of course this doesn't include unassessed need (nor does it count all the contributions of neighbors, kin, and informal local organizations who help people in times of crisis). But the fact is that humanitarian action, as a global enterprise, is poorly financed. Some of the available funding is diverted or ends up in the hands of the wrong people.[9] And some of it is simply not well spent, or can't reach the most vulnerable because of access constraints. The debate in the run-up to the 2016 World Humanitarian Summit, noted in Chapter 6, highlighted the question of whether humanitarian action is "broken" or just "broke." The truth is both, to some degree. But on the funding side, increased demand (in the form of people in assessed need) clearly is racing well ahead of the willingness of the international community to make resources available.

Considerable evidence shows that in a crisis, earlier action will prevent the slide into an extreme humanitarian emergency and thus require fewer resources to contain the overall impact of a major shock.[10] However, one of the long-standing challenges has been to mobilize funding and move it to the field quickly in the face of a rapidly worsening situation—the well named "early warning/late response" problem.[11] In theory, if earlier response has been shown to reduce expenditures, donors themselves would be eager to get money to a crisis as rapidly as possible.[12] But as the Somalia famine case study (Chapter 3) showed, this is not always the case. Somalia was an extreme but not unusual case and has led humanitarians to new attempts to synchronize information (early warning about a crisis) with finance (mobilizing resources) and rapid response (getting the resources to the field quickly enough to prevent widespread deterioration of humanitarian conditions).[13]

A humanitarian malaise?

The humanitarian world—and especially the UN/Red Cross/NGO backbone of the long-established system—has seen rapid growth, substantial institutionalization, and professionalization, but also increasing challenges. Much recent analysis has focused on the challenges—and labeled the current condition of the humanitarian community as ranging anywhere from a "malaise" to an "existential crisis."[14]

There are numerous reasons for this. The concerns about finance (and the need to maintain a good reputation for future financing) and humanitarian access that are discussed above are part of this. And a third concern is the rapid erosion of support for multilateral institutions in the face of increasing nationalist and populist political sentiments in Europe and North America. This erosion not only affects directly some of the UN agencies themselves, it undermines the general sense of collective responsibility for protecting vulnerable groups or populations on which an internationalized version of the humanitarian imperative is based.

This in turn leads to a fourth element of the malaise, the ability of humanitarian actors to learn from their own experience. Leading observers of humanitarian action noted concerns a decade ago about "learning challenged organizations" in humanitarian operations.[15] Despite widespread efforts since then to improve the evidence base, professionalize and internationalize the ranks of humanitarian workers, and build stronger normative guidelines, many of the same mistakes are made today that were made a decade ago. These challenges have had a demoralizing effect on the whole endeavor. A report by the London-based think tank, the Overseas Development Institute (ODI) in the run-up to the World Humanitarian Summit in 2016 referred to a humanitarian "groundhog day"—with reference to a popular movie in which the same characters continuously enact the same set of circumstances with the same results—underlining not only shortcomings but also the inability to overcome them.[16]

On the ground, a more personal kind of demoralization was noted in the aftermath of the Somalia famine—a sense of "damned if you do and damned if you don't." Not only had assistance arrived too late to save the lives of a quarter of a million people, but perhaps the long history of aid in Somalia, and the way in which aid played into the war economy of the country, had undermined resilience and in some ways helped to create the conditions that led to famine in the first place.[17]

Conclusion: towards the future of humanitarianism

Despite the challenges, there is little doubt that humanitarians and their activities—from service provision, to protection and advocacy, to solidarity, or what MSF simply calls *témoignage* (witnessing)—are more needed today than ever. As mentioned by one reporter, "There's one prediction … that most aid workers can make with confidence—that the New Year will usher in rising humanitarian needs."[18]

Humanitarians of all kinds will continue to play an increasingly important role for the foreseeable future. Humanitarian action will clearly be an "ecosystem" made up of multiple actors and multiple systems interacting with each other in the name of humanity. This calls for fresh approaches to (and understandings about) partnership—a concept and a practice that has been around for decades, but which has been determined largely by contractual-legal relationships.

The push for greater use of information and technology, for more evidence-based interventions, and for greater accountability among all stakeholders are all trends that will take on greater urgency as the gap between resources and demands widens (or even if the gap narrows somewhat). With the rise of localization and local actors, the need for both universal standards and context-specific analysis and response—and the challenge of striking the balance between them—will be greater than ever. And finally, the ongoing need for professionalization of humanitarian action while maintaining the spirit of voluntary citizen action and mutual aid that has always animated the humanitarian impulse will be equally imperative.

What changes and what remains the same (as in the "groundhog day" image) remains to be seen. If firm answers are few and every decision "depends," the challenge for humanitarians of the future will be to figure out the criteria and considerations on which making good choices depend. What is general and what is context specific? When does history and experience teach something? When does it teach the wrong thing? What will "the system" (or ecosystem) look like? What will define a "humanitarian actor" in the future? All these questions remain to be addressed.

Notes

1 Antonio Donini, to a meeting at Tufts University, November 2014.
2 Daniel Maxwell and Nisar Majid, *Famine in Somalia: Competing Imperatives, Collective Failures, 2011–12* (New York: Oxford University Press, 2016).
3 Clare Short, "Principles for a New Humanitarianism," (7 April 1998), https://publications.parliament.uk/pa/cm199798/cmselect/cmintdev/711/8042808.htm; David Rieff, *A Bed for the Night: Humanitarianism in Crisis* (New York: Simon & Schuster, 2002).
4 Sarah Collinson and Samir Elhawary, *Humanitarian Space: A Review of Trends and Issues*, HPG Report (London: Overseas Development Institute, April 2012), https://www.odi.org/sites/odi.org.uk/files/odi-assets/publications-opinion-files/7643.pdf.
5 The US- and France-based organization, Nonviolent Peaceforce, is one such agency, growing out of the anti-war movements of the late 20th century. See NVP, "About Nonviolent Peaceforce," Nonviolent Peaceforce, 2018, https://www.nonviolentpeaceforce.org/background/mission-history. From a more Dunantist perspective, the Swiss agency, Geneva Call, engages directly with armed non-state actors to educate them about—and call upon them to respect—IHL. See Geneva Call, "Mission," Geneva Call, https://genevacall.org/who-we-are/.
6 Antonio Donini and Daniel Maxwell, "From Face-to-Face to Face-to-Screen: Remote Management, Effectiveness and Accountability of Humanitarian Action in Insecure Environments," *International Review of the Red Cross* 95, no. 890 (June 2014): 383–413.
7 BBC News, "Oxfam Haiti Allegations: How the Scandal Unfolded," *BBC News*, 21 February 2018, https://www.bbc.com/news/uk-43112200.

8   UNHCR and SCF, *Sexual Violence & Exploitation: The Experience of Refugee Children in Guinea, Liberia and Sierra Leone Based on Initial Findings and Recommendations from Assessment Mission,* (London and Geneva: SCF and UNHCR, 2001), https://www.alnap.org/help-library/sexu al-violence-and-exploitation-the-experience-of-refugee-children-in-guinea-li beria.

9   For a particularly egregious contemporary case, see USIP, *The Unintended Consequences of Humanitarian Action in South Sudan,* (Washington, DC: United States Institute for Peace, 2018). For a more global overview see Transparency International, *Preventing Corruption in Humanitarian Operations,* (Transparency International, 10 December 2014), https://www.transparency.org/whatwedo/publication/preventing_corruption_in_humanit arian_operations.

10 Courtenay Cabot Venton, Tenna Shitarek, Lorraine Coulter, and Olivia Dooley, *The Economics of Early Response and Disaster Resilience: Lessons from Kenya and Ethiopia* (London: DFID, Conflict, Humanitarian and Security Department, June 2012), www.fao.org/fileadmin/user_upload/drought/docs/Econ-Ear-Rec-Res-Full-Report%20.pdf.

11 Rob Bailey, *Managing Famine Risk: Linking Early Warning to Early Action* (London: Chatham House, 2013); Maxwell and Majid, *Famine in Somalia: Competing Imperatives, Collective Failures, 2011–12;* Margaret Buchanan-Smith and Susanna Davies, *Famine Early Warning and Response: The Missing Link* (London: Intermediate Technology Publications, 1995).

12 Venton et al., *The Economics of Early Response and Disaster Resilience.*

13 For example, see the Famine Early Action Mechanism (FAM) proposed by the World Bank in 2018.

14 See Randolph Kent, Christina Bennett, Antonio Donini, and Daniel Maxwell, *Planning from the Future: Is the Humanitarian System Fit for Purpose?* (London; Medford, Mass.: Humanitarian Policy Group at the Overseas Development Institute; Feinstein International Center at Tufts University; The Policy Institute at King's College London, 2016), www.planningfrom thefuture.org/uploads/4/5/6/0/45605399/pff_report_uk.pdf; Michael Barnett and Peter Walker, "Regime Change for Humanitarian Aid," *Foreign Affairs,* July 2015, https://www.foreignaffairs.com/articles/2015-06-16/regim e-change-humanitarian-aid.

15 Thomas G. Weiss and Peter J. Hoffman, "The Fog of Humanitarianism: Collective Action Problems and Learning-Challenged Organizations," *Journal of Intervention and Statebuilding* 1, no. 1 (2007): 47–65.

16 HPG, *Time to Let Go: Remaking Humanitarian Action for the Modern Era* (London: Humanitarian Policy Group, ODI, 2016), https://www.odi.org/sites/odi.org.uk/files/resource-documents/10422.pdf.

17 Maxwell and Majid, *Famine in Somalia: Competing Imperatives, Collective Failures, 2011–12.*

18 Tom Esslemont, "These Are the Top Humanitarian Concerns for 2016," *World Economic Forum* (blog), 30 December 2015, https://www.weforum.org/agenda/2015/12/these-are-the-top-humanitarian-concerns-for-2016/.

Epilogue

We wrote this book for our students, current and future—those we formally teach and informally mentor, and those who (like us) are "students" of humanitarian action—whether formally registered for a class or not. Often times, at the end of a semester-long class, we get feedback like, "After taking this class, I don't see why anyone would go into humanitarian work? It is too daunting and too depressing" or, "The humanitarian system seems broken and maybe even part of the problem." And so, perhaps, it is at the end of a book too. We are not in the business of scaring people off; nor are we trying to recruit people. Humanitarians work under sometimes-horrific circumstances of violent conflict, corruption and *inhumanity*—and one's faith in humanity can be shaken to its core under these circumstances. So one has to be certain of what that core is and where it is to be found: In other words, after reading an introductory book of this nature, why *would* someone work in the humanitarian world?

People are drawn to humanitarian work for all kinds of reasons. Sometimes it is because of somewhat selfish reasons such as the "halo effect" that comes with being seen to help people, or for the "adrenaline" of working in rapidly changing and tension-charged environments, and for myriad other reasons. There is no hiding from all of these. But we continue our own engagement with the humanitarian world for another set of reasons.

First, the human demand is undeniable. Even though overall global statistics paint a picture of reduced poverty, of fewer and less-violent conflicts, and other indicators of improved human wellbeing, these global averages mask an ever-expanding number of people shunted aside by globalization, put at greater risk from climate change, and subject to horrific violence in warfare. Some observers—perhaps more cynical than ourselves—would say that humanitarian action is just the velvet glove or the "human face" of global capitalism, taking the roughest edge off the worst effects of a system that makes winners and losers. But, however one interprets the overall evidence, the fact remains that greater numbers of people are put at greater levels of risk with each succeeding year. A genuine concern for other people still drives humanitarian work.

Second, and perhaps more profoundly, is the effect that humanitarian action can have *on the humanitarian*. Burnout, engagement in dangerous behaviors like alcohol abuse, and cynicism are all part of the "malaise" outlined in Chapter 7 that some experience in this endeavor. Many expect that "doing good" will be rewarded by "doing well," and are disappointed by the comparison of their expectations with the realities they confront on the ground. But humanitarian action *can* be done well and can result not only in people having more to eat, or with roofs over their heads after their own homes have been destroyed—it can and does result in greater understanding, human solidarity, and rediscovery of what mutual assistance actually means—or even rediscovery of what being human means. When you learn these things from people you work alongside and are ostensibly there to "help," it can be a profound—even transformative—experience.

Third, let's face it: We are also drawn to the challenge. Something is intensely compelling about not just the "needs" but also the on-going search for how one can better address them. Is it possible to make sense of the plethora of information, of politics, of constraints, and of need—and come out with a better understanding and a better response? Can we do a better job of keeping people safe and ensuring that they have access to what they need for a dignified life—even if disrupted by crisis? The historical record that we have narrated here would suggest that the demands and the constraints have outpaced our ability to innovate, but we have learned, we have innovated, and we both have seen progress. Evidence and innovation can and do lead to better policies, better programs—and ideally, a more humane future. But evidence and innovation will only do so if we choose to make them do so.

Everyone has his or her own reasons for engaging in this endeavor, but understanding the humanitarian world is a prerequisite, and a solid foundation for positive engagement.

The Authors
September 2018

Bibliography

There are many good books on humanitarian action and humanitarian policy—a large number of which are referenced in the chapters of this book. Some major books in recent times that give a general overview of humanitarian history and contemporary humanitarianism include Peter Hoffman and Thomas Weiss, *Humanitarianism, War, and Politics: Solferino to Syria and Beyond* (London: Rowman and Littlefield, 2017); Didier Fassin and Mariella Pandolfi, *Contemporary States of Emergency: The Politics of Military and Humanitarian Interventions* (New York: Zone Books, 2013); and Michael Barnett, *Empire of Humanity: A History of Humanitarianism* (Syracuse, N.Y.: Cornell University Press, 2011).

On the critical topic of humanitarian principles and humanitarian ethics more broadly, the most important books in recent times are Hugo Slim, *Humanitarian Ethics: A Guide to the Morality of Aid in War and Disaster* (London: Hurst, 2014); and Jennifer Rubenstein, *Between Samaritans and States: The Political Ethics of Humanitarian INGOs* (New York/London: Oxford University Press, 2015).

Several recent books, and some classic older books explore the nature, causation and impact of famine as one particular form of humanitarian catastrophe. These include Alex de Waal, *Mass Starvation* (Cambridge: Polity Press, 2018); Daniel Maxwell and Nisar Majid, *Famine in Somalia: Competing Imperatives and Collective Failures, 2011–2012* (New York/London: Oxford University Press/Hurst, 2016); and de Waal's earlier book, *Famine Crimes: Politics and the Disaster Relief Industry* (Oxford: James Currey, 1997).

Some recent books look at humanitarian action from a particular perspective: For an economic perspective, see Gilles Carbonnier, *Humanitarian Economics: War, Disaster and the Global Aid Market* (London: Hurst, 2015). From the perspective of the politicization of humanitarian action, see Antonio Donini, *The Golden Fleece: Manipulation and Independence in Humanitarian Action* (Hartford, Conn.: Kumarian Press, 2012). And from the perspective of the dangers faced by humanitarian workers themselves, see Larissa Fast, *Aid in*

Danger: The Perils and Promise of Humanitarianism (Philadelphia: University of Pennsylvania Press, 2014).

Several books that convey a very first person sense of working in humanitarian crises include David Rieff, *A Bed for the Night* (New York: Simon and Schuster, 2002); Tony Vaux, *The Selfish Altruist: Relief Work in Famine and War* (London: Earthscan, 2002); Jessica Alexander, *Chasing Chaos: My Decade In and Out of Humanitarian Aid.* (New York: Broadway Books, 2013); and of course, Fiona Terry's *Condemned to Repeat? The Paradox of Humanitarian Action* (Ithaca, N.Y.: Cornell University Press, 2002).

Most importantly, books that aim to help give the perspective of the people caught in crisis include Ben Rawlence, *City of Thorns: Nine Lives in the World's Largest Refugee Camp* (New York: Picador, 2016); and Viet Thanh Nguyen, *The Displaced: Refugee Writers on Refugee Lives* (New York: Abrams, 2018).

Finally, there is a host of influential policy briefs and reports by humanitarian actors and think tanks. Specifically, these include the ALNAP's *State of the Humanitarian System* reports found at https://www.alnap.org/our-topics/the-state-of-the-humanitarian-system; the Development Initiatives *Global Humanitarian Assistance* reports found at http://devinit.org/post/global-humanitarian-assistance-report-2018/; and the wide ranging work by the Humanitarian Policy Group on humanitarian history, civilian security and protection, localization, displacement, and much more can be found at https://www.odi.org/our-work/programmes/humanitarian-policy-group.

Index

Abdirahman, Khalif 13n1
access to crisis-affected populations
174–5; constraints on 175–6
accountability, IASC and 125
Accountability to Affected Populations
(AAP) agenda 158
Action Learning Network for
Accountability and Performance
(ALNAP) 48, 101, 116n39,
116n47–8, 118n87, 162
actors at core of system 12, 88–114;
affected communities and responders of first resort 90–94; affected
people, local host communities and
91–2; Cambodia, responses to refugee crisis in (1980) 88; community-
based organizations 93; definitional
problems 88; development actors
111; diasporas 93–4; donor budgets,
stability of 88–9; faith-based organizations 109, 113; formal humanitarian assistance organizations
88; global poverty, fight against
113; grassroots organizations 108;
host-country governments 92–3;
humanitarian action, actors
carrying out 89–90; humanitarian
government donors 101–5; humanitarian response, globalization of
88–9; international financial institutions (IFIs) 112; International
non-governmental organizations
(INGOs) 97–100; learning networks
101; media 107–8; militaries 105–6;
national non-governmental organizations (NGOs) 93; NGO

coordination and advocacy bodies
100–101; numbers of actors,
growth of 88; peacekeeping
operations 107; philosophies and
objectives of humanitarians 112–14;
private donors 109–10; private
sector for-profit companies 110–11;
Red Cross and Red Crescent
Movement 95–7; regional inter-
governmental organizations 109;
religious groups 108–9; social
justice, commitment to 113;
traditional established humanitarian action 94–105; United Nations
(UN) Secretariat and specialized
agencies 97, 98–9; volunteer organizations 108; wider humanitarian
network 105–12; Yugoslavia,
responses to refugee crisis in
former (1995) 88
Adams, Lesley 168n36
Adan, Guhad 13n1
affected populations: local host
communities and 91–2; relief
through humanitarian system
120–21; responders of first resort
and 90–94
Afghanistan HRP 138
African Union (AU) 1, 101, 109
Agence France Presse (AFP)
142n18
Agenda for Humanity 171n81
Al-Assad, Bashar 76
Al-Assad, Hafaz 76
Al-Bashir, Omar 61
Alamgir, Mohiuddin 29n14

Alexander, Jessica 114n12, 115n17, 115n19, 119n90, 141n3, 166n1
Ali, Degan 85n48, 168n37–8
America Relief Administration (ARA) 24–5
American Red Cross (ARC) 25, 115n25
Amin, Mohamed 37, 38
Anderson, Mary B. 52n41
Ansari, Aimee 84n36
Armée Rwandaise (FAR) 46
Armenian genocide 24
Assistance Mission to Rwanda (UNAMIR) 44–5, 47, 107
Association of East Asian Nations (ASEAN) 109; Coordinating Centre for Humanitarian Assistance on Disaster Management (AHA Centre) 128
atrocities of war, limitation of 21–2
Emperor Augustus 15
Austin, Lois 171n76–7
Austrian Red Cross 128
Azarbaijani-Moghaddam, Sippi 82n11–83n12

Bailey, Rob 180n11
Bailey, Sarah 171n82
Balkan wars (1991–99) 40–43
Ballou, Stacey 83n18
Ban Ki-moon 13n10, 170n59
Barnes, John Robert 29n8
Barnett, Michael N. 51n31–2, 82n2, 102, 116n51, 142n15
Barre, Said 69
Barrett, Christopher B. 85n49, 85n51, 144n51, 168n32
BBC (British Broadcasting Corporation) 37, 38, 51n18; BBC News 83n24, 83n26, 86n60, 179n7
Belanger, Julie 171n82
Bell, Robert 85n49
Bellion-Jourdan, Jérôme 29n5
Belliveau, Joe 171n80
Bennett, Christina 29n2, 87n76, 141n4, 180n14; contemporary humanitarian actors 114n3–4, 114n7–8, 115n14, 115n16, 116n50, 117n62, 117n64–5
Benthall, Jonathan 29n5

Berlin airlift 27
Betts, Alexander 171n78–9
Beyoncé 140
Bhattacharjee, Abhijit 84n33
Biafra (1968–70) 31, 32–3
Billat, Céline 116n46
Black Death 16
Bloom, Louise 171n78–9
Bonard, Paul 84n40
Bonner, Michael 29n6
Bonwick, Andrew 52n40, 170n58, 170n65
Boon, Logan 141n6, 141n8
Borton, John 51–2n34, 52n37, 52n39, 118n75, 169n47
Bourns, Lesley 114n12, 115n17, 115n19, 119n90, 141n3, 166n1
Bourse, Francois 166n2
Bradbury, Mark 85n53
Bretton Woods institutions 26
Bromwich, Brendan 83n18
Buchanan-Smith, Margaret 50n15, 83n15, 83n18, 84n42
Buerk, Michael 37, 38, 51n18
Building a Better Response E-Learning 144n65
Burns, Kate 115n20–21
Bush, George W. 54

Cambodia, responses to refugee crisis in (1980) 88
Camp Coordination and Camp Management (CCCM) 131, 142n23–4
Cantor, Norman F. 29n3
Carbonnier, Gilles 82n1
CARE Canada 30n30
CARE International 69, 120
Caritas 108, 109, 118n76
Carstensen, Nils 50n16
cash-based assistance: Cash Learning Partnership (CaLP) 101, 118n45; cash transfer programming (CTP) 154, 155–6, 164; Cash Transfers, High Level Panel on 153–4; volume of 155–6
Catholic Relief Services (CRS) 49n2, 132, 143n40
Center for Global Development (CGD) High Level Panel on

Humanitarian Cash Transfers 168n30–31, 168n35
Center for International Stabilization and Recovery 116n42
Centers for Disease Control (CDCs) 35, 50n8
Central Emergency Response Fund (CERF) 65, 95, 135–6
Centre for Research on the Epidemiology of Disasters (CRED) 83n19
change: acceleration in pace of 146; continual change, challenge of environment of 165–6; drivers of 146–7; learning and 47–9; political change, agenda of 28; programming change, annual to multi-year contexts 149–51; response change, rural and camp to urban contexts 147–9; transformative agenda 68
charity: ideals of 16–17; Protestantism and ethic of 16; religious charity, humanitarian precursor 15–18; *waqf* Islamic equivalent of charitable foundation 17
Chasin, Bárbara H. 50n10
Checchi, Francesco 84n38
CHS Alliance 13n9, 169n51
Chudacoff, Danya 86n66
Clay, Jason W. 51n23
Clooney, George 60
cluster approach: beginning of 125–6; country-level representatives 127; Guidance Note on Using the Cluster Approach to Strengthen Humanitarian Response (2006) 141n7; inter-cluster working groups 127
Cole, Diane 118n72
Collinson, Sarah 179n4
Comerio, Mary C. 83n30–31
Communicating with Disaster Affected Communities (CDAC) initiative 157; CDAC Network 169n49
community-based organizations (CBOs) 93
Community World Service Asia 169n48
compassion, agenda of 27–8
Comprehensive Peace Agreement (CPA) for South Sudan 72–3

Connor, Phillip 166n6
Emperor Constantine 15–16
Constas, Mark A. 85n51
containment, agenda of 28
contemporary perspective on action 12, 53–81; CARE International 69; Central Emergency Response Fund (CERF) 65; Comprehensive Peace Agreement (CPA) for South Sudan 72–3; Darfur crisis (2002–2009) 57–61; Darfur crisis (2002–2009), "acute" or "frozen" crisis 60–61; Darfur crisis (2002–2009), impacts of conflict 59; Darfur crisis (2002–2009), response of international community 59–60; Darfur Peace Agreement (DPA) 60, 61; European Union (EU) 79–80; Famine Early Warning Systems Network (FEWSNET) 69; Haiti earthquake (January 2010) 65–8; humanitarian action, challenges for 81; humanitarian action, expansion of 81; humanitarian aid market 53; humanitarianism post-9/11, between "solidarity" and "governance" 54–7; Indian Ocean tsunami (December 2004) 62–5; Inter-Agency Standing Committee for Humanitarian Response (IASC) 65, 68; Inter-American Development Bank (IADB) 67; Intergovernmental Authority on Development (IGAD) 75; internally displaced persons (IDPs) 56, 59–60, 74, 75, 78–9; International Humanitarian Law (IHL) 76, 78; Islamic charities in Somalia famine 70; Islamic State in Iraq and Syria (ISIS) 76; Istanbul World Humanitarian Summit (2016) 80, 81, 178; Justice and Equality Movement (JEM) 58, 60; Médecins sans Frontières (MSF) 53; Mediterranean refugee crisis 78–81; Mediterranean refugee crisis, humanitarian response in Europe 80–81; MSF, Nobel Peace Prize for (1999) 53; multi-country crisis

in Indian Ocean 62–5; Operation
Lifeline Sudan (OLS) 72, 85n55;
Organization for Islamic Cooperation (OIC) 70; resonse to Haiti
earthquake, scale of 66–7; response
to tsunami, massive nature of 62–4;
Somali Transitional Federal
Government (TFG) 68; Somalia,
UN declaration of famine in 69;
Somalia famine (2011) 68–72;
Somalia famine (2011), actors,
multiplicity of 69–70; Somalia
famine (2011), early warning but
late response (again) 69; Somalia
famine (2011), innovative programmatic responses to scale 70–72;
Somalia Food Security and Nutrition Analysis Unit (FSNAU) 69,
84n39; South Sudan, disunity on
independence 72–5; South Sudan,
humanitarian impact of war 74–5;
South Sudan, new nation in crisis
(2011 onward) 72–5; Sudan People's Liberation Movement/Army
(SPLM/A) 72–3; Sudan People's
Liberation Movement-In Opposition (SPLM-IO) 73; Sudanese Liberation Army (SLA) 60; Sudanese
Liberation Movement/Army
(SLM/A) 58; Sudanese People's
Liberation Army (SPLA) 58, 72,
73–4; Syria, humanitarian nightmare in 78; Syria and UN, "whole
of Syria" approach, introduction
of 77; Syria "world's worst humanitarian crisis" 75–8; Syria
"world's worst humanitarian
crisis," impact of conflict 76–8;
Syrian Arab Red Crescent (SARC)
77; Syrian Democratic Forces
(SDF) 76; system-side reforms,
Haiti earthquake as trigger for 68;
system-side reforms, Indian Ocean
tsunami as trigger for 64–5; UN
Africa Mission to Darfur
(UNAMID) 60, 61; UN High
Commissioner for Refugees
(UNHCR) 79–80; UN Mission in
South Sudan (UNMISS) 74; UN
Office for the Coordination of

Humanitarian Affairs (OCHA)
66–7, 86n57, 86n61, 86n63; UN
Organization Mission in the
Democratic Republic of the Congo
(MONUC) 56–7, 82n10; UN
peacekeeping troops in Darfur 59;
UN peacekeeping troops in Haiti
67; United Nations (UN) Security
Council 60; United States Agency
for International Development
(USAID) 66; urban nature of
Haiti earthquake disaster 67–8;
World Food Programme (WFP)
69, 74
continuous support, agenda of 28
Convention on the Prevention and
Punishment of the Crime of
Genocide (1948) 51n29
Core Humanitarian Standard (CHS)
Alliance 156–7, 158; commitments
of 157
Cosgrove, John 83n22–3, 83n25,
83n28–9
Costello, Amy 169n54, 170n56
Coulter, Lorraine 180n10,
180n12
country-based pooled funds (CBPFs)
135–6
country-level coordination 122, 123;
UN involvement 126–7
crisis, world of 1–2, 3–5; Al-Shabaab
1, 2; climate-induced disasters,
frequency of 3; conflict, human
history of disaster and 2; Core
Humanitarian Standard (CHS)
Alliance 2; funding requests,
increases in 5; global health
threats, frequency of 3; human
suffering, scale and scope of 3;
humanitarian assistance, need for
(2018) 3–5; International Humanitarian Law (IHL) 2; natural
hazards, frequency of 3; Somalia,
Baidoa district in 1–2; Somalia
famine (2011), death toll in 2; UN
Consolidated Appeals Process
(CAP) 4; violence, displacement
by 3
crowd-sourced data 162
Currion, Paul 114n1

Dallaire, Lieutenant General Roméo 44, 45, 51n33

Danielson, Nora 167n8

Darcy, James 84n40, 170–71n70, 170n66

Darfur crisis (2002–2009): "acute" or "frozen" crisis 60–61; aftermath of 159–60; contemporary perspective on action 57–61; Darfur Peace Agreement (DPA) 60, 61; impacts of conflict 59; response of international community 59–60

data-driven programming, growth of 161–2

Davey, Eleanor 118n77–8

Davidson, Henry 25

Davies, Susanna 50n15, 84n42

De Torrente, Nicolas 82n7

De Waal, Alex 29n19–30n20, 39, 50n5, 51n19, 51n21–2, 83n13, 83n17, 84n43, 85n56, 86n59

Demir, Nilüfer 80

DesRoches, Reginald 83n30–31

Development Initiatives 13n3–4, 115n15, 144n45–6, 145n60–61, 167n21

Devereux, Stephen 35, 50n6, 50n11–12

DHL 110

Diasporas 70, 89, 93–4, 153

Dini, Shukria 84n40

Disaster Assistance and Response Teams (DARTs) 103

Disasters Emergency Committee (DEC) 136

Donini, Antonio 29n2, 49n3, 141n4, 170n63–4, 179n1, 179n6, 180n14; contemporary humanitarian action 82n3, 82n6, 82n8, 82n11–83n12, 84–5n47, 87n76; contemporary humanitarian actors 114n3–4, 114n7–8, 115n14, 115n16, 116n50, 117n62, 117n64–5

Dooley, Olivia 180n10, 180n12

Duffield, Mark 85n55

Dunant, Henri (and Dunantist tradition) 21–2, 30n21, 34, 112, 173, 179n5

dutiful charitable giving (*zakat*), Islamic notion of 16–17

Earle, Lucy 119n91

Eberhard, Marc 83n30–31

"eco-system" for humanitarians 5, 14; humanitarian world in 21st century 178–9

education, objectives and activities on 131

effective aid provision, incomplete and unfinished nature of 140–41

Egeland, Jan 84n46

Elhawary, Samir 179n4

Elizatethan attitudes to refugees 17–18

Elmi, Afyare Abdi 117n63

Emergency Capacity-Building (ECB) Project 101

Emergency Relief Coordinator (ERC) 97

emergency telecommunications, objectives and activities on 131

Emergency Telecommunications Cluster 143n31

"enabling environment," humanitarian system as 6–7

engagement with action, reasons for 181–2

Enhancing Learning and Research for Humanitarian Assistance (ELRHA) 101

Esslemont, Tom 180n18

ethical framework 9

Ethiopia (1984–85) 37–40

Europe: emergence of humanitarian activity in 17–18; postwar reconstruction of 28

European Civil Protection and Humanitarian Aid Operations (ECHO) 103

European Commission 142n20

European Recovery Program 26

European Union (EU) 101, 103, 148; contemporary perspective on action 79–80; Council of the European Union 142n20

European Universities on Professionalization of Humanitarian Action (EUPRHA) 142n21

evidence-based interventions, push for 178–9

evidence-based programming, growth of 161–2

Fabre, Cyprien 167n15, 168n23
Fadul, Abduljabbar Abdulla 83n15
faith-based organizations 109, 113
famine: action against 19–21; early
    warning of, beginnings of 35–6;
    Famine Codes of India (1883)
    20–21; Famine Early Action
    Mechanism (FAM) 180n13;
    Famine Early Warning Systems
    Network (FEWSNET) 69; Greek
    empire, famine amelioration in 15;
    India, famine relief in (1837–8) 19;
    Integrated Phase Classification
    (IPC) Famine Early Warning in
    South Sudan 86n58; Irish famine,
    relief for (1845–9) 19–20; Islamic
    charities in Somalia famine 70;
    "late response," problem of 36–7;
    Orissa famine, systematic attempt
    at relief of (1866) 20; regime
    change and global intervention
    (Ethiopia, 1984–85) 37–40; Roman
    empire, famine amelioration in 15;
    Sahel, famine in (1972–74) 34–7;
    Sudan famine, relief for (1920s) 21;
    see also Somalia famine (2011)
Ferguson, Niall 29n13
Ferris, Elizabeth 86n65, 166n4–5
Fiji, emergency shelter for 136
finance: concerns about 177–8; donor
    budgets, stability of 88–9;
    Financial Tracking System (FTS)
    136, 144n43–4; pooled funds
    135–6; private donors 109–10;
    see also funding
First Reponse Radio 118n74
Flowminder 170n67
food aid 42, 69, 74, 103, 134, 154;
    absence of 71
Food and Agriculture Organization
    (UN, FAO) 35, 115n32
food security, objectives and activities
    on 131
forecasting of likely conditions 134
formal humanitarian assistance
    organizations 88
Franco-Prussian War, Red Cross cash
    deliveries during 154
Franke, Richard W. 50n10
Frankenberger, Tim 85n52

funding: fund raising and fund
    management 135; gaps in, growth
    of 176–7; mechanisms and tools
    for 135–6
future challenges 178–9

Gaddafi, Muammar 57
Garang, John 73
Geldof, Bob 39
Gelsdorf, Kirsten 85n48, 168n37–8
Geneva Convention for the
    Amelioration of the Condition of
    the Wounded in Armies in the
    Field 22
Geneva Convention (IV) 10;
    humanitarian foundations 10;
    Protection of Civilian Persons in
    Time of War (1949) 105, 117n66
Geneva Society for Public Welfare 22
genocide, refugee crisis and 45–7
Ghannam, Jeffrey 118n73
Gilert, Heidi 171n76–7
Glenzer, Kent 50n7, 50n14, 51n17
Global Alliance for Humanitarian
    Innovation (GAHI) 163
Global Alliance for Urban Crises
    167n11, 167n13, 171n75
Global CCCM Cluster 142n23
Global Education Cluster 143n28
Global Emergency Telecommunica-
    tions Cluster 143n30
Global Food Security Cluster 143n25
Global Health Cluster 143n32
global humanitarian action, birth of
    24–7
"global humanitarian system" 3
global-level coordination 122, 123;
    UN involvement 122–5
Global Logistics Cluster 143n34
Global Nutrition Cluster 143n36
global poverty, fight against 113
Global Protection Cluster 143n38,
    170n57, 170n62
global sectoral responses 130–33
Global Shelter Cluster 143n40
global system, beginnings of 18–22
Global War on Terrorism (GWOT) 8,
    12, 54, 55, 57, 103
globalization, 19th century
    beginnings of 18

Good Humanitarian Donorship (GHD) 142n19
good nationhood, Vattel's precepts of 18
Gordon, Rachel 85n54
Gourevitch, Philip 13n8, 51n33
grassroots organizations 108
Great Depression 25–6, 28
Greek empire, famine amelioration in 15
Greenwood, F. 171n72
Ground Truth Solutions 167n7
Group URD 13n9

Habyarimana, Juvenal 43–4, 45
Emperor Haile Selassie 38
Hailey, Peter 171n71
Haiti earthquake (January 2010) 140; contemporary perspective on action 65–8; response to, scale of 66–7; system-side reforms, earthquake as trigger for 68; urban nature of disaster 67–8
Handicap International 86n64
Hansen, Greg 82n11–83n12
Harlet, Julie 167n14
Harmer, Adele 84n46
harmonized approach, aim for 135
Harvey, Paul 114n9–10
Haushofer, Johannes 118n82
health, objectives and activities on 131
Heath, J. Benton 141n9–10, 145n64
Hedlund, Kerren 168n39–40
Hepps, Jason 86n69
High Level Panel on Humanitarian Cash Transfers 168n30–31, 168n35
Hillbruner, Christopher 84n41
HIV/AIDS 150
Hoffman, Peter J. 180n15
Hofmann, Charles-Antoine 170–71n70
Holt, Julius 50n9
Hoover, Herbert 24
House of Commons International Development Committee 169–70n55
Howarth, C. 171n72
Howe, Kinberley 86n66–8
Howe, Paul 50n6

Høyen, Kristian 50n16
Human Rights Watch (HRW) 51n20, 86n62
Humanitarian Accountability Partnership-International (HAP-I) 48–9, 156
humanitarian action: Action Learning Network for Accountability and Performance (ALNAP) 48; actors carrying out 89–90; Armée Rwandaise (FAR) 46; Assistance Mission to Rwanda (UNAMIR) 44–5, 47, 107; Balkans wars (1991–99) 40–43; BBC (British Broadcasting Corporation) 37, 38, 51n18; Biafra (1968–70) 31, 32–3; boundaries of, 'fuzziness' of 8–9; Catholic Relief Services (CRS) 49n2; Centers for Disease Control (CDCs) 35, 50n8; challenges for 81; change, learning and 47–9; characteristics of 181–2; Cold War period and aftermath 12, 31–49; Convention on the Prevention and Punishment of the Crime of Genocide (1948) 51n29; crisis and reform, learning, change and 47–9; definition of 129–30; effects on humanitarians of 182; emergence of 7; engagement with, reasons for 181–2; Ethiopia (1984–85) 37–40; expansion of 81; famine, "late response," problem of 36–7; famine, regime change and global intervention (Ethiopia, 1984–85) 37–40; famine early warning, beginnings of 35–6; Food and Agriculture Organization (UN, FAO) 35, 115n32; genocide, refugee crisis and 45–7; High Commissioner for Refugees (UNHCR) 41–2, 46; Human Rights Watch (HRW) 51n20, 86n62; Humanitarian Accountability Partnership-International (HAP-I) 48–9; humanitarian imperative 9; humanitarian system 6; "humanitarian warfare," rise of 42–3; IFRC/NGO Code of Conduct 49; independent humanitarianism, rise of 32–3;

International Committee for the Red Cross (ICRC) 33, 45; International Federation of Red Cross and Red Crescent Societies (IFRC) 49; International Rescue Committee (IRC) 46; Joint Church Aid (JCA) 33; Joint Evaluation of Emergency Assistance to Rwanda (JEEAR) 47–9; Médecins sans Frontières (MSF) 34, 39, 46; non-governmental organizations (NGOs) 33–4, 35, 49n2; North Atlantic Treaty Organization (NATO) 41, 42–3; objective of 129; overlapping agendas 7–9; politically engaged humanitarian-ism 33–4; principles of 9, 10, 13n7, 95, 112–13, 175; Protection Force in Bosnia (UNPROFOR) 42; "Responsibility to Protect" (R2P), doctrine of 43, 56, 57, 175–6; responsiveness of 129–40; Review of Humanitarian Action (ALNAP) 48; Rwandan genocide and after-math (1994–96) 43–7; Rwandan Patriotic Front (RPF) 43–4, 45; Sahel, famine in (1972–74) 34–7; Security Council (UN) 45; televised action, competing ideologies in era of 40; Tigrayan People's Liberation Front (TPLF) 39; United Nations (UN) 32; World Food Programme (WFP) 35; World War II to end of Cold War, "golden era" for 31–2; *see also* actors at core of system; contemporary perspective on action; policy, practice and operational adaptations

humanitarian action, origins of 9–11, 14–28; America Relief Adminis-tration (ARA) 24–5; American Red Cross (ARC) 25, 115n25; Armenian genocide 24; atrocities of war, limitation of 21–2; Berlin airlift 27; Black Death 16; Bretton Woods institutions 26; charitable foundation, *waqf* Islamic equivalent of 17; charity, ideals of 16–17; charity, Protestantism and ethic of 16; compassion, agenda of 27–8;

containment, agenda of 28; continuous support, agenda of 28; dutiful charitable giving *(zakat),* Islamic notion of 16–17; Eliza-bethan attitudes to refugees 17–18; ethical framework 9; Europe, emergence of humanitarian activity in 17–18; Europe, postwar recon-struction of 28; European Recovery Program 26; famine, action against 19–21; Famine Codes of India (1883) 20–21; founding ideals, distortions of 14; Geneva Convention for the Amelioration of the Condition of the Wounded in Armies in the Field 22; Geneva Convention (IV) 10; Geneva Society for Public Welfare 22; global humanitarian action, birth of 24–7; global system, beginnings of 18–22; globalization, 19th century beginnings of 18; good nationhood, Vattel's precepts of 18; Great Depression 25–6, 28; Greek empire, famine amelioration in 15; history of 14–15; humanity, principle of 3, 9, 10, 13n7, 14, 18, 95, 112–13; impartiality, principle of 9, 10, 13n7, 21, 42, 47, 64–5, 71, 95, 109, 112–13, 175; indepen-dence, principle of 9, 10, 13n7, 21, 53, 95, 109, 112–13, 173, 175; India, famine relief in (1837–8) 19; Internal Displacement, Guiding Principles on 11; International Committee for the Red Cross (ICRC) 10, 12, 13n7, 21, 22, 24–5, 26, 30n22; International Commit-tee for the Relief of the Wounded 22; International Federation of Red Cross and Red Crescent Societies (IFRC) 25; International Humanitarian Law (IHL) 6–7, 10–11, 21, 22, 26; International Monetary Fund (IMF) 26; Inter-national Save the Children Union 23, 24; Irish famine, relief for (1845–9) 19–20; Islamic tradition 16–17; Judeo-Christian tradition 15–16; League of Nations 24, 25;

League of Nations Declaration of the Rights of the Child (1924) 23; Lisbon earthquake (1755), disaster-response strategy for 18; Macedonian Relief Fund 23; Marshall Plan 27; multiple agendas of humanitarianism 27–8; neutrality, principle of 9, 10, 13n7, 21, 25, 42, 95, 109, 111, 112–13, 175; "New Deal" agenda in US 26; non-governmental organizations (NGOs) 12; Organization for Economic Cooperation and Development (OECD) 26; origins and development of 11, 14–28; Orissa famine, systematic attempt at relief of (1866) 20; Ottoman Empire, dissolution of 24; political change, agenda of 28; political views on (19th century) 20; principles of humanitarian action 9, 10, 13n7, 95, 112–13, 175; Protestantism and ethic of charity 16; Red Cross Societies, League of 24, 25; Refugee Convention (1951) 11; religious charity, humanitarian precursor 15–18; Roman empire, famine amelioration in 15; Solferino, Dunant and beginnings of 22; Sudan famine, relief for (1920s) 21; United Nations (UN) Convention on the Rights of the Child (1989) 23; voluntary action (*sadaqa*), Islamic notion of 17; World Bank 26; World Humanitarian Summit (2016) 11; World War I and birth of NGOs 22–3; World War II, aftermath of 26–7
humanitarian aid market 53
Humanitarian Country Teams (HCTs) 120, 127, 134, 135, 138–9; Afghanistan HCT 143n29; Yemen HCT 142n13
Humanitarian Data Exchange (HDX) 161
humanitarian government donors 101–5
humanitarian imperative 9
Humanitarian Innovation Fund (HIF) 101

Humanitarian Needs Overview (HNO) 137–8
humanitarian operations 5–7, 12, 120–41, 181–2; accountability, IASC and 125; affected populations, relief through 120–21; Afghanistan HRP 138; Austrian Red Cross 128; Camp Coordination and Camp Management (CCCM) 131; challenges for 12, 172–9; cluster approach, beginning of 125–6; cluster approach, country-level representatives 127; coordination of global humanitarian network 121; coordination outside UN system 127–9; country-level coordination 122, 123; country-level coordination, UN involvement 126–7; early recovery, objectives and activities on 131; "eco-system" for humanitarians 5, 14; education, objectives and activities on 131; effective aid provision, incomplete and unfinished nature of 140–41; emergency telecommunications, objectives and activities on 131; "enabling environment" 6–7; Fiji, emergency shelter for 136; food security, objectives and activities on 131; forecasting of likely conditions 134; fund raising and fund management 135; funding mechanisms and tools 135–6; "global humanitarian system" 3; global-level coordination 122, 123; global-level coordination, UN involvement 122–5; global sectoral response 130–33; Haiti earthquake (January 2010) 140; harmonized approach, aim for 135; health, objectives and activities on 131; humanitarian action 6; humanitarian action, definition of 129–30; humanitarian action, objective of 129; humanitarian action, responsiveness of 129–40; humanitarian reform and beginning of cluster approach 125–6; Humanitarian Response Plans (HRPs) funding 138–9; "humanitarian world" 5–7,

181–2; information gathering 133–4; inter-cluster working groups 127; International Rescue Committee 140; local organizations, relief through 120–21; logistics, objectives and activities on 132; media perspective on 5; monitoring and evaluation (M&E) 139–40; multi-sector budgets, growth of 133; multi-sectoral assessments 134; needs assessment 133–4; NGO coalitions 124; nutrition, objectives and activities on 132; OIC Department of Humanitarian Affairs 128; organization of global humanitarian network 121; Pacific Humanitarian Team 127; partnership, IASC and 125; planning and programming 133–40; policy, practice and operational adaptations 12, 146–66; pooled funds 135–6; predictability, IASC and 125; procurement and logistics 136–7; programming and project management, implementation of 136–9; programming areas 133; protection, objectives and activities on 132; protection activities 137; rapid growth in 177; Red Cross Movement 121, 122, 127, 139; response planning, analysis and 134; shelter, objectives and activities on 132; South Sudan, mine clearance in 136; strategic choices for response 134; Sudan, fundraising for forgotten needs in 123; Sudan, medical attention for 136; Syria, technology in humanitarian aid and 123; Syria Regional Response Plan 133; United Nations (UN) - established coordination system 122–7; United Nations (UN) Global Humanitarian Overview 136; Water, Sanitation, and Hygiene (WASH), objectives and activities on 132; work in, demand for 181–2; World Humanitarian Day 140; Yemen, response to crisis in (2017) 120–21, 127

Humanitarian Practice Network 83n27
humanitarian principles: humanitarian action, principles of 9, 10, 13n7, 95, 112–13, 175; humanity, principle of 3, 9, 10, 13n7, 14, 18, 95, 112–13; impartiality, principle of 9, 10, 13n7, 21, 42, 47, 64–5, 71, 95, 109, 112–13; independence, principle of 9, 10, 13n7, 21, 53, 95, 109, 112–13, 173, 175; neutrality, principle of 9, 10, 13n7, 21, 25, 42, 95, 109, 111, 112–13, 175
humanitarian protection: activities, humanitarian system and 137; imperative of, recognition of 159–61; objectives and activities on 132; Oxfam scandal and 176; protection activities 137; recognition of imperative of 159–61
humanitarian reform: cluster approach, beginning of 125–6; process of 172
humanitarian response, globalization of 88–9
Humanitarian Response Plans (HRPs) 137–9; funding for 138–9; for Yemen 144n50
Humanitarian Response Review (HRR) 125
"humanitarian warfare," rise of 42–3
"humanitarian world," system, action and 5–7, 181–2
humanitarian world in 21st century 172–80; access to crisis-affected populations 174–5; access to crisis-affected populations, constraints on 175–6; competing imperatives 172–4; "eco-system" for humanitarians 178–9; evidence-based interventions, push for 178–9; finance, concerns about 177–8; funding gaps, growth of 176–7; future challenges 178–9; humanitarian protection, Oxfam scandal and 176; humanitarian reform, process of 172; humanitarian system, rapid growth in 177; institutionalization 177; learning

from experience, challenge of 178; multiple agendas 172–4; Oxfam scandal 176; partnerships, contractual-legal relationships and 178; professionalization 177; "remote management," rise in 176; Somalia famine (2011), aftermath of 178; *témoignage* (witnessing) 178

Humanitarianism in Question (Barnett, M. and Weiss, T.) 82n2

humanity, principle of 3, 9, 10, 13n7, 14, 18, 95, 112–13

Hussein, Saddam 55

Ibrahim, Barbara 29n7

IFRC/NGO Code of Conduct 49

impartiality, principle of 9, 10, 13n7, 21, 42, 47, 64–5, 71, 95, 109, 112–13, 175

in-kind assistance 153–4

independence, principle of 9, 10, 13n7, 21, 53, 95, 109, 112–13, 173, 175

independent humanitarianism, rise of 32–3

India, famine relief in (1837–8) 19

Indian Ocean, multi-country crisis in 62–5

Indian Ocean tsunami (December 2004) 62–5

information and communications technology (ICT) 131

information gathering 133–4

innovation agenda, emergence of 163–5

institutional bureaucracy and inertia, problem of 164

institutionalization 36, 53, 125–6, 164, 177

Integrated Phase Classification (IPC) Famine Early Warning in South Sudan 86n58

Inter-Agency Standing Committee for Humanitarian Response (IASC) 84n37, 95, 123–5, 127; Cluster Approach 125–6; contemporary perspective on action 65, 68; Guidance Note on Using the Cluster Approach to Strengthen Humanitarian

Response (2006) 141n7; *Introduction to Humanitarian Action* (2015) 141n5; membership and standing invitees 124

Inter-American Development Bank (IADB) 67

inter-cluster working groups 127

InterAction 116n43

Intergovernmental Authority on Development (IGAD) 75

Internal Displacement, Guiding Principles on 11

Internal Displacement Monitoring Centre (IDMC) 13n2, 161, 170n68

internally displaced persons (IDPs) 120, 137, 147, 159; contemporary perspective on action 56, 59–60, 74, 75, 78–9

international assistance, presumption of 151–2

International Commission on Intervention and State Sovereignty (ICISS) 82n9

International Committee for the Red Cross (ICRC) 95–6, 112, 115n24, 151–2, 177–8; humanitarian action 33, 45; humanitarian foundations 10, 12, 13n7, 21, 22, 24–5, 26, 30n22; humanitarian system 120, 121, 122, 132, 139; social impact bond for humanitarian action 163

International Committee for the Relief of the Wounded 22

International Council of Voluntary Agencies (ICVA) 100–101

International Development Department (DFID, UK) 85n50, 85n52, 104

International Federation of Red Cross and Red Crescent Societies (IFRC) 95, 96–7, 115n22, 124, 139; humanitarian action 49; humanitarian foundations 25

international financial institutions (IFIs) 105, 111, 112

International Humanitarian Law (IHL) 94, 95, 120, 123, 137, 173; contemporary perspective on action 76, 78; humanitarian foundations 6–7, 10–11, 21, 22, 26

International Monetary Fund (IMF) 26
International non-governmental organizations (INGOs): actors at core of system 94, 97–100, 108–9, 111; humanitarian system 120, 121, 122, 127; market-based programming, in-kind food assistance and 154–5; policy and practice, changes in 151–2, 153, 163, 165
International Organization for Migration (IOM) 98, 115n33, 124, 145n62
International Rescue Committee (IRC) 46, 99, 100, 163, 169n44, 171n74; humanitarian system 132, 140, 143n42
International Save the Children Union 23, 24
Ireton, Barry 117n54
IRIN News 107, 168n29, 169n50
Irish famine, relief for (1845–9) 19–20
Islamic charities in Somalia famine 70
Islamic State in Iraq and Syria (ISIS) 76
Islamic tradition, humanitarian foundations and 16–17
Istanbul World Humanitarian Summit (2016) 11, 80, 81, 159, 165, 178

Jackson, Michael 51n24
Jacobs, Dan 50n4
Jebb, Eglantyne and Dorothy 23
Joint Church Aid (JCA) 33
Joint Evaluation of Emergency Assistance to Rwanda (JEEAR) 47–9, 156
Jok, Madut 85n55
Judeo-Christian tradition, humanitarian foundations and 15–16
Justice and Equality Movement (JEM) 58, 60

Keen, David 85n55
Kennedy, Eilidh 166n2
Kent, Randolph 29n2, 87n76, 118n83–4, 141n4, 180n14; contemporary humanitarian actors

114n3–4, 114n7–8, 115n14, 115n16, 116n50, 117n62, 117n64–5
Khedouri, Adam N. 29n11
Kiir, Salva 73
Kim, Jeeyon Janet 13n1, 171m71
Kinealy, Christine 29n17–18
Kingsley, Patricia 87n73–4
Kirisci, Kemal 86n65
Kissinger, Henry 29n4
Kitching, George Tjensvoll 87n75
Knox-Clarke, Paul 171n83
Kolbe, Athena 84n34
Krebs, Hanna 117n59
Kuhn, Anthony 117n60–61
Kurdi, Alan 80, 107–8

Lasker, Romano 167n16–17, 168n24
Lattimer, Charlotte 169n43
Leader, Nicholas 52n42, 85n53
League of Nations 24, 25; Declaration of the Rights of the Child (1924) 23
learning from experience, challenge of 178
learning networks 101
Lee, Amra 170n63–4
Lenin, Vladimir 24–5
Lentz, Erin 85n49
Lisbon earthquake (1755), disaster-response strategy for 18
Lischer, Sarah Kenyon 82n8
Loane, Geoff 85n55
locally led action: affected populations, local host communities and 91–2; localization, MSF attitude towards 152; recognition of 152–3; relief through local organizations 120–21
logistics, objectives and activities on 132
Lossio, Roberta 84n33
Luther, Martin 16

Ma, Alexandra 87n71–2
Macedonian Relief Fund 23
Machar, Riek 73
MacKintosh, Kate 85n53
Macrae, Joanna 52n42, 114n11
Madete, Stella 114–115n13
Maietta, Michel 166n2

Majid, Nisar 13n1, 84n44–5, 118n88, 168n39–40, 179n2, 180n11, 180n17
Mamiya, Ralph 170n65
market-driven programming 153–6
Marrus, Michael Robert 30n24
Marshall, George C. 26
Marshall Plan 27
Massoud, Ahmed Shah 55
Maxwell, Daniel G. 28n1, 29n2, 84–5n47, 84n44–5, 85n49, 85n54, 87n76; contemporary humanitarian action 141n4, 141n11, 144n49, 144n51–2; contemporary humanitarian actors 114n3–4, 114n7–8, 115n14, 115n16, 115n26, 116n50, 117n62, 117n64–5, 118n88; humanitarian world in 21st century 179n2, 179n6, 180n11, 180n14, 180n17; policy and practice, changes in 168n32, 168n39–40, 169n42, 170n66, 171n71
McCloskey, Erin 171n71
McElvaine, Robert S. 30n29
Médecins sans Frontières (MSF) 143n33, 178; contemporary humanitarian action 120, 131; contemporary humanitarian actors 94, 99–100, 109, 112, 116n40; contemporary perspective on action 53; humanitarian action 34, 39, 46; localization, attitude towards 152; Nobel Peace Prize for (1999) 53
media: actors at core of system 107–8; perspective on humanitarian system 5
Mediterranean refugee crisis 78–81; humanitarian response in Europe 80–81
Meier, Patrick 84n35
A Memory of Solferino (Dunant, H.) 22
Metcalfe-Hough, Victoria 171n82
Miliband, David 140, 145n63, 163
militaries, humanitarian system and 105–6
Minear, Larry 82n8, 82n11–83n12, 83n14
Moghalu, Kingsley Chiedu 51n33
Moloney, Grainne 84n41

monitoring and evaluation (M&E) 139–40, 161
Mooney, Walter 83n30–31
Moore, Karen 83n18
Moorehead, Caroline 30n25
Morris, Roger 50n8
Morton, Bill 116n38
Mowjee, Tasneem 82n11–83n12
Muggah, Robert 84n34
Prophet Muhammad 16
multi-sector budgets, growth of 133
multi-sectoral assessments 134
multi-stakeholder accountability, calls for 156–9
multi-year planning (MYP) 150–51
multiple agendas 172–4; humanitarian foundations and 27–8
Murthy, Jaya 82n10

Nansen, Dr. Fridtjof 24
national non-governmental organizations (NGOs) 93
Natsios, Andrew S. 116n52
needs assessment 133–4
Network for Empowered Aid Response (NEAR). 101, 168n27
neutrality, principle of 9, 10, 13n7, 21, 25, 42, 95, 109, 111, 112–13, 175
Nicholson, Nigel 168n39–40
Niland, Norah 82n5, 170n63–4
non-governmental organizations (NGOs): contemporary humanitarian actors 88, 89, 90–91, 93; contemporary Western humanitarian, origins of 16; contributors to 109–10; coordination and advocacy bodies 100–101; Haiti as "NGO Nation" 66; humanitarian action 33–4, 35, 49n2; humanitarian foundations 12; humanitarian system 120, 124, 135; humanitarian world, rapidity of growth in 177–8; IFRC/NGO Code of Conduct 49; Islamic charities in Somalia famine and 70; learning networks 101; Mediterranean refugee crisis 81; Network for Empowered Aid Response (NEAR). 152–3; NGO coalitions 124; NGO coordination

and advocacy bodies 100–101;
post-World War II creation of new
family of 26; World War I and
birth of 22–3
Nonviolent Peaceforce 179n5
North Atlantic Treaty Organization
(NATO) 41, 42–3
Norwegian Refugee Council 86n64
nutrition, objectives and activities
on 132

Ó Gráda, Cormac 29n15–16
Obama, Barack 60
O'Brien, Stephen 166n1
O'Callaghan, Sorcha 170n60–61
Office of Food for Peace (FFP) 103
Office of US Foreign Disaster
Assistance (OFDA) 102–3
official development assistance
(ODA) 104
Olsen, Gorm Rye 50n16
Operation Lifeline Sudan (OLS) 72,
85n55
O'Reilly, Fiona 85n55
Organization for Economic Coop-
eration and Development (OECD)
88, 102, 104, 117n55, 117n57, 150;
humanitarian foundations 26
Organization for Islamic Cooperation
(OIC) 109, 142n16–17; con-
temporary perspective on action
70; Department of Humanitarian
Affairs 128
Orissa famine, systematic attempt at
relief of (1866) 20
Osman, Abdalmonium el Khider
83n18
Ottoman Empire, dissolution of 24
overlapping agendas 7–9
Overseas Development Institute
(ODI) 118n77, 178; High Level
Panel on Humanitarian Cash
Transfers 168n30–31, 168n35;
Humanitarian Policy Group
(HPG) 180n16
Oxfam International 84n36, 99,
158–9; Oxfam scandal 159, 176

Pacific Humanitarian Team 127
Pallardy, Richard 166n3

Pantuliano, Sara 168n28, 170n60–61
Paras, Andrea 29n10
Parker, John 144n52, 169n42
Parrish, Cloe 169n43
partnerships: contractual-legal relationships and 178; IASC and 125
Patenaude, Bertrand M. 30n28
Patton, Anna 168n25
Saint Paul 16
peacekeeping operations 43, 44, 56,
59, 60, 67, 97, 105, 107, 137
People In Aid 156
Pflanz, Mike 143n37
philosophies and objectives of
humanitarians 112–14
planning and programming 133–40
Polastro, Riccardo 170n63–4
policy, practice and operational
adaptations 12, 146–66; acceleration in pace of change 146; cash-
based assistance, volume of 155–6;
"cash transfer programming"
(CTP) 154–6; Cash Transfers,
High Level Panel on 153–4;
change, acceleration in pace of
146; change, drivers of 146–7;
continual change, challenge of
environment of 165–6; Core
Humanitarian Standard (CHS),
commitments of 157; crowd-
sourced data 162; Darfur crisis,
aftermath of 159–60; data-driven
programming, growth of 161–2;
evidence-based programming,
growth of 161–2; food aid 154;
Franco-Prussian War, Red Cross
cash deliveries during 154; Humanitarian Accountability Partnership
156; humanitarian system 12,
146–66; in-kind assistance 153–4;
innovation agenda, emergence of
163–5; institutional bureaucracy
and inertia, problem of 164; international assistance, presumption of
151–2; locally led action, recognition of 152–3; market-driven
programming 153–6; multi-
stakeholder accountability, calls
for 156–9; "New Way of Working"
165; operational and policy trends

147; People In Aid 156; post-crisis reflection 161; programming change, annual to multi-year contexts 149–51; protection, recognition of imperative of 159–61; response change, rural and camp to urban contexts 147–9; Response Innovation Labs 163; sexual abuse and exploitation 158–9; Somalia famine (2011), cash transfers and market based programming during 154–5; Sphere Project 156; Syrian White Helmets 160; technological approaches, critiques of 164–5; technology, emergence of use of 163–5; World Humanitarian Summit in Istanbul (2016) 159, 165

Polman, Linda 114n2
Pombal, Sebastiano José, Marques de 18
Poole, D.N. 171n72
Poole, Lydia 171n82
pooled funds 135–6
post-crisis reflection 161
Pottier, Johan 51n33
Powell, General Colin 54, 60
Power, Samantha 30n23, 51n33
predictability, IASC and 125
principles of humanitarian action 9, 10, 13n7, 95, 112–13, 175
private donors 109–10
private sector for-profit companies 110–11
procurement and logistics 136–7
professionalization 177
programming: change in, annual to multi-year contexts 149–51; in humanitarian system 133; project management and, implementation of 136–9
Protection Force in Bosnia (UNPROFOR) 42
protection *see* humanitarian protection
Protestantism and ethic of charity 16
Purushotma, Karina 82n11–83n12

Quinn, Barry 117n56

Rashid, Ahmed 82n4
Raymond, N.A. 171n72
Red Cross and Red Crescent Movement 95–7
Red Cross Movement 121, 122, 127, 139
Red Cross Societies, League of 24, 25
Redvers, Louise 168n29
Refugee Convention (1951) 11
regional inter-governmental organizations 109
Regional Organisations Humanitarian Action Network (ROHAN) 109
religious charity, humanitarian precursor 15–18
religious groups as actors at core of system 108–9
"remote management," rise in 176
response change, rural and camp to urban contexts 147–9
Response Innovation Labs 163
response planning, analysis and 134
response to tsunami, massive nature of 62–4
"Responsibility to Protect" (R2P), doctrine of 43, 56, 57, 175–6
Reuters 143n39
Review of Humanitarian Action (ALNAP) 48
Rieff, David 51n26–8, 52n35, 52n38, 174
Robinson, W. Courtland 84n38
Rochdi, Najat 127
Roman empire, famine amelioration in 15
Roosevelt, Franklin D. 25–6
Rwandan genocide and aftermath (1994–96) 43–7
Rwandan Patriotic Front (RPF) 43–4, 45

Sahel, famine in (1972–74) 34–7
Santschi, Martina 85n54
Save Darfur Coalition 83n16
Save the Children Fund (SCF) 99, 180n8
Scarnecchia, Daniel P. 171n72
Schenkenberg, Ed 168n26
Schopper, Doris 142n22

Schreeb, J. Von 169n45–6
Schuller, Mark 84n32
Seaman, John 50n9
Security Management Initiative
   118n77
Seferis, Louisa 169n41
Sen, Amartya 35–6, 50n13
Serhan, Yasmeen 114n6
sexual abuse and exploitation 158–9
Shaer, Matthew 171n74
Shaikh, Salman 86n65
Shaping the Humanitarian World
   (Walker, P. and Maxwell, D.G.)
   28n1, 49n1, 82n2
Shapiro, Jeremy 118n82
Sheeran, Scott 170n65
Sheets, Hal 50n8
shelter, objectives and activities
   on 132
Sherif, Dina H. 29n7
Shitarek, Tenna 180n10, 180n12
Short, Clare 13n6, 52n42, 174, 179n3
Simpson, Sir John Hope 30n27
Singer, Amy 29n9
Slawson, Nicola 169n53
Slim, Hugo 52n40, 170n58, 170n65
Smillie, Ian 49n3, 82n11–83n12
social justice, commitment to 113
Solferino, Dunant and humanitarian
   foundations 22
Solnit, Rebecca 13n5
Somalia: CCCM Cluster 142n24;
   Food Security and Nutrition
   Analysis Unit (FSNAU) 69,
   84n39; Transitional Federal
   Government (TFG) 1, 68; UN
   declaration of famine in 69
Somalia famine (2011): actors, multi-
   plicity of 69–70; aftermath of 178;
   cash transfers and market based
   programming during 154–5; contemporary perspective on action
   68–72; early warning but late
   response (again) 69; innovative
   programmatic responses to scale
   70–72; innovative programmatic
   responses to scale of 70–72
South Sudan: Comprehensive Peace
   Agreement (CPA) for 72–3;
   disunity on independence 72–5;

humanitarian impact of war in
   74–5; independence 73–4;
   Integrated Phase Classification
   (IPC) Famine Early Warning in
   86n58; mine clearance in 136; new
   nation in crisis (2011 onward)
   72–5; warfare, renewal of 74
Spearin, Christopher 119n89
Special Inspector General for
   Afghanistan Reconstruction
   (SIGAR) 117n69
Spencer, Alexandra 169n43
Sphere Project 13n9, 169n52; policy,
   practice and operational
   adaptations 156
Steering Committee for Humanitarian
   Response (SCHR) 100, 101
Stirk, Chloe 118n80–81
Stites, Elizabeth 82n11–83n12, 86n66
Stobaugh, Heather 144n52, 169n42,
   170n66
Stockton, Nicholas 52n36
Stoddard, Abby 84n46, 119n95
Sudan: famine in, relief for (1920s)
   21; fundraising for forgotten needs
   in 123; medical attention for 136
Sudan Liberation Army (SLA) 60
Sudan People's Liberation Army
   (SPLA) 58, 72, 73–4
Sudan People's Liberation Movement/
   Army (SPLM/A) 58, 72–3
Sudan People's Liberation Movement-
   In Opposition (SPLM-IO) 73
Sustainable Development Goals
   (SDGs) 8
Svoboda, Eva 168n28
Swithern, Sophia 116n49
Syria: humanitarian nightmare in 78;
   impact of conflict in 76–8; Regional
   Response Plan 133; technology in
   humanitarian aid 123; UN and,
   "whole of Syria" approach, intro-
   duction of 77; "world's worst
   humanitarian crisis" 75–8
Syrian Arab Red Crescent (SARC) 77
Syrian Democratic Forces (SDF) 76
Syrian White Helmets 77, 91, 160
system-side reforms: Haiti earthquake
   as trigger for 68; Indian Ocean
   tsunami as trigger for 64–5

Tan, Y.S. Andrew 169n45–6
technology: emergence of use of 163–5;
  technological approaches, critiques
  of 164–5
televised action, competing ideologies
  in era of 40
Telford, John 83n22–3, 83n25,
  83n28–9
Emperor Tiberius 15
Tigrayan People's Liberation Front
  (TPLF) 39
Tomlinson, Brian 116n38
traditional established humanitarian
  action 94–105
Transparency International 180n9
Truman, Harry S. 26
Turkish International Cooperation
  and Development Agency
  (TIKA) 105

Umutesi, Marie Beatrice 51n33
Union of Syrian Doctors
  (UOSSM) 94
United Nations (UN) 5, 6, 12, 44–5,
  88, 89, 90–91, 117n70, 120, 121,
  151–2, 177–8; Africa Mission to
  Darfur (UNAMID) 60, 61;
  Assistance Mission to Rwanda
  (UNAMIR) 44–5, 47, 107; Charter
  of, Chapters concerned with
  peacekeeping 107; Children's Fund
  (UNICEF) 98, 110, 115n29,
  118n86, 131; China and 104; Consolidated Appeals Process (CAP)
  4, 95; Convention on the Rights of
  the Child (1989) 23; coordinated
  appeals 138; coordination systems
  121–5, 126–7, 128, 136; country-
  level coordination 126–7; Development Programme (UNDP) 99,
  111, 116n35, 131, 143n27, 150;
  Yemen 141n2; Emergency Relief
  Coordinator (ERC) 122–3, 125;
  Entity for Gender Equality and
  Empowerment of Women (UN
  Women) 98; established coordination system 121, 122–7; Food and
  Agriculture Organization (FAO)
  35, 98, 115n32; funding appeals
  149; General Assembly Resolution

46.18294–5; General Assembly
  Resolution 46/18294–5, 115n20–21,
  122, 123–4, 125, 175; Global
  Humanitarian Overview 136;
  global-level coordination 122–5;
  High Commissioner for Refugees
  (UNHCR) 41–2, 46, 79–80, 98,
  115n28, 119n92, 133, 148–9, 164,
  167n9–10, 167n18, 180n8;
  "Common Cash Facility" in
  Lebanon, establishment of 164;
  humanitarian action 32; Humanitarian Air Service 132; Humanitarian Coordinator (HC) 120;
  Humanitarian Coordinators (HCs)
  126–7, 135; Humanitarian Needs
  Overviews 4; market-based programming, in-kind food assistance
  and 154–5; Mission in South
  Sudan (UNMISS) 74; Office for
  the Coordination of Humanitarian
  Affairs (OCHA) 66–7, 86n57,
  86n61, 86n63, 97, 99, 111, 114n12,
  115n23, 115n27, 116n37, 116n44,
  117n68, 118n79, 118n85, 120, 122,
  142n12, 142n14, 144n47–8,
  144n53–7, 145n58–9, 149, 166n1,
  167–8n22, 167n19–20, 171n73;
  Yemen 141n1; Organization Mission in the Democratic Republic of
  the Congo (MONUC) 56–7,
  82n10; peacekeeping 118n71;
  peacekeeping forces 105, 107;
  peacekeeping troops in Darfur 59;
  peacekeeping troops in Haiti 67;
  Population Fund (UNFPA) 99,
  116n36; Protection Force in
  Bosnia (UNPROFOR) 42; Resident Coordinators (RCs) 126–7;
  Secretariat and specialized agencies
  97, 98–9; Security Council 45, 60,
  107, 123; Somalia, declaration of
  famine in 69; Syria and, "whole of
  Syria" approach, introduction of
  77; UN Women 115n34
United States: Agency for International Development (USAID) 66,
  102–3, 116–17n53, 131, 143n26,
  168n33; Commander's Emergency
  Response Program (CERP) 106;

Institute for Peace (USIP) 180n9;
"New Deal" agenda in 26
Universal Intervention and Develop-
ment Organization (UNIDO) 93
unmanned aerial vehicles (UAVs) 134
Urban Refugees 167n12
Uvin, Peter 51n30

Valente, Rodolpho 167n16–17,
168n24
Vattel, Emmerich 18, 29n12
Vaux, Tony 51n25
Venton, Courtenay Cabot 117n55,
167n15, 168n23, 180n10, 180n12
Vieira de Mello, Sérgio 55–6
voluntary action (*sadaqa*), Islamic
notion of 17
Voluntary Organizations in Cooperation in Emergencies (VOICE) 100
volunteer organizations 108

Walker, Peter 28n1, 82n8, 115n26,
117n67, 141n11, 142n15, 170n66
Water, Sanitation, and Hygiene
(WASH) 126; objectives and
activities on 132
Waters, Liz 114n2
Watkins, Benjamin 144n49
Weiss, Thomas G. 82n2, 102, 116n51,
180n15
Weissman, Benjamin M. 30n26
Weissman, Fabrice 115n18
Weller, Marc 170n65
Wheeler, Heather Y. 86n70

Willmot, Haidi 170n65
Wilson, Woodrow (and Wilsonian
approach) 25, 113
World Bank 119n93–4, 180n13;
humanitarian foundations 26
World Food Programme (WFP) 98,
115n30, 131, 168n33; con-
temporary perspective on action
69, 74; humanitarian action 35;
Logistics Cluster and 143n35
World Health Organization (WHO)
98, 115n31
World Humanitarian Day 140
World Humanitarian Summit in
Istanbul (2016) 11, 80, 81, 159,
165, 178
World Vision International (WVI) 99,
100, 109, 116n41
World War I and birth of NGOs
22–3
World War II to end of Cold War,
"golden era" for 31–2
Wrabel, Maria 171n71

Xi Jinping 104

Yemen, response to crisis in (2017)
120–21, 127
Young, Helen 83n18, 83n20–21
Yugoslavia, responses to refugee
crisis in former (1995) 88

Zeebroek, Xavier 82n11–83n12
Zyck, Steven 118n83–4